Democracy, Education, and the Schools

Democracy, Education, and the Schools

Roger Soder, Editor

Jossey-Bass Publishers • San Francisco

Substantial discounts on bulk quantities of Jossey-Bass books are available to corporations, professional associations, and other organizations. For details and discount information, contact the special sales department at Jossey-Bass Inc., Publishers (415) 433–1740; Fax (800) 605–2665.

For sales outside the United States, please contact your local Simon & Schuster International Office.

Manufactured in the United States of America on Lyons Falls Pathfinder Tradebook. This paper is acid-free and 100 percent totally chlorine-free.

Library of Congress Cataloging-in-Publication Data

Democracy, education, and the schools / Roger Soder, editor. — 1st
ed.
    p. cm. — (The Jossey-Bass education series)
    Includes bibliographical references and index.
    ISBN 0–7879–0166–0 (acid-free paper)
    1. Education—United States—Aims and objectives. 2. Democracy—
Study and teaching—United States.   I. Soder, Roger, date.
II. Series.
LA217.2.D44   1996
370'.973—dc20
                                                 95–30986
                                                  CIP

FIRST EDITION
HB Printing   10 9 8 7 6 5 4 3 2

The Jossey-Bass Education Series

Contents

Preface   xi
Acknowledgments   xvii
The Editor   xix
The Contributors   xxi

1. **The Meanings of Democracy**   1
    Nathan Tarcov
2. **Democracy, Nurturance, and Community**   37
    Donna H. Kerr
3. **Democracy, Ecology, and Participation**   69
    Mary Catherine Bateson
4. **Democracy, Education, and Community**   87
    John I. Goodlad
5. **Public Schooling and American Democracy**   125
    Robert B. Westbrook
6. **Democracy and Access to Education**   151
    Linda Darling-Hammond and Jacqueline Ancess
7. **Curriculum for Democracy**   182
    Walter C. Parker
8. **Oratory, Democracy, and the Classroom**   211
    John Angus Campbell
9. **Teaching the Teachers of the People**   244
    Roger Soder

Afterword   275
Name Index   279
Subject Index   287

Preface

Taken together, the essays in this book address fundamental questions of democracy (specifically, democracy in the United States), education, and the schools, and the interrelationships among the three. The underlying propositions advanced in the essays present an argument that runs along the following lines: of all the ways in which people can constitute themselves politically, American democracy holds the best promise for freedom and the betterment of human beings.

Several conditions must be met in order to secure, maintain, and improve American democracy. One set of those conditions, brilliantly articulated by Robert Putnam in his study of Italian regional government, *Making Democracy Work*,[1] is trust, exchange, and social capital. Another condition is a citizenry educated to carry out its moral and political responsibilities for living and working in the American democracy. The American schooling system is necessary to ensure an educated citizenry. As such, how might the American schooling system, and education more broadly conceived, best ensure the development of an educated citizenry? How might participants in the schooling system best learn to understand and participate critically in the American democracy?

Put another way, the questions are: To what extent should the enculturation of the young into the American democracy be the major function of the schools? If a major purpose of schools is to teach the young their rights and responsibilities as citizens in a democracy, then what should the schools teach? And what must teachers know in order to teach these rights and responsibilities in effective and responsible ways?

Over the years, many colleagues and friends have debated these questions and have long considered writing a book addressing the challenges to democracy. The immediate impetus for

Democracy, Education, and the Schools stems from the work of the Center for Educational Renewal at the University of Washington. John Goodlad, Ken Sirotnik, and I came together to create the center in 1985 with the agenda of focusing on the simultaneous renewal of schools and the education of educators. That agenda was, and continues to be, derived from four basic notions of education and schooling: enculturating the young into a social and political democracy, ensuring responsible stewardship of schools, practicing pedagogical nurturing, and providing access to knowledge for all children and youths, with moral considerations underlying all four. These notions have been explored elsewhere in the center's publications; in its related not-for-profit organization, the Institute for Educational Inquiry; in *The Moral Dimensions of Teaching,*[2] edited by Goodlad, Sirotnik, and myself; and in Goodlad's *Teachers for Our Nation's Schools*[3] and his *Educational Renewal: Better Teachers, Better Schools.*[4] A book dealing with the interplay of democracy, education, and schooling was thus a natural extension of our work.

The appearance of a volume bearing on the relationship of democracy, education, and schooling might well elicit modest surprise from those who believe the arguments and questions are redundant. Surely, they will say, the relationship between public schools and democracy was established two hundred years ago, that these are matters that have been talked about many times over, matters that are settled and done with. From the perspective of the authors, the objection on grounds of redundancy is in one sense positive, in that it implies support for (or at least leaves untouched) the book's basic argument. To be redundant is not to be wrong. Still, is the volume redundant, serving little purpose but to rehearse what everybody already knows?

It will be acknowledged that notions of democracy and schooling have been linked, have long been a staple of American rhetoric, from George Washington's farewell address on down to the barn-burner Fourth of July addresses that some of us might remember. Education is a bulwark against tyranny; it is the source of freedom; and it leads to good citizenship (indeed, report cards used to include marks for "citizenship" as well as academics). This acknowledgment notwithstanding, a theme of this book, argued in various ways by the several authors, is that these matters of democracy, education, and schooling may have been talked about, but rarely have they been addressed critically together. Moreover, as found throughout the organizational change literature (and as experienced by those who have attempted organizational change), these fundamental notions need to be reenacted and reevaluated by each group of people in each of the many parts and subparts of the American democracy. Thus, it surely helps to review the major terms—*democracy, education,* and *schooling*—and their interrelationships as part of that reenactment.

Another, quite different kind of reaction might be provoked by the appearance of a book on the democracy-education-schooling relationship. There are those who will hold the view that what is stressed and argued in this book is just plain wrong. They will argue that public schools have no relationship to the American democracy, that if public schools are indeed necessary, their primary function is not the preparation of active and alert citizens in a democracy, but something quite different, namely, either the production of workers capable of gaining and sustaining primacy in international economic competition, or the inculcation of basic academic skills.

And standing quietly by are those who will question whether having an alert and engaged and critical citizenry is necessary, desirable, or even possible. It is in this part of the political and social landscape that we find spokespeople for authoritarianism, for benevolent despotism, for oligarchies of one sort or another, for fascism and irrationality in all sorts of guises. First among these people is Dostoevsky's Grand Inquisitor, who argues that people do not want freedom, cannot live with freedom, and are unwilling and unable to govern themselves; all they want is "miracle, mystery, and authority."[5] If this book has a reason, a purpose, and a place, it is to construct persuasive and compelling responses to the arguments quietly flung at us by the Grand Inquisitor.

Overview of the Contents

Democracy, Education, and the Schools has three parts. The first part, Chapters One through Three, addresses the several meanings of democracy, the relationship between democracy and nurturance of the self, and the relationship between democracy and ecology. Nathan Tarcov begins the discussion in Chapter One with the argument that democracy is not simply an empowerment of people, but a challenge for the people. Tarcov considers ancient Greek understandings of classical democracy, the standards of democracy at its best and its defects, and the virtues required for the preservation of democracy. He then moves to a consideration of modern democracies, first by examining the mixed republic advocated by Machiavelli, moving then to a consideration of Locke's liberalism, and concluding with a discussion of the American representative democracy through an interrogation of *The Federalist.*

In Chapter Two, Donna Kerr continues the examination of democracy by considering the relationship between democracy and the nurturance of self. She argues that democratized family relations and civic society are instrumental to the nurturance of self, and that we should encourage whatever particular associations, including families and communities, bring specifically mutual respect and trust to human relationships. Kerr concludes with a critical examination of myths that surround nurturance, and makes important distinctions between nurturance, caring, and intervention.

Mary Catherine Bateson, in Chapter Three, considers the relationship of democracy and larger ecological understanding, arguing that "changes in human treatment of the biosphere, slowing and reversing existing patterns of degradation and exploitation, must be rooted in childhood learning." Bateson calls for a new attitude toward the living world, and suggests that this new attitude will require "a new kind of common sense, fundamental assumptions, and aspirations, and a rethinking of both education and the processes and institutions of democracy." She also calls for increasing the voice of children in civic society and a better understanding of ecological injustice, stating that equity issues are intergenerational in terms of children's future interests.

The second part of the book, Chapters Four, Five, and Six, shifts from an examination of democracy to a consideration of education and schooling in relation to democracy. In Chapter Four, John I. Goodlad develops an understanding of education as an instrument versus education as a good in itself, and considers education as it relates to political democracy, social democracy, and democracy of the human spirit. He then moves to a discussion of the simultaneous protection and cultivation of individuality and the common good, and the cultivation of the moral arts of democracy, and concludes with a discussion of the need to shore up social and health agencies to ensure the readiness of all children to participate in the educational process and the human conversation.

Robert B. Westbrook, in Chapter Five, focuses specifically on the relationship between public schooling and American democracy. Arguing that both freedom and democracy are at stake, he considers why American schools have not educated people for democratic citizenship, and how schools might be reconstructed so that they would do so. Westbrook critically analyzes the rise of "occupational competence" as the school's major purpose, and concludes with a rejection of the "neo–Hamiltonians," who actually prefer that people do little with the franchise, in favor of a neo–Jeffersonian or Deweyan approach to citizenship, and thus democratic education, with a greater focus on critical participation.

In Chapter Six, Linda Darling-Hammond and Jacqueline Ancess address fundamental matters of access to education and the relationship between access and full participation in the rights and benefits of democracy. They discuss the nature, history, and costs of educational inequality and its relationship to democracy, and conclude with an examination of proposed policies for resource equalization, of standards for delivery systems and for practice, and of school restructuring.

The third part of the book, Chapters Seven through Nine, centers on what happens and what needs to happen in schools, given the connections between democracy, education, and schooling. In Chapter Seven, Walter C. Parker considers curricula for democracy and discusses curriculum deliberation, including content selection and curriculum access/differentiation. He connects seven basic curriculum principles to a fresh formulation of democratic aims, within the frameworks of participatory democracy, creative democracy, and multicultural democracy.

In Chapter Eight, John Angus Campbell considers the school classroom as an arena for democratic practice and argues for a "model of democratic practice based on the ancient art of rhetoric—the civic language of democratic order and the embodiment of democratic epistemology." He shows how the classroom is the place for the cultivation of the ability to deliberate—to talk in productive ways and to move attitudes in new directions—and concludes with specific examples of speech classes as ways to create deliberating communities.

In the final chapter, Chapter Nine, I argue that if teachers are to ensure that students assume their rights and responsibilities as citizens in a democracy, then the preparation of teachers must focus much more than it has in the past on what should be the liberal arts education of those who intend to become teachers. I conclude with a bibliography of prescribed texts that must be part of the basic working knowledge of all teachers in a democracy.

Seattle, Washington   Roger Soder
August 1995

Notes

1. Robert Putnam, *Making Democracy Work: Civic Traditions in Modern Italy* (Princeton, N.J.: Princeton University Press, 1993).
2. John I. Goodlad, Roger Soder, and Kenneth A. Sirotnik, *The Moral Dimensions of Teaching* (San Francisco: Jossey-Bass, 1990).
3. John I. Goodlad, *Teachers for Our Nation's Schools* (San Francisco: Jossey-Bass, 1990).
4. John I. Goodlad, *Educational Renewal: Better Teachers, Better Schools* (San Francisco: Jossey-Bass, 1994).
5. Fyodor M. Dostoevsky, *The Brothers Karamazov* (New York: Random House, 1990).

Acknowledgments

General consideration of a volume addressing the relationship between democracy, education, and schooling started early on in the course of work at the Center for Educational Renewal and, subsequently, at the Institute for Educational Inquiry. As already stated, John Goodlad, Ken Sirotnik, and I had edited, with contributions from other colleagues, *The Moral Dimensions of Teaching*, and it was clear to us that looming around and about the moral issues were political issues. Many of the subtle and important shifts in the fundamental argument and structure of this book are due to guidance and suggestions from John and Ken. We have worked closely together for a decade in a collaboration both congenial and exciting. What is there, is there, and I would have it no other way.

My sense is that the contributing authors might well have been persuaded to prepare chapters without expectation of financial reward. However, the matter is moot, thanks to the generosity of the AT&T Foundation, whose grant covered all costs for this undertaking. Nor were powers of persuasion needed in working with contributing authors in revising, sometimes substantially, early drafts. I deeply appreciate their helpful cooperation and amiability in responding to suggestions and in meeting deadlines.

Many colleagues at the Institute for Educational Inquiry, the Center for Educational Renewal, and other institutions were patient and giving of their time and insights. I owe them a great deal.

Special thanks are extended to Mary Louise Hartline, who worked diligently on preparing the manuscripts for editorial production and keeping track of the details. Thanks are extended, too, to Paula McMannon, whose continuing assistance is always reassuring.

Another kind of thanks is due my wife, Jane. For many years, all delightful, she has by precept, and even more by the way she lives, helped me begin to understand what democracy is all about.

—R. S.

The Editor

Roger Soder is associate director of the Center for Educational Renewal at the University of Washington and vice president of the independent Institute for Educational Inquiry. He is coeditor (with John I. Goodlad and Kenneth A. Sirotnik) of *The Moral Dimensions of Teaching* and *Places Where Teachers Are Taught*. His articles in professional journals center on education, politics, professionalization, and rhetoric. His research interests continue to focus on the ethics and politics of rhetoric and education and the role of the university in a free society. Prior to joining with Goodlad and Sirotnik in creating the Center for Educational Renewal in 1985, Soder was an administrator in the Cape Flattery School District on the Makah Indian Reservation at Neah Bay, Washington, and was education director of the Seattle Urban League.

The Contributors

Jacqueline Ancess is a senior research associate with the National Center for Restructuring Education, Schools, and Teaching (NCREST) at Teachers College, Columbia University. Her research has been in the areas of accountability, authentic assessment in secondary schools, and restructuring of schools. Prior to joining NCREST, Ancess was director of Secondary School Change Services for the Center for Collaborative Action, a New York affiliate of the Coalition of Essential Schools, and spent twenty-three years in the New York City school system, as an English teacher in a South Bronx junior high school and finally as an administrator responsible for innovation and restructuring in three New York City school districts. In 1985, Ancess received the Schools and Culture Award from the New York Alliance for the Arts for her work as the founding director of Manhattan East Junior High School in East Harlem.

Mary Catherine Bateson is a cultural anthropologist who divides her time between teaching in Virginia and writing in New Hampshire. She is currently Clarence J. Robinson Professor in Anthropology and English at George Mason University in Fairfax, Virginia. She received her B.A. degree (1960) from Radcliffe College in Semitic languages and history and her Ph.D. (1963) from Harvard in Middle Eastern studies and linguistics. Her books include *Our Own Metaphor: A Personal Account of a Conference on the Effects of Conscious Purpose on Human Adaptation* (1972; second edition 1991); *With A Daughter's Eye: A Memoir of Margaret Mead and Gregory Bateson* (1984); *Composing a Life* (1989); and *Peripheral Visions: Learning Along the Way* (1994), as well as *Angels Fear: Towards an Epistemology of the Sacred* (1987, with Gregory Bateson) and *Thinking AIDS* (1988, with Richard Goldsby).

John A. Campbell is professor of communication at the University of Memphis. He received his B.A. degree (1964) in speech communication from Portland State University and his M.A. (1967) and

Ph.D. (1968) degrees from the University of Pittsburgh. Campbell's numerous essays have focused primarily on the rhetorical dimensions of Darwin's campaign for evolution. Two of these essays, "Darwin and the Origin of Species: The Rhetorical Ancestry of an Idea" (published in *Speech Monographs*, March 1970) and "Scientific Revolution and the Grammar of Culture: The Case of Darwin's Origin" (published in the *Quarterly Journal of Speech*, November 1986), received the Golden Anniversary Award of the Speech Communication Association. His essays have also appeared in *Victorian Studies, Studies in Burke and His Time, Rhetorica, Argumentation,* and *Rhetoric Society Quarterly* and as chapters contributed to nine books. In 1990, he gave the Van Zelst Lecture in Communication at Northwestern University. In 1993, he received the Distinguished Teaching Award and, in 1994, the Dean's Recognition Award, both from the University of Washington, where he taught from 1968 to 1995. He is currently at work on a book, *Charles Darwin: A Rhetorical Biography.*

Linda Darling-Hammond is currently William F. Russell Professor in the Foundations of Education at Teachers College, Columbia University, and co-director of the National Center for Restructuring Education, Schools, and Teaching (NCREST). She received her B.A. degree (1973) from Yale University, magna cum laude, and her Ed.D. degree (1978) in urban education from Temple University. She is actively engaged in research, teaching, and policy work on issues of school restructuring, teacher education reform, and educational equity. She is the author or editor of six books, including *Professional Development Schools: Schools for Developing a Profession* (1994); *A License to Teach* (1995); *Building a Profession for Twenty-First Century Schools* (1995), and *Authentic Assessment in Action: Studies of Schools and Students at Work* (1995). In addition, she has authored more than one hundred journal articles, book chapters, and monographs on educational policy issues.

John I. Goodlad has held professorships at Agnes Scott College, Emory University, the University of Chicago, the University of California, Los Angeles, and the University of Washington, where he now serves as director of the Center for Educational Renewal. He holds a Ph.D. (1949) in education from the University of Chicago and honorary doctorates from sixteen universities in Canada and the United States. He has authored or coauthored more than thirty books, has written chapters and papers in more than one hundred other books and yearbooks, and has published more than two hundred articles in professional journals and encyclopedias. Through his work at the Center for Educational Renewal and as president of the Seattle-based Institute for Educational Inquiry, he continues to direct a comprehensive nationwide program for the simultaneous renewal of schooling and the education of educators.

Donna H. Kerr is professor of education at the University of Washington and senior fellow of the Institute for Educational Inquiry. Formerly vice provost of the university and dean to launch its branch campuses, Kerr now focuses on philosophical questions regarding domination and nurture in interpersonal relations and institutional structures. She is writing a popular book on education and dignity, with the working title "Packaging the Soul." In an effort to ensure that this work will cross cultural boundaries, Kerr has been garnering reactions to pieces of that work from diverse audiences in both Russia and the United States. Earlier works include *Educational Policy: Analysis, Structure, and Justification* (1976) and *Barriers to Integrity* (1984).

Walter C. Parker is professor of education at the University of Washington. His interests include democratic citizenship education and social studies curriculum development. He is the editor of a collection of curriculum theorizing on democratic education, *Educating the Democratic Mind* (1996), and the author of *Renewing the Social Studies Curriculum* and *Social Studies in Elementary Education* (1993, with John Jarolimek). His research on teaching children to think critically about public issues has appeared in *Social Education* and *Theory and Research in Social Education.*

Nathan Tarcov is professor in the Committee on Social Thought, the Department of Political Science, and the College at the University of Chicago. He has also taught at Harvard University and has served on the policy planning staff of the Department of State and as a Secretary of the Navy Senior Research Fellow at the Naval War College. He received his B.A. degree (1968) in history from Cornell University and his Ph.D. degree (1975) in political science from Harvard University. He is the author of *Locke's Education for Liberty* (1984) and of articles on Machiavelli, Locke, *The Federalist*, Leo Strauss, American political thought, and American foreign policy, and is editor and translator with Harvey C. Mansfield, Jr., of Machiavelli's *Discourses on Livy* (1996), and editor with Ruth Grant of an edition of Locke's *Some Thoughts Concerning Education* and *Of the Conduct of the Understanding* (1996).

Robert B. Westbrook teaches American history at the University of Rochester. He is the author of *John Dewey and American Democracy* (1991), as well as numerous articles and essays in American cultural and intellectual history.

Democracy, Education, and the Schools

The Meanings of Democracy

Nathan Tarcov

To think clearly about democratic education, we must reconsider the meaning and the goodness of democracy.[1] It is sometimes said, and even believed, that democracy is the ultimate political criterion, good, or aspiration, and that all political evils should be attributed to the absence of full democracy and their cure sought in more democracy. That view is usually accompanied by an understanding of democracy that insists on the maximum of immediate and unlimited popular rule and the exclusion of any elements of other forms of government. Such a view sees democratic education as directed toward the propagation and actualization of such an understanding of democracy. The textual, typological, and terminological historical investigation of democracy presented in this chapter, however, is intended to help us relearn the lesson that the beginning of political wisdom for democratic citizens, statesmen, and educators is the sober recognition that democracy has its own characteristic defects and excesses. On the basis of that recognition, we can seek to remedy the diseases incident to democratic government and embrace an understanding of democracy that includes limits to popular rule and incorporates elements of other forms of government. If democracy is to be not simply an empowerment, but also a challenge for the people, then the people and their chosen leaders need education in order to be prepared to rise to that challenge.

This investigation of the meanings of democracy does not claim to be a comprehensive survey of all the classics of political

1

thought. It does not attempt to trace the roots of faith in unlimited democracy. It is limited instead to some of those friendly critics or critical friends of democracy whom the author judges most likely to help us appreciate the limits of democracy.

It is customary to begin an examination of the meaning of democracy with the undeniable etymological observation that the term comes from the ancient Greek word for rule (*kratos*) by the people (*demos*) and with the more questionable historical claim that what is meant today by democracy is of ancient Greek origin. It is indeed useful to begin this consideration of the meaning of democracy and its implications for education with the ancient Greeks, not so much because they were democrats in whom we can see ourselves, but because the differences between their democracy and the modern democracies that have come into being since the late eighteenth century help to clarify both what democracy may mean generically and what our modern and especially American democracy may mean specifically. Also, their political philosophers offer critiques of democracy that can make us both more self-critical and more capable of defending democracy. Self-defense may depend upon self-criticism—in that a clear understanding of the limitations, weaknesses, or dangerous propensities of democracy may be a prerequisite for the preservation as well as for the improvement of our own democracy and for an education conducive to those purposes.

Pericles' Praise of Athenian Imperial Democracy

The most famous praise of democracy is that of the Athenian leader Pericles in a funeral oration delivered in the first year of the Peloponnesian War (431 B.C.), as presented in Thucydides' history of that war (II 34–46).[2] It is a praise, however, not of democracy in general but of a particular democracy, the Athenian polity. What we might consider the democratic character of that polity, that it was managed by (or for) not few but many, was only one of its aspects, albeit the first mentioned by Pericles. He proceeds to mention two other aspects: equality before the law in private disputes, and the distribution of honor and office in public affairs on the basis not of class or wealth but of virtue or the ability to do some good for the city. (The Greek conception of *arete*, virtue or excellence, referred to the qualities that enable human beings to benefit the community, do their jobs, fulfill their functions, or achieve their own perfection. The virtues were commonly conceived to be justice, courage, moderation, and prudence or wisdom.) Whereas equality before the law appears to be a corollary of democracy, the distribution of honor and office on the basis of virtue seems to stand in some contrast or tension with equality and democracy; but it would be incompatible with democracy only if the people were incapable of such distribution, or if the virtuous were incapable of managing public affairs for the people, or if democracy meant direct rule by all the people equally or the distribution of office strictly on the basis of equality without any regard for virtue. Distribution of honor and office on the basis of virtue is compatible with democracy if democracy means only the distribution of honor and office by the people or the management of public affairs for the people. Democracy might then allow a kind of elective public-spirited aristocracy[3] in which the virtuous, emerging out *of* the people, are selected *by* the people, and govern *for* the people.

Pericles suggests that distribution of honor and office on the basis of virtue is a kind of freedom or liberality, and that the Athenians also showed their freedom or liberality in their tolerance of each other in daily private affairs. Pericles balances this freedom in private life with public fear of lawlessness and with obedience to those in office and to the laws. There seems to be a tension between lawfulness and freedom, yet Pericles claims that Athens managed to combine them. There is a hint of defensiveness here, as if democracies need to show that they do not sacrifice in law-abidingness what they grant in liberty.

Pericles turns from specifically political considerations to praise the recreations Athens offered the mind: contests, festivals, elegant private homes, and imports from all over the world. It is not enough to praise a political community for its political characteristics; in the words of Edmund Burke, "To make us love our country, our country ought to be lovely."[4]

Pericles commends Athens for its openness (in sharp implicit contrast with Spartan secrecy and exclusiveness), its allowing foreigners to look and learn. This openness appears to be praiseworthy at first merely as a sign of reliance on courage rather than on covert preparations and deceptions. Pericles acclaims Athenians for showing courage despite their free way of life and without the severe training and harsh laws of their Spartan opponents. The place of education in Athenian democracy therefore seems problematic: instead of praising Athens for an education (or legislation) directly designed to produce or enforce military or civic virtue, its great leader applauds his city for managing to elicit outstanding virtue without such education (or legislation).

Yet it would be a grave mistake to conclude that this splendid praise of the exemplary ancient democracy disparages education. The very next clause, probably the most famous in the oration, suggests the contrary: "We love beauty with thrift and we love wisdom without softness." Athenian life, civic as well as private, was a kind of higher education. Pericles praises the Athenians' willingness to participate in debate, to be taught by speeches before engaging in deeds. The heart of Athenian democracy, the popular decision making of the assembly, was not a mere mechanism for satisfying popular preferences, but an arena of teaching and learning. It is therefore all the more appropriate that Pericles shortly thereafter calls his city "the school of Greece." The openness of Athenian democracy thus is praiseworthy not only as a sign of reliance on courage but also as a mark of its exemplary and educative status, not only for its own citizens but for all the Greeks. Still, we must note that this education is achieved not through direct public control over the upbringing and training of children (which was characteristic of nondemocratic Sparta), but through democratic politics itself and the city's general way of life. Pericles' oration nearly concludes by asserting that "where the greatest prizes are offered for virtue, there the best men will be citizens." It is above all through the democratic distribution of honor and office on the basis of virtue that democracy is supposed to educate its citizens toward virtue.

This examination has so far ignored the dominant note of the funeral oration that colors all its other points: pride in the *power* of Athens. The climax of the speech is Pericles' invitation to his listeners to gaze upon the power of the city and become lovers of it. Its democratic polity is presented as part of what enabled Athens to acquire and enlarge its empire. The citizens of Athenian democracy are presented as reconciling their private and public concerns primarily through sharing in the fame acquired by the Athenian empire. The Athenian democracy of Thucydides' Pericles is emphatically *imperial* democracy.

Although Pericles holds forth for the Athenians a potentially universal naval empire commanding eternal fame (II 41, 62, 64), his praise of democracy is not universalist in the mode of modern democracy. It does not depart from the general expectation derived from Greek political experience that individual cities would continue to have different *politeiai* (regimes, constitutions, or forms of government) and ways of life. It exemplifies the particularist concern with having the best regime for one's own city and with spreading the city's power and renown rather than its form of government around the world. It regards democracy not as a matter of principle but as the form of government with more advantages than disadvantages for Athens. It appeals to the Athenian sense of natural superiority, rather than to any doctrine of universal human equality or individual natural rights.

It would be seriously misleading to treat Pericles' beautiful funeral eulogy as Thucydides' last word on Athenian democracy. Thucydides turns directly from the eulogy to the plague that devastated Athens, which introduced there a lawlessness and devotion to bodily pleasure that contrast darkly with the lawfulness and public-spirited pursuit of glory praised by Pericles (II 47–53). When shortly thereafter Thucydides recounts Pericles' death, Thucydides' eulogy for him reveals that while in speech the city was a democracy, in deed it was a "rule by the first man" (II 65). Pericles restrained the multitude while respecting its liberty, leading it rather than being led by it. In retrospect, Pericles' praise of the Athenian people for distributing honor and office on the basis of virtue and for being willing to be instructed by speech before engaging in action seems to be a praise of them for allowing him to rule them under the form of a democracy. After his death in 429 B.C., in the absence of his monarchic rule, based on his recognized ability and honesty, Athens succumbed to private ambition, private greed, and private quarrels, resulting in its defeat by Sparta. Furthermore, the toleration Pericles praised gave way to the intolerance behind the politically disastrous inquisition in 415 B.C. into the mutilation of the Hermae (statues of Hermes) and the reported profanation of the Eleusinian mysteries (religious rites) (VI 15, 27–29, 53, 60–61), and the trial and execution of Socrates in 399 B.C. In both of these cases, impiety was prosecuted not as a matter of private religious belief but as a challenge to democracy itself. The most glorious moment in the history of ancient democracy seems to have been based not only on a dedication to imperial power, but on intolerant fanaticism as well as a precarious departure from democracy in the direction of monarchy.[5]

Plato's Criticism of Democracy

The most famous criticism of democracy is that by Plato in his *Republic* (555b–561e).[6] He describes democracy as the polity resulting when the poor put an end to oligarchy by defeating the rich through civil strife, killing, or exiling some but sharing the regime and the ruling offices on an equal basis with those who are left, with offices for the most part given by lot. An ambiguity lies at the heart of ancient democracy: the *demos* that rules means especially the many rather than all, the poor or common people rather than the whole people, but they share rule on an equal basis with the few or rich. The inclusive democratic principle of equality can be at odds with the exclusive rule of the *demos*, but if the poor or common people are many and the rich are few, an equal share in rule by vote or lot tends to result in the rule by the *demos* in the narrow sense.

But Plato also describes regimes less institutionally by what they regard as good, stating that democracies regard freedom as good. He accordingly attributes to democracies freedom and free speech, even license for all to live as they please, the absence of any compulsion to rule or be ruled, gentleness toward criminals, and the distribution of honor and office on the basis of favorable disposition toward the multitude, without any regard to upbringing or occupation. Plato judges each regime ultimately by its effect on the souls of its citizens, by the kind of individual it tends to produce. The individual most characteristic of democracy, Plato seems to say, lives on the basis of an equality of pleasures and desires without any order or necessity in his life. But that is the individual who resembles a democratic regime as a whole, not the actual individual citizens within a democracy. Plato says that democracies contain the widest variety of human types, presumably including the most excellent as well as the worst, the philosophical as well as the tyrannical.

After describing democracy and the democratic individual, Plato turns to describing how tyranny arises out of democracy (562a–566d). What are often quoted as Plato's harshest criticisms of democracy actually occur in this account of the degeneration of democracy into tyranny rather than in the preceding description of democracy as such. It is in this context that he argues that the insatiable desire for freedom destroys democracy and leads to tyranny. It supposedly leads to lack of obedience to rulers by the ruled, to parents by children, to teachers by students, to masters by slaves, and even to humans by beasts.[7] Democratic citizens end up, he says, "paying no attention to the laws, written or unwritten, in order that they may avoid having any master at all" (563d).[8]

This extreme democracy is transformed into tyranny through the interaction among its three classes: the rich who have become bankrupt and idle; the hardworking super rich; and the *demos* themselves, "all those who do their own work, don't meddle in affairs, and don't possess very much," who whenever they assemble constitute the most numerous and most sovereign class in a democracy (565a). Members of the first class usually become the leaders of the *demos*, confiscating the wealth of the second class to distribute some of it among the *demos* and to keep the greatest part for themselves. As class conflict intensifies, the *demos* set up one man as their leader who resorts to judicial murder of his enemies, hints at cancellation of debts and economic redistribution, establishes a bodyguard to protect himself from his enemies, and if not killed or exiled by his enemies, ends by becoming a complete tyrant who instigates continual wars, purges all the best elements in the city, and impoverishes and enslaves the *demos*. Thus the failure to moderate the democratic desire for freedom leads to its opposite for the *demos*.

The *demos* are therefore more the victim than the villain in Plato's sad story of the degeneration of democracy into tyranny. Plato does not encourage statesmen or citizens of a democracy to attempt to replace it with a superior regime; he frightens them into trying to prevent its degeneration into tyranny. He indicates that this can be done by such means as regulating the extravagance of the rich, letting contracts be at the contractors' own risk, promoting obedience to law, resisting the divisive appeals of demagogues, and moderating class conflict, especially through holding democracy to its principle of equality that includes rich as well as poor.

Plato's emphasis on the dangers of excessive freedom within democracy may, however, be a paradoxical part of his effort to soothe the multitude by diverting attention away from the graver opposite danger of democratic intolerance. Like other regimes, democracy threatens to kill those who would disturb the city's constitution; it punishes with dishonor, fines, and death whoever does not praise and blame the same things as the many; the many blame whoever seeks true intellectual freedom and would kill whoever tries to lead men out of the cave of opinion into the realm of truth (426bc, 492bd, 494a, 499d–500a, 517a). Plato does not attribute to democracies a scheme of public education like that of Sparta, but describes democratic education as a private or family affair.[9] Yet he doubts that any private education is likely to hold out against the experience of popular praise and blame obtained through participation in democratic assemblies, courts, theaters, and army camps (492b–492e).

Plato's focus in *The Republic,* however, is not on democracy or any other actual regime, but on what he considers the best regime, the rule of philosopher-kings, which is far from democratic. This regime consists above all in a scheme of public education designed to foster the moral virtues of courage, truthfulness, and moderation required by good citizens; the prudence, patriotism, and incorruptibility needed in good rulers; and the philosophic knowledge and virtue essential for good human beings. In this regime, education serves the requirements of politics, but ultimately, politics serves the highest kind of education. The best regime, however, is not meant to be universally actualized; on the contrary, it exists only in speeches, in heaven, or in the souls of human beings (592b). In Plato's more democratic, second-best regime of the rule of law, described in his *Laws,* a scheme of public education plays a similar dual role.

The distinction between moderate or healthy and extreme or degenerate democracy is clarified in Plato's *Statesman,* in which the Eleatic Stranger laments that there is only one term, *democracy,* for both the regime in which the many rule by law and with consent and the regime in which they rule without law and by violence, whereas the corresponding forms of rule by one or few are distinguished by different terms—kingship rather than tyranny, and aristocracy rather than oligarchy.[10] The Stranger suggests that because democracy divides power into small portions among many, it is not only the most tolerable of the lawless and violent regimes, but also the least tolerable of the lawful and consensual regimes. Yet his argument for the very rule of law that distinguishes among regimes is that a number of persons have carefully deliberated and persuaded the multitude to enact the laws, an argument that presupposes a regime more democratic than monarchic.[11] In Plato's *Laws,* the Athenian Stranger argues that although excessive liberty leads to lawlessness, the moderate liberty of the *demos* is essential for friendship and community, and that a good regime must mix the liberty and friendship of democracy with the prudence of monarchy.[12]

Aristotle's Mixed Polity

Aristotle's *Politics* offers a much more systematic treatment of democracy as a regime. Regimes or constitutions are not only different arrangements of and ways of distributing ruling offices, but different ends, ways of life, and conceptions of justice (III 6 1278b7–10, 9 1280a7–9, IV 1 1289a15–18, 11 1295a40–1295b1, V 1 1301a25–28).[13] Aristotle's basic typology of regimes is produced by the intersection of two distinctions: rule by one, few, or many and rule in the common interest versus rule in the private interest of the ruler. This yields six basic kinds of regime: the right regimes of kingship, aristocracy, and polity, and the wrong regimes of tyranny, oligarchy, and democracy (III 7 1279a22–1279b10). Aristotle characterizes democracy by its conception of justice as equality in the distribution of honor and office (though that equality is limited to the freeborn and not extended to slaves) and by its conception of liberty as doing whatever one wishes (III 9 1280a7–11, V 9 1310a28–38, VI 2 1317a40–b17). He thus uses the term *democracy* to denominate a bad regime, the rule of the many in their private interest rather than in the common interest. It would be misleading, however, to conclude that he was therefore simply antidemocratic. First of all, democracy is the least bad of the three bad regimes, the ones most commonly existing (IV 2 1289b2–5). Second, he uses another term, polity (*politeia,* the generic term for regime or constitution) to denominate a good regime, the rule of the many in the common interest. Although it is apparently inferior to kingship or aristocracy, he favors polity not only in contrast to what he calls democracy but as the best practicable regime for most political communities and perhaps even the simply best regime (IV 11, VII 14 1332b12–41). He argues that the many, each of them bringing his own share of virtue and prudence, may collectively surpass even the few best as judges in exercising sovereign power (III 11). We may be inclined to disregard Aristotle's terminology and consider him to be an advocate of good or healthy democracy ("polity") and a critic only of bad or degenerate democracy. But he differs sharply from any doctrinaire democrat who deems democracy as such to be good and the defects of any particular democracy to be only the results of its not being fully democratic. Aristotle encourages us to believe that democracy as the rule of the many can be either a good regime or a bad one.

Aristotle does not, however, only distinguish what he calls polity from what he calls democracy as right rule of the many from wrong rule of the many. He also presents polity as a mixture of democracy and oligarchy, a good regime resulting from the mixture of the two most common bad regimes (IV 8–9). Aristotle's dual definition of polity as both right rule of the many and a mixture of democracy with oligarchy exemplifies the enduring relationship between democracy and the mixed regime. The term republic and the related equivalents of *politeia* in Latin and Romance languages possess the same dual meaning of both rule by the people and mixed regime. The implication of Aristotle's dual definition of polity is that rule of the many as such (which we today might call democracy) is defective and needs to be mixed with rule of the few to remedy its defects. The democratic conception of justice as equality in the distribution of honor and office is defective (as is the oligarchic conception of justice as inequality on the basis of wealth) in its failure to recognize that political virtue has a superior claim to rule (III 9). Similarly, the democratic conception of liberty as doing whatever one wishes fails to recognize that living according to virtue and the law does not detract from liberty. Aristotle also makes the middle class the predominant element in the polity or mixed regime, so we could think of it as middle class democracy (IV 11–12). The predominance of the middle class introduces a kind of virtue. Whereas the rich tend toward hubris and unwillingness to obey and the poor toward excessive humility and slavish obedience, the middle class tend toward moderation and a willingness both to rule and to obey (IV 11 1295b1–34).

Aristotle's critical stance toward democracy as a defective regime in need of mixture with its opposite is not simply anti-democratic. He judges ultimately not by the standard of the good citizen of any regime but by that of the good human being. He criticizes *every* regime—each has its defects that can be remedied by mixture with elements from other regimes. Democracy seems to be more open than other regimes or even more inclined to mixture with other regimes. Furthermore, some of the models Aristotle offers for the mixture of democracy and oligarchy may seem to us more like familiar or feasible features of modern democracy than like archaic departures from democratic principle or practice. For example, whereas democracies select officials by lot without a property qualification and oligarchies do so by election with a property qualification, well-mixed polities would do so by election without a property qualification (IV 9 1294a36–b13). I am suggesting not that we should consider Aristotle's mixed regime as simply democratic, but rather that we might consider some of the features of what we currently think of as democracy to be instead a mixture of democracy with other regimes. Election, in particular, perhaps the most characteristic feature of modern democracy, is presented by Aristotle in contrast to democratic lot as oligarchic when it favors wealth and as aristocratic when it favors virtue (IV 7 1293b7–12). Only when election is conducted so as to approximate lot by selecting officials typical of the common people (usually in conjunction with short terms and term limits, VI 2 1317b17–25) should it be considered democratic in Aristotle's sense, rather than an attempt to include within democracy elements of oligarchy or aristocracy.

Aristotle's stance toward democracy is clarified by his sub-typology of the kinds of democracy. The most important distinction for him is between those kinds of democracy in which the law rules and those in which not the law but the multitude are sovereign, ruling by decree and swayed by demagogues rather than by the best citizens, who take the lead in lawful democracies. The people usually rule according to law since they do not have the leisure to assemble in constant session, unless or until the political community acquires revenues sufficient to enable them to do so (IV 4 1291b30–1292a10, 6 1292b25–1293a10). Aristotle is not an enthusiast of participatory democracy; the advantage of democracy is that its rulers are usually too busy to rule and therefore let the laws rule most of the time. The preoccupation of the people with their farms may leave the way open for tyranny (V 5 1305a18–21), but increased popular participation may also be a mark of the degeneration of democracy rather than a solution for its problems.

For Aristotle, the political art or science culminates in knowing what is simply the best regime, which he does not expect to become universal but considers as dependent on various social, geographical, and other conditions that are regarded as a matter of prayer. The political art or science also includes knowing the best regime for most communities, the best regime for a particular community, and how to preserve the regime of a given community (IV 1–2). The most practical parts of the *Politics*, Books V and VI, concentrate on that last task, preserving an existing regime. A prudent statesman cannot be expected to attempt to establish in his own community the simply best regime or even the best regime for most communities; he cannot even be expected to aim directly at establishing the best regime for his own community. His first job must be to preserve the present regime. According to Aristotle, however, the fundamental cause of regime change is the injustice of a regime, the inadequacy of its conception of justice, and its tendency to treat unjustly those who might prefer another regime and thereby drive them to revolution. Oligarchy thus tends to perish through oppressing the *demos,* and democracy tends to perish through oppressing the rich. The best way to preserve a given regime therefore turns out to be to moderate its tendency to take its principle to an extreme, to correct the inadequacy of its conception of justice, and to restrain its tendency toward injustice (V 1, 5–6, 8–9). Preserving a democracy, in particular, is not a matter of making it as democratic as possible, but rather involves such policies as seeing to it that the multitude is not excessively poor, through ensuring long-term prosperity and enabling the poor to start out in trade or farming rather than keeping them on the dole (VI 5). There turns out, therefore, not to be such a great difference between trying to preserve a given regime and trying to establish the best regime for that community. In particular, there turns out not to be such a great difference between preserving a democracy and turning it into a polity or mixed regime.

For Aristotle, the greatest means of preserving a regime is through education for that regime, for example, democratic education to preserve a democratic regime. Being educated for a regime, however, means learning to do not the things that please the partisans of that regime, but the things that maintain it (V 9 1310a12–36). Democratic education therefore would not be education for liberty, defined as doing whatever one wishes, but would approximate the education for virtue of a polity or even of the best regime. Aristotle's best regime, like Plato's, consists above all in a scheme of public education designed to foster the virtues not only of good citizens of that regime but of good human beings, virtues understood not merely as qualities supportive of the regime but as the perfection of the soul (III 4, VII 13–15, VIII 1). Education for virtues that preserve democracy leads to a concern for virtues that transcend democracy.

It is tempting to say that for Aristotle the best democracy is the least democratic, yet being faithful to the democratic principle of equality dictates inclusion of the wealthy and the middle class, a kind of mixture of regimes (IV 4 1291b30–38). Some of the aspirations of modern democracy, such as rule of law, rule by all rather than by one part, or elections in which the best man is supposed to win, may remind one of features of Aristotle's best democracy, his polity, or even his aristocracy. In their dedication to liberty, however, modern democracies resemble Aristotle's democracy rather than his polity or aristocracy, while their frequent preoccupation with security and prosperity rather than with virtue, and their related vast size, would make them in Aristotle's judgment not true political communities at all (III 9, VII 4–5). Also, their universalization of equality distinguishes them from any of Aristotle's regimes, in which slaves, women, and usually the foreign-born are excluded from political life.

Consideration of these ancient Greek understandings of democracy may lead us to ask whether modern democracies as well are liable to such possible defects as a tendency to distribute honor and office solely on the basis of equality or popularity; rule by popular decree and even mob violence and general lawlessness; intolerance and conformism; imperialism; privatism; oppression of the

rich or of whoever is seen as not being part of the people; dema-
goguery and eventual degeneration into tyranny; and conceptions
of equality and liberty that foster indifference to excellence. We
may also be led to hold modern democracies to the classical standards of democracy at its best: a willingness to teach and learn in
debate before taking action; a collectivity that surpasses even the
few best in deliberation by each bringing his own share of virtue
and prudence; rule of law as a product of popular deliberation; a
liberal tolerance and openness; encouragement of virtue through
distribution of office and honor on the basis of ability to benefit
the community; the flourishing of a fundamental diversity of
human types; a receptivity to elements of other regimes; and a liberty that fosters sentiments of friendship and community.

This consideration should also help us to distinguish clearly
between democracy as the rule by one part or class of the people
(the poor or common people) in their own interests and the rule
of every part or class of the people equally (including the rich and
those from famous families) in the common interests. The more
inclusive meaning can claim to be more democratic at the same
time that it approximates a mixed regime by incorporating oligarchy or even aristocracy within democracy. We should also be able
to distinguish more clearly between democracy as direct rule by the
people and as distribution of honor and office by the people.

Consideration of these ancient Greek understandings of democracy also enables us to distinguish among democratic equality as
equality before the law, which of course entails inequality between
the lawful and the lawless; equality as an equal share in rule; and
equality as only an equal share in distributing honor and office and
equal eligibility for honor and office, resulting in an unequal share
in honor and office, compatible with elective aristocracy. Similarly,
we can distinguish between democratic liberty as allowing complete
liberty to live as one pleases and as allowing only as much liberty as
is compatible with lawfulness and the virtues required for the
preservation of democracy.

Machiavelli's Tyrannical Imperial Republic

In his *Discourses on Livy*, Machiavelli is the first great modern advocate of republican government and defender of the multitude,

which he says has been "accused by all the writers" (I 58, 59, II 2, III 9).[14] He writes that "a people is more prudent, more stable, and of better judgment than a prince," that "governments of peoples are better than those of princes," and that "the people will be seen to be by far superior [to princes] in goodness and in glory." He argues that "the common good is not observed if not in republics," and he concludes that "a republic has greater life and has good fortune longer than a principality." Even in *The Prince*, which is often thought to be nonrepublican, he offers the Roman republic as *the* model.[15]

Even in the *Discourses*, however, Machiavelli is not exactly an advocate of democracy. First of all, he appears to adopt a version of the classical typology of regimes: he notes that the writers who in the opinion of many are the wisest say that principality, aristocracy, and a popular state are the good states, and tyranny, oligarchy, and license are the bad states (I 2). Each of the good states is so easily corrupted and so "similar to the one next to it," however, that "they easily jump from one to the other" and they can all be declared "pestiferous," or bearing a potentially fatal defect. He concludes, therefore, in favor of "one that shares in all" as firmer and stabler since "the one watches the other." Furthermore, in the *Discourses*, as in *The Prince*, Machiavelli actually employs a simpler dichotomy of principalities and republics instead of a version of the sixfold classical typology. By republics he means any nonmonarchic state, whether aristocratic, oligarchic, popular, licentious, or mixed, and it is republics rather than democracies in particular that he endorses over principalities in the *Discourses*.

The particular kind of mixed republic Machiavelli endorses in the *Discourses* is, however, more of a democratic than an aristocratic mixed republic, Rome rather than Sparta (I 3–6).[16] In the Roman republic, popular tumults and refusals to enlist in the army made it necessary from the start to satisfy popular desires at least partially. Later, the creation of the tribunes (officials who were elected in and presided over the plebeian assembly, who exercised a veto over the acts of consuls and other magistrates, and who could initiate prosecutions or legislation) provided an institutional way to frighten the nobles, suppress their pride and insolence, elicit a popular spirit among them, and induce them to act humanely toward the plebs, or common people. The Spartan kind of mixed republic, in which the nobles predominate, promises greater stability through satisfying the ambition of the nobles, while not stimulating the restless spirits of the plebs to demand more and more authority. The Roman kind of mixed republic, in which the people predominate, seems more reasonable: whereas the nobles desire to dominate, the people desire not to be dominated but to live in freedom. Machiavelli finally favors a more democratic republic, however, because to acquire and maintain a great empire, it is necessary to employ the people in war and therefore to accept the dynamism and instability entailed by satisfying their demands. And the only alternatives to successful expansion are being conquered by others, being compelled to acquire an empire without the ability to hold it, or falling prey to the "effeminacy" (presumably aversion to war) and division that result from prolonged peace. Machiavelli's democratic mixed republic is at least as imperial as Periclean democracy.

Although the mixed republic Machiavelli favors is more democratic than aristocratic, it is still far from being simply rule by the people. The people have a share in ruling and are represented by such institutions as the tribunes; they also get a share of the booty of empire, enjoy a measure of security from the assaults of the nobles, and relish the satisfaction of being able to take revenge on their enemies. The people are often manipulated, however, by the nobles for their own purposes through the skillful use of religion, rhetoric, and electoral and other devices (I 7, 13, 37, 47, 48, 51, 54, II 6, III 34, 49). Although modern democracies perhaps may be less manipulative, they too are not the simple rule of the many over the few but rather a complex set of institutions and incentives designed to produce a popular spirit among the rich and powerful and to provide the common people with security.

The people in Machiavelli's mixed republic are dependent on the leadership of princely or tyrannical individuals. Machiavelli argues that ordering or reforming a republic must depend on the mind of one individual who should "contrive to have authority alone" (I 9). He justifies the need for such a founder or reformer to take actions outside the order he seeks to found or reform, such as Romulus' murder of his brother, so as to achieve sole authority. His ambition is to be gratified, however, not through establishing a hereditary principality or tyranny, but through founding or reforming a republic. Though "one individual is apt to order, the thing is ordered to last long not if it remains on the shoulders of one individual, but rather if it remains in the care of many" (I 9). Machiavelli's formula is one to order, many to maintain.

The need for such princely or tyrannical men and means arises not only once at the founding, but repeatedly for reforming or refounding. Machiavelli frequently refers to the leaders of republics as "princes," and says that republics need new orders "every day" (I 49, III 49). For a republic to live long, it is necessary "to draw it back often toward its beginning," to restore esteem for virtue through fear (III 1). This can be done through some terrifying external danger, through the virtue of a citizen who rushes spiritedly to execute orders against the power of those who transgress them, through "excessive and notable" executions, or through the simple virtue of one man. One citizen who wants to do any good work in his republic by his authority must first "eliminate envy" (III 30). This can be achieved either through an accident that makes each individual face imminent death and "put aside every ambition and run voluntarily to obey him whom he believes can liberate him with his virtue," or through the deaths of the envious, either by natural causes or otherwise. Modern democracies often continue to incorporate such princely or tyrannical elements in their strong executives and emergency powers.[17]

Machiavelli recommends tyrannical policies as well as tyrannical leaders for republics. Republics distribute honors and rewards on the basis of merit, but people do not feel obligated for receiving what they think they deserve (I 16–18). Republics secure the common utility of not fearing for one's property, one's family, or oneself, but people do not feel obligated for not being injured. The problem with republics, in short, is that they are just, and justice is not appreciated. Machiavelli's implied solution is for republics to behave less justly, more tyrannically, so that the benefits they confer and the security they provide will be more appreciated and better defended.

Machiavelli's very endorsements of republics over principalities in the *Discourses* reveal the imperial and princely or tyrannical elements in his republicanism. The advantage of a well-ordered republic is that election provides "infinite most virtuous princes" (I 20). In the *Discourses,* as in *The Prince,* Machiavelli encourages his readers to understand virtue not in the classical way, as the perfection of the soul (which he never mentions), but as those qualities conducive to security and expansion, goals that he regards as threatened by that classical conception of virtue. He says that "a republic has greater life and has good fortune longer than a principality" because it can accommodate to the times by choosing which of its citizens to employ as princely leaders (III 9). The chapter that says "a people is more prudent, more stable, and of better judgment than a prince" ends up repeating the formula of one to order, many to maintain (I 58). The argument that the common good is only observed in republics depends on the view that the common good is the good of the many, which may "turn out to harm this or that private individual" and go "against the disposition of the few crushed by it" (II 2). Peoples have affection for republics because they expand more not only in dominion but also in riches and population. Individuals in republics seek to acquire and multiply those goods they believe they can securely enjoy once acquired; and they freely procreate children, confident that their patrimonies will not be taken away and that they are born free and can "through their virtue become princes." Thus, even the most liberal element of Machiavelli's republicanism, the reliance on security of life, family, and property to stimulate growth through the pursuit of private and public advantages, is interwoven with imperial expansion and princely aspiration.

Machiavelli's famous call for the conquest of fortune[18] laid the groundwork for the modern expectation that the best regime, understood to be republican or democratic, should become universal instead of depending on rare chance favorable conditions. He presents republican government as dependent on a social structure of equality, the absence of a class of gentlemen who live in leisure and have subjects who obey them. He regards that social precondition, however, not in Aristotelian fashion as a matter of prayer, but as a condition that a man "rare in brain and authority" can bring about by eliminating the class of gentlemen (I 55). In this way, Machiavelli prepares both some of the greatest horrors of our century (against which his understanding of virtue offers us no defense), committed in the name of eliminating those classes regarded as impediments to equality or the right order, and our common expectation that in the process of modernization, democracy should and will become universal.

Locke's Liberalism

Machiavelli inspired a modern neoclassical tradition of seventeenth- and eighteenth-century political thought that celebrated republics for their promotion of the common good, preservation of liberty, and cultivation of virtue.[19] Like Machiavelli, this tradition tended to be more democratic and less aristocratic (though not always less monarchic) than Plato or Aristotle, and to define virtue as the qualities supportive of the common good, understood as prosperity and security of life, family, and property, rather than to define the common good in the classical way as the cultivation of virtue, understood as the perfection of the soul. This tradition did try, however, to establish a higher moral tone than Machiavelli's emphatic republican imitation of tyranny.

The eighteenth-century Anglo-American form of neoclassical republicanism combined republican politics with the principles of Lockean liberalism.[20] Although whether or to what extent Locke advocated a republican or democratic form of government remains controversial, he certainly developed many of the fundamental principles of liberalism that distinguish modern liberal democracy from ancient democracy.[21] These principles include the natural liberty and equality of human beings; rights to life, liberty, and property; government by consent; limited government; rule of law; supremacy of society over government; and the right of revolution.

The fundamental hypothesis of Locke's *Second Treatise of Government* is what he calls the state of nature, his claim that all human beings are naturally in a condition of freedom and equality. Thus, it is supposed that by nature human beings are free to act, constrained only by their own reason (the dictates of which Locke called the law of nature) and not by the will of any other human being (I 67, II 4, 6).[22] This hypothesis contrasts sharply with Aristotle's view that human beings are by nature members of a political community and that natural inequalities subordinate some human beings to be ruled or even enslaved by others.

Since adult human beings are by nature free and equal, for Locke all rightful political power exists only by consent, and governments that do not enjoy the consent of the governed are not entitled to obedience (II 95, 104, 134, 189, 192). Thus, the origin or basis of government, as distinguished from the form of government, is democratic: the consent of all the members of society. This contrasts with any justification derived from conquest, as well as with the classical view that superiority in wisdom or virtue carries with it a right to rule (II 54, 70). By consenting to membership in a society, individuals give up the liberty they enjoyed there only as far as is necessary to preserve themselves and the other members of society (II 87–89, 129–130).

Locke regards the end of government as the protection of the lives, liberties, and properties of all the members of society as far as possible (II 88, 123, 131, 134, 159). He defines the public good as "the good of every particular member of that society, as far as by common rules, it can be provided for" or "the preservation of every man's right and property" (I 92). Thus, not only the basis but the end of government, as distinguished from its form, is democratic, securing the rights of all the members of society. Governments may deprive individuals of life, liberty, or property only as required by that end, and may protect individuals only from violation of those rights by others, not from their own negligence or prodigality (II 131, 135).[23] This limited end of government is the heart of modern liberalism that makes modern democracy liberal democracy. It contrasts sharply with classical and medieval conceptions of the end of government as the improvement or salvation of souls, the punishment of vice or sin, the propagation of the truth, or the glorification of God, as well as with Periclean or Machiavellian emphasis on human glory.

Although the end of government, according to Locke's *Second Treatise*, is the protection of rights rather than education toward virtue, Locke is directly concerned in other works with education for liberty, and therefore with teaching the virtues required to make human beings able and willing to avoid both tyranny and slavery. In *An Essay Concerning Human Understanding*, he argues against the doctrine of innate ideas, which he regards as a justification for subservience to prejudice, superstition, and intellectual tyranny. He encourages his readers to question the opinions others would impose on them by authority and to refrain from imposing their own opinions on others by authority.[24] In *Some Thoughts Concerning Education*, he shows how children could be educated in the virtues necessary in a free society: civility, liberality, humanity, self-denial, industry, thrift, courage, truthfulness, and justice as respect for the rights of others. These virtues, reminiscent of those of Aristotle's middle class, are to be inculcated not through coercion but above all through appealing to love of liberty, pride in human rationality, and a sense of what is suitable to the dignity and excellence of a rational creature.[25]

Lockean liberalism limits the power as well as the end of government (II 131, 135–140, 221–222). Government may not possess absolute arbitrary power over the lives and property of the people. This follows from the limitation of end: a power given for the end of preserving its subjects' life, liberty, and property cannot be used to destroy, enslave, or impoverish them. Government may not rule by decree, without promulgated laws and authorized judges; rule of law distinguishes civil society from a state of nature in which the law of nature is unwritten and unrecognized by human beings swayed by passion and interest. Nor may government take any part of one's property without one's consent, which Locke equates with the consent of the majority or their representatives. This limitation inspired the American Revolutionary slogan of "no taxation without representation."[26]

One of the most obviously democratic elements of Locke's political theory is that once individuals have consented to government, political power belongs to the people acting by majority decision, constituting what Locke calls "a perfect Democracy," unless or until they establish another form of government (II 95–99, 132). Even in a form of government other than direct democracy, political power should be ultimately derived from democratic action. The people acting through the majority are prior and ultimately superior to the government. Locke, however, avoids saying that the people are sovereign; the limitations he sets on the end and power of government limit even the people, and counter any doctrine of sovereignty understood as absolute arbitrary power. So, in a liberal democracy the end and power of democratic government are limited.

Locke's principles of government by consent with limited end and power and ultimate popular supremacy laid the ground for liberal constitutionalism. By majority decision, the people establish the form of government by a voluntary grant which Locke calls the original constitution (II 134, 141, 153–158). He establishes the basis of the position that a constitution is paramount over ordinary laws on the grounds that it is prior to them, it authorizes the legislature to make them, and it is the act of the people themselves rather than of the legislature. Locke is a constitutionalist rather than a populist in that, for him, once the people delegate their authority through the constitution to the authorities it constitutes, they do not resume that authority as long as that constitution and government last (II 168, 243). Locke is not, however, a doctrinaire constitutionalist in that he recognizes that the uncertainty and variableness of human affairs may prevent the framers of a government from settling important questions in the original constitution by a steady fixed rule and compel them to entrust such matters to the prudence of later governors (II 156).

Locke propounds what we may call democratic conceptions of the basis and end of government, and limited and constitutional conceptions of the powers of government, as universal criteria of the legitimacy of government, but he does not require a simply democratic form of government. His political theory is concerned less with sketching a best form of government in the fashion of Plato or Aristotle than with delineating the basis and limits of government and thereby distinguishing legitimate governments that subjects are obligated to obey from illegitimate ones they are entitled to resist. His claim (II 132) that the majority may consent to a democracy, an oligarchy, a monarchy, or a mixed form, as they think good, seems to suggest almost an indifference to forms of government, the central subject matter of classical political philosophy. Allowing the majority to consent to the form of government they think good might seem both more democratic and less democratic than insisting that they establish a democracy and regarding any other form of government as illegitimate.

But Locke allows the majority less latitude in choosing a form of government than first appears. First, he rules out absolute monarchy as inconsistent with civil society, since uniting all legislative and executive power in one man leaves him still in the state of nature with those under his dominion (II 90–94). Second, the rule of law requires that the same persons should not have in their hands the legislative and executive powers, that the legislature should include a number of persons, and that it should be supreme over the executive (II 134, 143, 150). Third, Locke's stipulation that government may not take property without the consent of the majority or their representatives effectively requires every form of government to include one democratic branch for purposes of taxation (II 138–140, 142, 213, 221–222). Indeed, the breadth with which Locke sometimes uses the term "property" (including life and liberty) suggests that all legislation may require the consent of a representative body (II 87, 192, 221). Thus, while Locke does not insist on a government composed entirely of democratic elements, he does require that whatever form of government the majority establishes in the original constitution must include at least one representative democratic component.

Although Locke's conception of civil society requires the supremacy of a legislature with a number of persons and the rule of law, there are nonetheless monarchic and extralegal elements in Lockean government. Where the executive shares in the legislative power (as the English monarch then did and the American president still does through the veto), Locke allows that the executive may also be called supreme (II 151–152). Locke also argues that since it is impossible to foresee and provide by law for all accidents and necessities, the good of the society requires that many things be left to the discretion of the executive to be ordered for the public good, both where law is silent and sometimes even against the law (II 156–168). This monarchic doctrine of executive prerogative is in tension with legislative supremacy and even with the rule of law, but it remains within a legal and popular framework, for the people may judge whether the exercise of such prerogative tends toward their good, and may if necessary limit it through laws passed by the legislature.

In addition to the legislative and executive powers familiar from later versions of the theory of the separation of powers, Locke also discusses what he calls the "federative" power, the power over war and peace, leagues and alliances, and all transactions with persons and communities outside the commonwealth (II 145–148). The executive and federative powers are almost always united in the same hands since they both involve control over the armed force of the society. Although the executive power is in itself subordinate to the legislative power, the federative power must be left to the prudence of those whose hands it is in. The actions of foreign powers, unlike those of subjects, cannot be directed in advance by general laws; foreign policy must instead flexibly take account of the varying actions, designs, and interests of foreign powers. Executive prerogative and "federative" discretion constitute monarchic qualifications of the democratic tendencies of Lockean government.

Lockean liberalism is democratic in a more fundamental respect. Although the legislative is the supreme power within any form of government, it is given by the people as a trust to be employed for their good, and they retain the supreme power to remove or alter it when used contrary to that trust (II 149, 171, 221–222, 240). This supremacy of the people or society over the government or state is expressed ordinarily in the election of representative legislative bodies and ultimately in the right of revolution. Transgression of its limits dissolves a government and the obligation of its subjects to obey it. Political power reverts to the society acting through its majority, which must remove the offending rulers and establish a new government before society itself dissolves (II 220).[27] The people must be sure that the violated right is worth the trouble and cost of vindicating it and therefore may well tolerate great mistakes and even many wrong and harmful laws or overlook the oppression of one or a few unfortunate individuals. However, if acts of injustice or oppression extend to the majority or to a few individuals in such a way that the precedent and consequences seem to threaten all, resistance becomes a moral necessity (II 168, 205, 208–210, 225, 230). This justification of resistance was echoed by Thomas Jefferson in the Declaration of Independence.

American Democracy

The Declaration of Independence affirms the fundamental principles of Lockean liberalism, including human equality; individual rights to life, liberty, and the pursuit of happiness; the end of government as the securing of those rights; the derivation of the powers of government from consent of the governed; and the right of the people to alter or abolish any government that becomes destructive of these ends and institute new government on such principles and in such form "as to them shall seem most likely to effect their Safety and Happiness." It thus accepts Locke's both more and less democratic position of allowing the people to establish the form of government that they think good, instead of insisting that they establish a democracy and regarding any other form of government as illegitimate. Like Locke, the Declaration of Independence also rules out absolute despotism or tyranny and asserts the popular right of representation in the legislature as "a right inestimable to them, and formidable to tyrants only." Thus, it also requires that whatever form of government the people establish must include at least one representative democratic component.

American political leaders had inclined to accept the British mixed constitution of king, lords, and commons as more or less consistent with the fundamental principles of human equality, individual rights, and popular consent, until the outbreak of armed conflict and the ensuing decision for independence made practically inevitable a republic without a hereditary monarchy or aristocracy. Thomas Paine's *Common Sense,* published in January 1776, was probably the first public systematic rejection of monarchy and hereditary succession and call for independence and republican government, though without much explanation of the nature of that form. John Adams's *Thoughts on Government,* written in January and published in April 1776, announced that "there is no good government but what is republican."[28] Adams explains that whereas the end of man is the happiness of the individual, which consists in virtue, so the end of government is the happiness of society, which consists in ease, comfort, and security for the greatest number of persons in the greatest degree. He suggests that republics have virtue as their principle and foundation, and defines a republic as "an empire of laws, and not of men." He leaves unclear whether the essence of a republic is to "depute power from the many, to a few of the most wise and good," or to have a representative assembly that should be, "in miniature, an exact portrait of the people at large" and "think, feel, reason, and act like them." Adams does make clear that "Laws for the liberal education of youth, especially of the lower class of people, are so extremely wise and useful, that to a humane and generous mind, no expence for this purpose would be thought extravagant." He makes equally clear that republican government itself is a form of education that introduces knowledge among the people, inspires them with a conscious dignity befitting freemen, encourages a general emulation and elevation of sentiment that make the people brave and enterprising as well as sober, industrious, and frugal. Just how democratic the American republic would be, and whether any monarchic or aristocratic elements would be incorporated, remained to be determined.

Given that the Articles of Confederation were only "a firm league of friendship" rather than a government, the definition of the form of government for the American people as a whole did not come until the Constitution, for which *The Federalist* may serve as an authoritative guide.[29] *The Federalist* adheres to the fundamental Lockean principles of the Declaration that the consent of the people is the "original fountain of all legitimate authority" and that the people retain "the transcendent and precious right" to "abolish or alter their governments as to them shall seem most likely to effect their safety and happiness" (no. 22, p. 152; no. 28, p. 180; no. 40, p. 253; no. 43, p. 279; no. 49, p. 313; no. 78, p. 469).[30] It focuses, however, on how the people should exercise that right, on what sort of government they should consent to.

The Federalist distinguishes between republics and democracies, but that should not lead us to regard its republicanism as antidemocratic. Writing in *The Federalist,* Madison's distinction is that "in a democracy the people meet and exercise the government in person; in a republic they assemble and administer it by their representatives and agents" (no. 10, pp. 81–82; no. 14, pp. 100–101; no. 39, p. 241). These forms are two species of what he calls popular government. (This is in sharp contrast to most earlier usage that denominated as republics all nonmonarchic governments, including aristocracies and mixed governments.) His distinction might be reworded in our contemporary terminology as one between two kinds of democracy: direct and representative.[31] Madison insists that the proposed American republic is "wholly popular" and "unmixed," not a departure from democracy in the direction of monarchy or aristocracy or the classical or British mixed constitution. The electors of the federal representatives are "not the rich, more than the poor; not the learned, more than the ignorant; not the haughty heirs of distinguished names, more than the humble sons of obscure and unpropitious fortune." They are "the great body of the people of the United States." And the candidates are any citizens whose merits may recommend them to the esteem of their fellow citizens without any qualification of wealth, birth, religion, or profession (no. 57, p. 351).

The Federalist emphasizes the defects of (direct) democracies in part because (representative) republics are meant to cure them.

The "petty republics of Greece and Italy" were in "a state of perpetual vibration between the extremes of tyranny and anarchy," and their "momentary rays of glory" were "overwhelmed by the tempestuous waves of sedition and party rage" (no. 9, pp. 71–72; no. 14, p. 100; no. 28, p. 179). Instability, injustice, and confusion have been "the mortal diseases under which popular governments have everywhere perished" (no. 10, p. 77). Popular government enables a majority moved by a common passion or interest adverse to the rights of others or to the public good to have its way (no. 10, p. 80).

The inclusion of both republics and democracies within popular government does not mean that they differ only technically in the means by which the people govern. Representation need not be a simple equivalent of direct popular government. Its effect may be "to refine and enlarge the public views by passing them through the medium of a chosen body of citizens, whose wisdom may best discern the true interest of their country and whose patriotism and love of justice will be least likely to sacrifice it," so that "the public voice, pronounced by the representatives of the people, will be more consonant to the public good than if pronounced by the people themselves." When representation works in this way, it approximates what Aristotle means by calling election aristocratic. Conversely, its effect may instead be that "men of factious tempers, of local prejudices, or of sinister designs" betray the interests of the people (no. 10, p. 82).

The meaning of American representative democracy seems to hinge on the working of representation. For the interests and feelings of the different classes to be understood and attended to and for there to be true sympathy between the representative body and its constituents, it is not necessary to have actual representation of all classes of the people by persons of each class (no. 35, pp. 214–217; no. 57, pp. 350–353). *The Federalist* argues that such a mirroring representation ("a government that looks like America," we might say) can never happen under any properly republican arrangement that leaves the people free to vote for those who they think have the ability as well as the sympathy to effectively promote their interests. Such a mirroring is not necessary because it is natural that a person dependent on the votes of fellow citizens for continuance in office should learn about and be influenced by their dispositions and inclinations even if he does not share them. Not any shared class or group identity but this electoral dependence and the fact that the representatives are bound, along with their posterity, by the laws they make are the truly republican and strong "chords of sympathy" between representatives and constituents.

The fundamental maxim of republican government is that the sense of the majority should prevail (no. 22, p. 146); but that does not require "unqualified complaisance to every sudden breeze of passion" of a popular majority (no. 71, p. 432). On the contrary, it requires only that "the cool and deliberate sense of the community" ultimately prevail over the views of its rulers, who must therefore resist the "temporary errors and delusions" of their constituents (no. 63, p. 384; no. 78, pp. 469–70). Republican government thus makes it possible for "the reason, alone, of the public . . . to control and regulate the government," while their passions are "controlled and regulated by the government" (no. 49, p. 317). This ideal of republican rule of reason over passion is far, however, from implying the achievement of uniformity through the suppression of diversity. Its expression was promptly followed by the statement, "When men exercise their reason coolly and freely on a variety of distinct questions, they inevitably fall into different opinions on some of them," whereas only "when they are governed by a common passion" will their opinions be the same (no. 50, p. 319; see also no. 10, p. 78).

Republican government thus presupposes a portion of wisdom, patriotism, love of justice, courage, and magnanimity among the government sufficient to discern the right course and withstand popular pressure (no. 10, p. 82; no. 71, p. 432). It also presupposes sufficient good sense among the governed for their errors to be only temporary, so that "reason, justice, and truth can regain their authority over the public mind" upon "more cool and sedate reflection" (no. 63, p. 384; no. 71, p. 432). In short, republican government is a political experiment that requires us to "view human nature as it is, without either flattering its virtues or exaggerating its vices," and rests upon "the capacity of mankind for self-government" (no. 39, p. 240; no. 55, p. 346; no. 76, p. 458).

Republics differ from democracies not only in the use of representation but in "the greater number of citizens and greater sphere of country" and therefore the greater diversity of interests representation makes it possible to include. Madison gives great weight to this diversity as "the best security, under the republican forms, for the rights of every class of citizen," making it less likely for a majority to coalesce on any other principles than those of justice and the general good or to have a common motive to invade the rights of other citizens (no. 10, pp. 82–84; no. 51, pp. 324–325).

The Federalist emphasizes the defects of democracies only in part to distinguish them from republics, for the defects of democracies are potentially those of republics as well. The "pleasure and pride we feel in being republicans" should lead us not to regard a republic as the perfect form of government, but to welcome the extent and structure of the union as "a republican remedy for the diseases most incident to republican government" (no. 10, p. 84). In The Federalist, Madison praises his friend Jefferson for his equal display of "a fervent attachment to republican government and an enlightened view of the dangerous propensities against which it ought to be guarded" (no. 49, p. 313). The Federalist presents a conception and a demonstration of democratic statesmanship that exemplify Aristotle's prudent statesman who corrects the defects of his regime.

The Federalist starts by invoking not republican or popular but "good government" (no. 1, pp. 33, 35). The Federalists, as the proponents of ratification of the Constitution called themselves, first appear in the papers as advocates of energetic, efficient government, accused, therefore, of being "hostile to the principles of liberty." Energy is far from incompatible with liberty, however: "The vigor of government is essential to the security of liberty . . . their interests can never be separated" (no. 1, p. 35). There are certain things any government, whatever its form, must be able to do if it is to be any good: collect taxes, enforce the laws, win wars, put down rebellions, and protect property. If a free or republican government is incapable of doing these things, it will not remain free or republican for long. Advocates of free or republican government must not only make sure that their government secures liberty or is strictly republican; they must make sure that it is a good government.

Good government must be powerful government. It must possess without limitation the powers essential to the common defense, including that of taxation, because foreign danger knows no limitation (no. 23, pp. 153–154, 156–157; no. 26, p. 168, 170; no. 30; no. 31, pp. 193–195; no. 34, pp. 207–209; no. 41, pp. 256–257).

Good government must also be smart government. Good government must not only be faithful to the object of government, the happiness of the people, but also know the means by which it can best be obtained (no. 62, p. 380).

Good government is especially bound up with able administration and an energetic executive. *The Federalist* declares that "the true test of a good government is its aptitude and tendency to produce a good administration" (no. 68, p. 414). Energy in the executive must also be "a leading character in the definition of good government," for the sake of protection against foreign attacks, steady administration of the laws, protection of property, and the security of liberty (no. 70, p. 423; no. 37, p. 226). Alexander Hamilton warns that "a government ill executed, whatever it may be in theory, must be, in practice, a bad government." Hamilton's ambitious single executive, moved by "the love of fame, the ruling passion of the noblest minds" (no. 72, p. 437), resembles Pericles, Machiavelli's princes, and Locke's prerogative-wielding executive. Madison reminds readers that "you must first enable the government to control the governed" (no. 51, p. 322). Hamilton expects a good government to be able also to undertake "liberal or enlarged plans of public good" and "extensive and arduous enterprises for the public benefit" (no. 30, p. 191; no. 72, p. 437).

Another crucial ingredient of good government is stability (no. 37, pp. 226–227; no. 62, pp. 380–382), which is needed for respect abroad and confidence at home. Stability both prevents the clever, enterprising, and moneyed few from reaping profits from constant change, and encourages prudent merchants, farmers, and manufacturers to engage in useful undertakings, great improvements, and laudable enterprises. Even the wisest and freest government needs the veneration time bestows to acquire stability and to have the prejudices of the community on its side (no. 49, p. 314).

One lesson we can learn from *The Federalist* is that democratic government does not exhaust the definition of good government, and that the effort to make our government democratic cannot exhaust the effort to achieve good government. The salience of energy and stability as ingredients of good government leads *The Federalist* to articulate the problem of American constitutional statesmanship as the effort to combine energy and stability with liberty and republican government (no. 26, p. 168; no. 37, pp. 226–227;

no. 63, p. 385). This effort appears most difficult because republican liberty seems to demand short terms of office and many officers, whereas stability requires long terms and energy requires a single hand. The American constitutional combination involves long terms for the executive, the Senate, and the judiciary, and a unitary executive. This combination recalls elements of Aristotle's mixed regime.

The Federalist also invokes free government, which appears for Hamilton and Madison to be exemplified, however imperfectly, by the nonrepublican British constitution (no. 9, p. 72; no. 53, pp. 331–332; no. 63, p. 389; no. 70, p. 429; no. 71, p. 435; no. 73, p. 444). Free government involves both political and civil liberty, that is, both the presence of at least one popular branch of government and the security of private rights under the rule of law. It also requires the separation of legislative, executive, and judicial powers, that is, the effectual prevention of the exercise of the whole of any one of those powers by the same body that exercises the whole of another, to protect the life and liberty of individuals from arbitrary control (no. 47, pp. 303–304, 308; no. 48, p. 308). *The Federalist* expects its readers to be devotees of liberty and free government as well as of popular government, to be liberals as well as republicans. They are expected, however, not to give way to a "zeal for liberty more ardent than enlightened," but to remember that power is as necessary as liberty and that "liberty may be endangered by the abuses of liberty as well as by the abuses of power" (no. 26, p. 168; no. 63, p. 387).

Free governments are not necessarily wholly popular, though the popular branch in a free but not republican government does tend to prevail (no. 58, p. 361; no. 63, p. 384, 389; no. 66, p. 403). Popular governments provide the political liberty involved in free government, but they do not necessarily secure civil liberty; they are therefore not necessarily free governments. Making a government more democratic does not necessarily make it more free.

The Federalist advocates not only good government, free government, and republican government, but constitutional government. Madison makes the "important distinction so well understood in America between a Constitution established by the people and unalterable by the government, and a law established by the government and alterable by the government" (no. 53, p. 331). This Lockean distinction is the essence of constitutional government. Hamilton defends the further implication that laws contrary to the constitution are void and can be declared so by the courts—the doctrine of judicial review (no. 78, pp. 467–469). He does so on the democratic ground that the people is superior to the legislature, and the constitution is made by the people, whereas the laws are made only by the legislature. His constitutionalism is not, however, simply democratic; judicial review serves to guard the constitution and the rights of individuals not only from a legislature that ignores the intention of the people, but also from the "ill humors" of the people themselves, though only until they give way to "better information, and more deliberate reflection," or until the people by "some solemn and authoritative act" amend or annul the constitution.

According to *The Federalist*, republican government is neither free from defects nor the only political feature to be sought. Statesmen and citizens must seek to ensure that republican government is also good government, free government, and constitutional government.

The Federalist resembles the Aristotelian statesman in its concern for remedying the defects of its own regime, and it reflects the classical concern with wisdom and virtue. It differs, however, from ancient practice and theory in its emphatic universalism. It begins by appealing to the philanthropy as well as the patriotism of the American people, to their concern for mankind as well as their own true interests and the public good (no. 1, p. 33). Hamilton holds out the possibility of America's vindicating the honor of the human race by teaching Europe moderation and challenging its claims to racial superiority and world dominion (no. 11, pp. 90–91). Madison hopes that American political innovations will benefit the whole human race, and he seems to look forward to the day when the peoples of Europe will shake off their yokes, overturn every tyranny in Europe, and rescue their rights from the hands of their oppressors (no. 14, p. 104; no. 46, pp. 299—300). *The Federalist*'s invocations of the principles of the Declaration of Independence remind us that the United States is the first of the modern democracies founded on explicitly universal principles of human equality, individual rights, and popular consent.

The Federalist's concern with the defects of democracy and

democracy's need for wisdom and virtue is not limited to Federalists such as Hamilton, whom Jefferson came to consider a "mono-
crat." Jefferson himself considers that "the natural aristocracy" of
virtue and talents, as opposed to the artificial aristocracy of wealth
and birth, is nature's way of providing "virtue and wisdom enough
to manage the concerns of the society," and that "that form of government is the best, which provides the most effectually for a pure
selection of these natural aristoi into the offices of government."
Democracies could "leave to the citizens the free election and separation of the aristoi from the pseudo-aristoi, the wheat from the
chaff. In general they will elect the really good and wise." He proposes a system of public education to seek out persons of "worth
and genius" from every condition of life and prepare them to
defeat the competition of wealth and birth for public trusts.[32] And
the Jacksonian Democrat (and founder of the American novel)
James Fenimore Cooper, in his work of political theory, *The American Democrat*, stresses the disadvantages of democracy, which he
prefers "on account of its comparative advantages, and not on
account of its perfection." He knows it has evils; great and increasing evils, and evils peculiar to itself; but he believes that monarchy
and aristocracy have more. He cautions that, "under every system it
is more especially the office of the prudent and candid to guard
against the evils peculiar to that particular system, than to declaim
against the abuses of others."[33]

This historical investigation is intended to question the view
that democracy is the sole political good, and to remind us that
democracy has its own defects. The dependence of democracy on
a portion of wisdom and virtue among both governors and governed dictates the need for education to prepare both statesmen
and citizens. Such education ought not simply to promote democracy or democratic qualities, but must remember that ours is a liberal constitutional democracy, and that democracy is not simply
the liberation of the people from the power or oppression of the
few, but a responsibility, even a burden for the people. One cannot understand virtue merely as those qualities that are useful to
society, or aim education at the promotion of the qualities needed
to preserve democracy. Thoughtful students ultimately want to
know that the qualities they are acquiring are needed not merely

to preserve their form of government but to improve their own souls. Education for wisdom and virtue does not simply serve democracy, but can be an end in itself.

Notes

1. This essay benefited from comments on an earlier draft from James Dunn, David Ericson, Paul Franco, Paul Friedrich, Francois Furet, Stephen Holmes, John Kenny, Jonathan Lear, Ralph Lerner, Bernard Manin, Peter Miller, Robert B. Pippin, John Ray, James Redfield, Richard Ruderman, John T. Scott, Cass Sunstein, and Eduardo Velasquez.

2. Parenthetical notes in this section are to the standard book and chapter numbers in Thucydides. On Thucydides' political thought, I am indebted to Clifford Orwin, *The Humanity of Thucydides* (Princeton, N.J.: Princeton University, 1994) and (also for Plato and Aristotle) Leo Strauss, *The City and Man* (Chicago: University of Chicago Press, 1964, 1977).

3. The Greeks tended to distinguish aristocracy, as rule of the best, excellent, or most virtuous, from oligarchy (literally rule of the few), as rule of the rich. In practice, oligarchies claimed to be aristocracies, and aristocracies included elements of oligarchy.

4. Edmund Burke, *Reflections on the Revolution in France,* edited by J.G.A. Pocock (Indianapolis, Ind.: Hackett, 1987), p. 68.

5. Compare Alexander Hamilton, James Madison, and John Jay, *The Federalist Papers,* edited by C. Rossiter (New York: New American Library, 1961), no. 9, pp. 71–72.

6. Parenthetical notes in this section are to the standard Stephanus numbers in *The Republic of Plato* (2nd ed.), translated by A. Bloom (New York: Basic Books, 1968, 1991).

7. Plato includes equality between men and women in this catalogue of the consequences of extreme democracy, but in that respect it resembles his best regime; compare 563b to 451d–457c and 540c.

8. *The Republic of Plato,* 563d.

9. But compare Plato, *Crito,* 50d.

10. Plato, *Statesman,* 291d–292a, 302d–303b.

11. Plato, *Statesman,* 300b.

12. Plato, *Laws,* 693b–e, 697cd, 698ab, 700a–701b, 701e.

13. The parenthetical notes in this section are to Aristotle's *Politics,* by book and chapter numbers, and where further specificity is necessary, the standard Bekker numbers included in most editions.

14. Although Machiavelli has been called a classical republican by many writers, this discussion will show that his republicanism is modern rather than classical. The parenthetical notes in this section are by book and chapter number to Niccolò Machiavelli, *Discourses on Livy,* translated by H. C. Mansfield and N. Tarcov (Chicago: University of Chicago Press, 1996).

15. Machiavelli, *The Prince,* translated by H. C. Mansfield, Jr. (Chicago: University of Chicago Press, 1985), Chapters Three, Four, and Five.

16. Compare Machiavelli, *The Prince,* Chapter Nine.

17. Harvey C. Mansfield, Jr., *Taming the Prince: The Ambivalence of Modern Executive Power* (New York: Free Press, 1989).

18. Machiavelli, *The Prince,* Chapter Twenty-five; see also, *Discourses* II 29 and III 9.

19. See J.G.A. Pocock, *The Machiavellian Moment: Florentine Political Thought and the Atlantic Republican Tradition* (Princeton, N.J.: Princeton University Press, 1975); Thomas L. Pangle, *The Spirit of Modern Republicanism: The Moral Vision of the American Founders and the Philosophy of Locke* (Chicago: University of Chicago Press, 1988); and Paul A. Rahe, *Republics Ancient and Modern: Classical Republicanism and the American Revolution* (Chapel Hill: University of North Carolina Press, 1992).

20. On recent scholarly efforts to dichotomize republicanism and liberalism and the resulting controversy, see Gordon S. Wood, *The Creation of the American Republic, 1776–1787* (New York: Norton, 1969); Ralph Lerner, *The Thinking Revolutionary: Principle and Practice in the New Republic* (Ithaca, N.Y.: Cornell University Press, 1987); Isaac Kramnick, *Republicanism and Bourgeois Radicalism: Political Ideology in Late Eighteenth-Century England and America* (Ithaca, N.Y.: Cornell University Press, 1990); Joyce Appleby, *Liberalism and Republicanism in the Historical Imagination* (Cambridge, Mass.: Harvard University Press, 1992); and David F. Ericson, *The Shaping of American Liberalism: The Debates over Ratification, Nullification, and Slavery* (Chicago: University of Chicago Press, 1993).

21. This discussion of Locke draws on my article on Locke for the *Encyclopedia of Democracy,* edited by Seymour Martin Lipset (Washington, D.C.: Congressional Quarterly Books, 1995), and other of my writings on Locke. See also, Ruth W. Grant, *John Locke's Liberalism* (Chicago: University of Chicago Press, 1987).

22. Parenthetical notes in this section are by treatise and section number of John Locke, *Two Treatises of Government,* edited by P. Laslett (Cambridge: Cambridge University Press, 1988).

23. See also, John Locke, *Epistola de Tolerantia/A Letter on Toleration,* edited by R. Klibansky, translated by J. W. Gough (Oxford: Oxford University Press, 1968), pp. 66, 90.

24. John Locke, *An Essay Concerning Human Understanding,* edited by P. H. Nidditch (Oxford: Oxford University Press, 1975), Ep. Ded. 6–7, I 4.22, III 5.16, IV 15.6, 16.1–4, 19.2, 20.4.

25. Nathan Tarcov, *Locke's Education for Liberty* (Chicago: University of Chicago Press, 1984).

26. See James Otis, "The Rights of the British Colonies Asserted and Proved," and [Samuel Adams?], "A State of the Rights of the Colonists," both quoting from *Two Treatises* II 135–142, in *Tracts of the American Revolution 1763–1776,* edited by M. Jensen (Indianapolis, Ind.: Bobbs-Merrill, 1967). pp. 26–27, 239.

27. See Nathan Tarcov, "Locke's *Second Treatise* and 'The Best Fence Against Rebellion,'" *The Review of Politics,* 1981, 43(2), 198–217.

28. John Adams, *Thoughts on Government.* In *The Founders' Constitution,* Vol. I, edited by P. B. Kurland and R. Lerner (Chicago: University of Chicago Press, 1987), pp. 107–110.

29. This treatment of *The Federalist* leans on *As Far as Republican Principles Will Admit: Essays by Martin Diamond,* edited by W. A. Schambra (Washington, D.C.: AEI Press, 1992), and on David F. Epstein, *The Political Theory of The Federalist* (Chicago: University of Chicago Press, 1984). The whole of this essay is indebted to the spirit of Diamond's teaching and writing.

30. Parenthetical notes in this section are to *The Federalist* by paper and page number in the Rossiter edition cited above.

31. Hamilton may have coined the phrase "representative democracy" as a synonym for republic; see Gerald Stourzh, *Alexander Hamilton and the Idea of Republican Government* (Stanford, Calif.: Stanford University Press, 1970), p. 49.

32. Letter to John Adams, October 28, 1813, in *The Portable Jefferson,* edited by M. D. Peterson (New York: Viking Press, 1975), pp. 534–535. For the thoughts of Jefferson and other American founders concerning education, see Lorraine Smith Pangle and Thomas L. Pangle, *The Learning of Liberty: The Educational Ideas of the American Founders* (Lawrence: University Press of Kansas, 1993).

33. James Fenimore Cooper, *The American Democrat* (Indianapolis, Ind.: Liberty Fund, n.d.), Author's Preface, "On the Disadvantages of Democracy," and Conclusion, pp. xxiv–xxv, 80–86, 243.

Chapter Two

Democracy, Nurturance, and Community

Donna H. Kerr

I have some prickly things to say, and I will say them in ways that offend even my own academic philosopher's ear. The problem, for me, is that they cannot be said by doing what I usually do: sort out the arguments, identify their historical antecedents, write on a yellow legal pad the points that would need to be established in each paragraph, and follow my plan to its tight, inexorable conclusions. Arguments of that sort simply cannot convey what needs to be said. The topic is too fundamental, too important, too laden with moral meaning, too uncharted, too rich to fit on my old legal pad. Instead, I must resort to stories and metaphors. Occasionally, I shall willingly, knowingly violate a cardinal rule of academic writing: I will say some things of a personal nature, and I will feel exposed, vulnerable. These would be utterly silly things to do if my purposes were purely academic.

In 1973, I took a position as an assistant professor; five years later I wore the rank of full professor. In 1983, I accepted the position of academic vice provost of the university. Highly organized, politically adept and pleased to be so, somehow always focused and energetic, clear of purpose, and persuaded of the importance of my work, I was able to assume responsibility for, coordinate, and carry to successful conclusions projects of extraordinary complexity.

Then, in 1985, a curious thing happened. I hesitate to tell it, for fear that you will label what I have to say as a women's issue. If you do that, you will be dead wrong. Nor should what I say be misconstrued to be somehow against men. I myself grew up culturally male. I loved sports and played on the boys' teams until it was disallowed. I excelled at mathematics and science. It was not uncommon for me to be the only woman in philosophy courses at Columbia University. I sometimes just fell into and sometimes sought leadership positions, which I undertook with confidence, toughness, and great pleasure. And yes, what I am about to tell you is something that in one sense happens only to women, but if you focus on that fact, you will entirely miss the point of this paper.

After many years of deciding not to have children, my husband and I changed our minds. I became pregnant, and eight months later our daughter was born—eight months, not nine. There remained on my desk, piled high but well-organized, a full month's work to be completed prior to the baby's birth. The amniotic sac had torn, but I resisted the birth for three days while I conducted business by telephone from my hospital bed between and even during labor pains. This was the first time in my life that I had collided head on with a project that could not be put in a file folder or delegated. There was simply no way to set it aside until the time was right. There I was, almost forty-two, for the first time feeling directly, unavoidably, the crushing weight of my fundamental misunderstanding. How could I have lived so long and have become so successful in a world of intellectual and political acumen and yet so basically have misunderstood the requirements of nurture?

I am not talking here of the traditional tasks women have shouldered in the rearing of children. The issue is one of where and when one human being can nurture another. It can take place only in the concreteness, the immediacy, of a particular time and place, in a particular moment of a particular life, within particular human relationships. If nurture admits of design, it does so only vaguely. It can never be done by policies or other directives. Nor does one nurture another in the way one might program a computer. Nor can legislative decrees and institutional reshuffling nurture children, as perennial, doomed efforts to remake our society by reforming our schools attest. Nurture demands more—and less. It is possible only where one life meets another, and then only beyond the grasp of nurture's nemesis, domination.

Nor am I preparing a paean to the family. Adults using children for their own purposes, compulsions, and other private or domestic forms of domination can just as surely visit harm near the hearth as can tyrants at large in the state and market. That is, the antidote to the dominating rules and roles of our public lives is not to simply yield to private lives.

To understand the requirements of nurture, we shall need to make a map. From where I stand, the forest is dark and deep. In a clearing, rays of light illuminate only a few things. One is that we understand well many forms and techniques of domination. Numerous writings and practices, from the works of Machiavelli to institutional means for labeling people, attest to our powerful insights into how to dominate others. Happily, the liberal democratic tradition has evolved as a shield against domination. The liberal line that "you may not unjustifiably interfere in my life" sets you and me apart as potential combatants, neither one of whom is to be allowed to dominate the other on specified grounds (for example, race and sex) that have evolved historically. (Notice that on grounds on which some dominate others, such as property, liberalism remains silent.) Unhappily, however, liberalism does not know what to do when politically incorrect domination has legally been ended.

Liberalism does not help us understand how to nurture our own lives, or the lives of others. Put another way, liberalism can help us see our way clearly to fight the evils of politically identified domination. For example, I may justifiably interfere with your activities if they keep me from getting a job because I am a woman. Liberalism cannot, however, help us know how to cultivate meaning in our lives, how to nurture ourselves and others.

The noninterference rules of liberalism are designed to keep us out of one another's reach. To find nurture, we must be concerned instead about how one person's presence is essential to another's developing a sense of self—a presence that if tainted by any measure of domination may deeply harm the other person's prospects for psychological wholeness and moral agency. Further, liberalism cannot by itself help us decide when a form of domination or "interference" should be regarded as unacceptable. Nor can liberalism by itself require any one of us to offer nurture to another. Instead, as Rawls's *Theory of Justice* exemplifies, it can only wish that somehow, somewhere, we all have been nurtured.[1] To get on with the task of mapping the requirements of nurture, we shall have to avoid the underbrush of this liberal fantasy.

In the darkness, we sometimes countenance activities that could never survive in the light of day. We allow it to be proclaimed, for example, that the focal purpose of our schools, presumably nurturing institutions, should be to prepare the young for the "information age," to train participants in a democratic society, or to make the nation economically competitive. Much as some would use children for adult purposes, so too we often fail to see the evil in using schools as instruments for such miscast "ultimate" purposes. Such purposes must be abandoned as ultimate. They cannot be morally ultimate, because they can be at most only instrumental to and not constitutive of our selves. By treating such external purposes as if they were morally ultimate, we visit harm upon our children and upon one another. If information technologies, democracy, or the economy are to have any moral meaning, it can only be in the context of the nurture of ourselves and one another, for nurture is morally primitive. Morally, technologies, democracy, and the economy can be no more than instruments. If our schools are to have moral meaning, they can do so only as instruments for the nurture of our children.

Here in the dense forest where we must travel, others have already in some measure mapped the character and forms of domination, but we collectively know little of the nature and conditions of nurture. Sometimes nurture takes place, sometimes it does not. We are commonly hard pressed to discern the difference. It has something to do with love, but then domination sometimes masquerades in the cloak of love. Nurture seems somehow related to caring, but then well-intended acts undertaken in the name of caring can damage persons—witness: "This hurts me more than it hurts you," or "I'm doing this for your own good."

As I think about nurture, old maps that chart other features of the terrain evoke questions and seem confounding. If others' efforts are indeed essential to our development as selves (if, as Alasdair MacIntyre put it, we are "co-authored"[2]), how can the noninterference, low-obligation doctrine of liberalism be helpful? Nurture seems connected to concern, but that connection has been severed in our expressing concern as curricular and in other "solutions" to our children's lives. Nurture has something to do with listening carefully to each others' stories, but how can we even begin to listen through the noise of our own narratives, which are born in part as defenses against cruelties—born in part of our not having been nurtured so well ourselves. Are we even capable of not wreaking evil as we attempt to nurture others?[3] Just listening to one another will surely not be enough. Family and community would seem to have something to do with growing souls, but families and communities can and do commonly stunt the development of selves. As a broader context, a political or even economic democracy may be, generally speaking, a favorable condition for cultivating lives, but it does not by itself provide the conditions for nurturing selves.

So, how then can we understand nurturance? What follows is intended to be less definitive than suggestive. The philosophical and psychological expanses of the topic, in addition to its moral undergrowth, suggest that mapping nurture will require a much greater exploration than I can attempt here. As I gaze into the dense forest at this complex, sometimes treacherous terrain, I stand humbled and grasping for courage to set out. I shall be pleased if my trek maps a few major features.

What There Is to Nurture

I remember once looking into the mirror on the door of a medicine chest that was, unbeknownst to me, slightly ajar. My God, I was not there. Even though it was early in the morning and I was not fully awake, the experience sent a swift and icy chill through my being. While the reason for my "absence" became apparent just as quickly as I had disappeared, the horror of the memory can still send a shudder through my soul.

What possibly could be so horrific about looking in a mirror and not seeing oneself? Let us engage in a small thought experiment. Imagine that you have accepted an offer of some treatment that will render you invisible to yourself in all mirrors, though when others look in your direction they will still be able to see you. Here I have in mind not optical mirrors, but social mirrors. That is, when you feel pain, no one will acknowledge your discomfort. When you feel ebullient, no one will smile back. When you grieve, no one will acknowledge your loss. When you report what you experience on reading a poem, no one will acknowledge your report, much less your experience. Others talk only of their own experiences and the facts of matters. And so on, surely ad nauseam.

If you are confident that you will once again become visible, and if this demonic experiment does not exceed your amusement, you may walk away unscathed, save for the memory of an unpleasant, jolting invisibility. That is, you may still be there. If you imagine, however, that such a fate will endure until your death, your future is most likely doomed. That with which you touch the world—your experience of the world—is lost. Your self, your soul, is lost.

Now, thank goodness such hypothetical cases, which philosophers are so prone to invent, are just that: hypothetical. Sadly, however, affronts to the self abound in schools and other institutions. Students are subjected to instructional packages that tell them how to regard what they see. For example, "Here is a dogfish. Look at the anatomical chart to see where everything is inside, cut it open to identify all the parts, and fill in names of the various parts on your worksheet as you find them." This, dear student, will be your experience of a dogfish. Actually, student, your experience is irrelevant. What matters here are the facts of the dogfish and that you learn them. We are talking about zoology. This is science! Thoughts of selves and souls are irrelevant. But could one perhaps take a few minutes to observe a dogfish in the water, or even to just encounter one washed onto a beach? Could one just watch for a time? Could one just mess around with it? Could one allow oneself to be curious, to somehow experience the dogfish? Dare a student but for a moment stand in awe of a dogfish? Dare a student poke around at the dead, split fish upon the beach, marveling at how things connect and trying to surmise why?[4]

Packaged dissections in zoology laboratories are commonplace, their educational "value" established. They are obviously highly efficient ways to teach the parts of a dogfish. They are also, I should add, excellent examples of how to forget that science is a human enterprise—an engagement that makes sense only if a single person's experiencing of a dogfish matters. One might protest, "But a single person's experience of phenomena does not make for scientific findings"; and the rejoinder may be that there is so much more to science than its "findings," and that such talk diverts us from the main point: if science must (no thoughtful researcher would countenance such tunnel vision) be conducted in denial of the self, then it is inherently immoral and should be banished. Morally, nothing is so primitive as acknowledging and respecting the self that has experiences; morally, nothing is so important as nurturing the self. Without a self, there can be no agency, hence no morality.

There may be no harder place to see, to comprehend this thing called the self or the soul, than in a society in which the computer metaphor, instrumental thinking, and consumerism prevail. Indeed, in contemporary America, the metaphor of the computer so pervades thinking that it rarely is given a second thought. Many otherwise serious cognitive scientists talk in computer language about the mind processing information, about how the mind can be programmed. So, reduced to a bundle of procedures, protocols, and programs, the self is no more than the intersection of information, skills, and abilities.[5] One might wonder: Well, what harm done? Science has always run on metaphors, yes? But the literal treatment of the metaphor bespeaks tragedy.

Thoughtful, sincere teachers in a highly respected private school who talk of students as computers to be programmed, and seemingly caring parents and a secretary of education who talk of programming children for the "information age," are not harmless. A mournful bell tolls when language forecloses consideration of "acts of meaning" or of the self that would shape, texture, and color the world in its own way. Without that art, we are left with the tragic realization that life is not worth living. Like John Stuart Mill as a young man, we are left groping for something or someone to save us. Coleridge rescued Mill.[6] Can we avoid the disaster that requires our being saved?

The computer metaphor of mind turns even more dangerous as it fades into the literal, powerful world of the market, in which people serve a dual purpose as instruments of production and consumption.[7] Here we find a Kantian nightmare. Instead of a world in which persons would always be treated as ends, as selves or souls, and never as means, we face the specter of a world in which persons are treated only as means and never as ends. Where the market is allowed to totally dominate our shared lives, we have only to return to our demonic thought experiment to imagine the horror;

but this time we would not be totally invisible. We would see something mirrored back, but only our experiences as they would enhance production and consumption. Any shaping, texturing, or coloring of experience would fall under the purview of the corporate divisions of worker motivation and Madison Avenue.

The art of living would be reduced to the arts of worker motivation and advertising for consumption. Visions of product-design teams so totally defined by their work that they sleep on office cots and images of social gatherings designed to sell plastic containers for the household, of greeting cards that "express your true feelings," of tours that package the sites of the world, and of corporate sponsorship of museum exhibits are early warning signs of a society becoming gradually more hostile to the soul. In such a world, it is ever harder even to see one's own self. In this Kantian nightmare of a "real" world, where there is nothing of serious import to nurture, the very notion of nurture is either marginalized as "maybe nice, but not necessary" or subverted as programming for instrumental purposes.

It is so easy to be misunderstood when one talks against a totalitarianism of the market. Do I not understand that a strong market increases the standard of living and so makes a "better" life possible? Yes, I appreciate the role of a vibrant economy in augmenting our material lives. However, the market must be placed in the context of a civic society if it is to make sense for human purposes. That discussion will come, but first, we need to think a bit more about the character of the self or soul.

The Nature of the Self

In *Lost in Translation,* Eva Hoffman tells of having moved with her family at age thirteen from Cracow, Poland, to Vancouver, British Columbia.[8] The loss, while somehow related to geography and climate, had more to do with moving from hearing and speaking Polish to hearing and speaking English, from an apartment building filled with familiar cooking aromas and voices to the less obvious human connectedness of a suburban house, from music warmed by particular human relationships to a colder music of performance before strangers. In the "translation," it was not Hoffman herself who was lost. It was, instead, the familiar mirroring of her self. Her piano teacher, the housekeeper, her friends, her family's neighbors, the aromas and language through which lives connected—Hoffman still held these in her being. The self nurtured through these other lives did not disappear. Hoffman held securely in her memory those with whom her self was constituted; but in her new land there were no mirrors in her presence that would reflect back the immediate strangeness of it all, that would reflect back the pain of having left Cracow, that would reflect back the awkwardness and inadequacies of her new tongue.

The pain, the awkwardness, the inadequacies Hoffman had to experience as the "stranger in a strange land" placed her in isolating loneliness. She became the consummate clinical observer, standing outside of the new world she observed. While this may be an ideal position for certain "scientific" endeavors, it is an impossible place for the soul to flourish. Removed from the old mirrors of her experience and not yet having learned to express her experience in ways that would be visible or comprehensible to others, Hoffman's reflection of her new experiences was simply not available in translation.

Eva Hoffman would not, nor could any of us, emerge in the new culture the same person, but her experiencing, expressive self survived and thrived. (Doubtless there are scars.) Circumstances have not been so kind to all who have experienced a clash of cultures.[9] Consider the Tlingit Indians of what is now Southeast Alaska, whose civic society was radically diminished by the arrival of a U.S. territorial government, schools of the Bureau of Indian Affairs (BIA), and the Presbyterian Church. The content and purposes of the government's and church's schools, for example, reflected a culture and language that did not mirror life as the children experienced it at home. Such young souls so relegated to marginality sometimes survived, sometimes not.

The scenes from early in the twentieth century in the Mt. Edgecombe BIA School and in Sheldon Jackson School in Sitka, Alaska, and the great efforts to "correct" the young Tlingit and other native children reminds me of Richard Rodriguez, in his autobiographical *Hunger of Memory*, sitting in the British Museum trying to write a dissertation.[10] Incredibly able academically, fully equipped with all intellectual instruments for producing a reasonable dissertation, he sat there. Yet he could not and would not write it. He walked out the door, never to return to the project. Wildly and successfully "adjusted" to the expectations of an academic world divorced from life as he had experienced it as an outsider both in his Mexican-American home and in school, and highly skilled in the ways and arguments of the academic world, Rodriguez was programmed to cocktail-party perfection. Yet the packaged learning at which he had become so successful could not give meaning to his life.

To be sure, many things Rodriguez learned could be instrumentally useful to him in the marketplace and in giving expression to what his experience might mean to him, but these academically honed instruments could not themselves provide for artful living, for living in ways that render meaning in his own life. As Rodriguez learned, such tools themselves cannot enable one to write a dissertation that makes sense to oneself. The expectations of his Catholic schools mirrored back not life as Rodriguez experienced it—not his fears, his longings, his pain, his joy—but a notion of how life "ought" to be experienced. Likewise, the Tlingit students in government and church schools looked in the mirror and saw reflected only "corrected" selves, who were supposed to feel gratitude instead of pain, and so could apparently not trust the feelings of their own "defective" experiences.

It would be a nightmare to look into a mirror and see nothing reflected back. Such was the horror of the earlier thought experiment. Perhaps even more destructive of the self would be to look into the mirror and see an image that distorts oneself. If, in a revised demonic experiment, you gazed into the mirror and saw yourself as a defective, marginal person, needful of correction, you would be less likely to survive, your soul more likely to be colonized. Imagine for a moment that what you experience has nothing to do with "reality" as you know it. Your life could have no meaning. Your self could not grow, much less flourish.

Historically, many dominated persons have in fact been able to avoid destruction of the soul. A glimpse at one view of how this could happen may cast light on the nature of the self. In *Domination and the Arts of Resistance,* James Scott talks of the importance of the "hidden transcript" of the dominated.[11] In their stories, songs, and other ways of obscuring themselves for safety's sake, the dominated are able to recognize one another, to provide authentic mirrors for their pain and joy, so that the marginalizing, distorting mirrors of those in political power can be revealed for what they are: ersatz. For example, in the antebellum United States, it was in the relative autonomy of slave quarters that the hidden transcript "found expression in folktales, dress, language, song, and religion."[12] The social site of the slave quarters provided space for recognition and nurture that the public or dominant transcript would not allow. In medieval Europe, Michael Bakhtin argues, the marketplace provided such a "privileged site of antihegenomic discourse."[13] It is in the richness of these associations, the civic culture of the hidden transcript, that the self finds the sanity of authentic reflections. For its survival, the soul requires a space in which reflections are authentic. Only in such a space can the soul dance. Only in that space can one find comfort.

Social spaces, civic spaces, a safe, shared place to play with life as one actually experiences it; a place where others recognize, acknowledge, respect one's experiences—the self requires these and is constituted in them. One finds one's self, then, not by retreating to the solitude of ponds, mountains, gardens, or deserts. Those may be places to go to clear one's head, but they cannot provide the wellsprings of the soul.

For the infant, such a space may be provided by "good enough" mothering, which, according to D. W. Winnicott, occurs in the mother's recognizing and acknowledging the baby's self by accurately mirroring back the discomforts, curiosities, fears, satisfactions that the baby experiences.[14] Such an early self is nurtured by having a place to learn to recognize and cherish one's own experiences. Selves denied, selves incapable of holding their own experiences, would psychologically be no more than a point in space. They would have no volume to experience taking others into their own being and to treasure that experience. Socially, such tragic lives could be no more than instruments for others' purposes. Such persons could have no moral capacity. They would be utterly isolated from others and could, at best, stand aside as clinical observers, sometimes curious, but never able to enter into life with other persons.

The widespread association of nurturing with babies, mothers, and nurseries is in some ways nice, I suppose. Good mothering of babies does sometimes take place in nurseries, as women care for their young. Such circumstances are nice, but severely limiting. This is why I have often taken to talking of not the nurture but the cultivation of selves. The change in term generally frees the concept from gender and age limitations. Although when thoughts of bonsai creep in, the cultivation metaphor carries its own risks. Understanding the potential problems, let us continue to talk of nurturing the soul, as we move from the domestic spaces of infancy to the public spaces of schools.

If we focus on the subjects in the curriculum, on the standard sorts of achievement expectations, on the future world of work that we expect our children to enter and in which we want them to succeed, we shall totally miss seeing how teachers or other adults might attend to nurturing young children. Nurture requires that we attend to the content and ways in which the children, as selves, experience their lives. It has perhaps become fashionable, maybe dangerously fashionable, to say that teachers can do so by listening to the stories of their students' lives.

When the young, or for that matter any of us, tell a story from their own lives, a personal something, even in the best of conditions they feel exposed, vulnerable. There are understandable reasons for this sense of vulnerability. A story told may offer an opportunity for nurture, but it also offers a splendid opportunity for harm, great and small. It is sad but true that persons who withhold their own stories, who "play it close to the vest," tend to collect power. Likewise, persons to whom others "open up" collect power—the power to harm as well as to nurture. Sharing implies the most basic trust. If I trust you enough to share a personal story with you, I trust you with a piece of my self. If you violate that trust, you harm me. Between adults, that may be the worst it gets, though that is bad enough.

When an adult uses a child's story to bring harm, intentionally or not, the child may be damaged for life. When the doors to children's fragile narratives are opened, evil is all too ready to enter. Lest it be thought that nurturing is not a highly risky endeavor, demanding of great skill, competence, and love, remember the path of unintended child abuse. It is strewn with lives of persons both young and old.[15] We need not revisit it here.

How, then, might one nurture children with their own stories? Vivian Paley offers a beautiful, skillful example in *The Boy Who*

Would Be a Helicopter.[16] The teacher for a group of four-year-old children, Paley could simply have provided standard sorts of stories, used packaged language materials to promote letter and word recognition, and worked on counting skills. If additionally she had shown kindnesses toward the children, most parents and others who care would likely have been satisfied—but not Paley. Curious about each child's experience and expression of that experience, Paley listened to the stories, the extended metaphors through which each child structured life and with which each child expressed and dealt with feelings of, for example, fear or vulnerability or comfort. Just hearing the stories required a disciplined dedication. Every night the classroom tapes had to be transcribed and pieced together before they would start to yield the particular stories through which the children lived their lives.

By listening, Paley heard that Jason, a boy who isolated himself and tended to act with hostility, talked of himself as a helicopter. How did Paley know not to use that information misguidedly to encourage Jason's interest in helicopters or aircraft more generally? Some teachers or parents might have seen a recalcitrant kid who alternatively kept to himself and, other times, "acted out" his anger by knocking down other kids' blocks and so might have opted for the socially more acceptable isolation—but not Paley, who saw the helicopter as Jason's defense in a frightening world. When Jason did not feel well, the helicopter's blades were broken; when he felt better, he would fly into other children's play areas; when he became frustrated, his helicopter would become an instrument for destruction. These "facts" were not written on Jason's behavior. Where did Paley get them?

Paley's work did not stop with the listening. She told the children's stories back to them. She made the stories important. They became the basic stuff of the curriculum. Then, she invited each child to direct a play of his or her own. Not surprisingly, the basic metaphors of the children's stories carried over into the plays, in which they were elaborated as a social enterprise. For example, a participating child might request that the child director alter a role, or the child director might invite a character from another child's story into his or her own play. Thus, Paley provided a context that encouraged the children themselves to be attentive to one another's stories and that invited the children to elaborate or even change their own stories in ways that would invite others in. In short, she gave herself permission, before anything else, to be curious about the children as selves, about what they each experienced and about what their stories expressed. She also gave the children a context in which to develop and the means by which to act on their curiosity about one another.

Parenthetically, it is of interest here to note that along the way Paley discovered something that perhaps we all know in our bones: that one child considers another a friend when the second child includes the first by name or by metaphor (such as a helicopter) in his or her own story. Yes, if with my consent you include me or a part of my story in your life story, I will doubtless regard you as my friend. I will feel "connected" to you.

Paley's curriculum stands on the strongest of justifications: a moral one. It assumes that we value the self above all else—the self as that which experiences a life. Paley's curriculum also requires an understanding of the role of social mirrors and dialogue in the formation of a self of agency and connectedness.

I understand full well that some (nay, many) do not call for curricular or other policies in the so-called nurturing institutions to be morally justifiable. It is commonly thought to be sufficient if policies are designed to lead to a "better life," where the standards are material well-being and physical survival. Some who experienced the Great Depression might, in their understandable confusion, believe that the greatest loss one can suffer is material. After all, for many it caused human suffering so great that it is taking generations to express the pain. How much greater is the loss of self. Morally speaking, creature comforts are instruments in the life of a creature, and not the obverse—that is, selves cannot be instruments in the provision of creature comforts.

Theoretically, where is this self that calls for nurture? "Well, it's over there." What I can sketch on this trek may have to be a little more satisfying than that. I beg your indulgence as I turn briefly to psychological and literary theories that seem highly pertinent to understanding the nature of the self. My hope is that even cursory remarks may suggest how I think we could construct a compass to find our way about. I refer to four works: Eli Sagan's *Freud, Women, and Morality;*[17] Michael Bakhtin's essay, "The Epic and the Novel";[18] Alan Roland's book *In Search of Self in India and Japan;*[19] and *The Transformation of Intimacy* by Anthony Giddens.[20]

I have been talking about the moral meaning of life. Clearly, I am not interested in the punishing "moralities" demanded by angry gods. When I talk here of morality, I do not refer to packages of externally imposed rules that might contain "the" rules for moral living. Instead, I am trying to shine my lantern on the moral significance and power of the soul or self as it can be cultivated through relationships of unfailing respect and trust. With Eli Sagan, I would agree that Freud's notions of the moral import of the Oedipal complex are confused. It is more likely that adults are trying to kill children, not that children seek to kill adults; or, more to the point, it is more likely that a psychology that bases morality on fear and terror under the threat of punishment grossly underestimates the power of early nurture, of love, in the formation of a moral self.

It is through consistent respect for and recognition of the particular child's particular experiencing that the child develops a self who, in turn, can recognize, respect, and trust others. If we fail to understand this, we risk becoming caught in "solution syndromes," desperate attempts to promulgate policies to fix the outcomes: more prison beds, tougher standards in schools, more rules about the control of handguns, more locks on more gated communities. In other words, if we embrace a morality based on fear, then we shall constantly be faced with figuring out how to control the moral damage. My point here is not that we should recognize and respect one another in order that we can mend *our social fabric*, but simply that recognition and respect are themselves the woof and warp of our moral lives. They also provide the threads for what we sometimes call the social fabric of our society, especially when we sense its disintegration.

The self calling for nurture is the character not of an epic but of a novel. The difference, as Bakhtin sees it, represents a development in human consciousness. The character of an epic is "completely externalized. . . . All his potential, all his possibilities are realized utterly in his external social position, in the whole of his fate and even in his external appearance; outside of this predetermined fate and predetermined position there is nothing." Bakhtin continues: "He is entirely externalized in the most elementary, almost literal sense: everything in him is exposed and loudly expressed." Tellingly, "his view of himself coincides completely with others' views of him."[21] The epic character is, in short, stuck and completed. In sharp contradistinction, we find the character of the novel, at whose core "lay personal experience and free creative imagination"[22]—a character not immune to but made in dialogue with others.

Notice that the character described by some cognitive scientists, a "soul" literally reducible to protocols and computer programs, would resemble the epic figure far more than a character of a novel, inasmuch as he could be "entirely externalized." (Almost painfully, I am reminded here of the preoccupation in our schools with a narrow standardization of the curriculum, often to the total exclusion of the recognition of differences in children's experiences.) That is, in the novel, the self evolves through its experience with others, in dialogue (to use Bakhtin's language), and requires a space for its art, which derives from the open-ended personal nature of experiencing.

If we focus exclusively either on the dialogic character of the self or on the individually experiencing, creative self, we unwittingly divide the psychic house against itself. Alan Roland, a psychiatrist who has had the extraordinary experience of practicing in India and the United States and of working closely with therapists in Japan, attempts the development of a "cross-cultural psychology." More particularly, his interest is in "changes in the structure of the self that take place when persons are in intense contact with both Eastern and Western cultures."[23] Without any intention of summarizing this rich work, I do want to draw out a point that regards the dialogic yet individually creative aspect of the self.

Roland notes that while the traditional cultures of India and Japan provide especially rich social-psychological grounds for the cultivation of a dialogic self with its "personal emotional needs for sociability, dependence, security, and status" fulfilled through "the strongly affective intimacy relationships in the extended family" and to some extent in the community,[24] the autonomy and individuation required of Bakhtin's novel character appear to find richer soil in America. The East's and the West's imbalances in nourishing the different aspects of the self carry with them their own pathologies. For example, the traditional Indian adult male whose mentor in the workplace dies falls into a most serious crisis. So it is with the young person experiencing the distinctly Western demand to "self define" during adolescence.[25] In sum, for Roland, the self that we seek to nurture has a psychic need for *both* the we-self (or, familial self) and the I-self. To try to escape the basic tension between the dialogic or we-self and the creative or I-self is to run from the human condition of an intrapsychic drama.

And finally, let us turn to Anthony Giddens who argues that if we are to transform our public world in ways that provide for the nurture of the self, we shall have to import democracy, a heretofore public form, into the private spaces of our most intimate relationships. I agree with Giddens when he argues that not all love can nurture the self. What Giddens labels romantic love serves to develop codependencies, stifling selves with a suffocatingly mutual narrative. For example, "the heroine tames, softens and alters the seemingly intractable masculinity of her love object, making it possible for mutual affection to become the main guiding-line of their lives together."[26] The stultifying dependencies or domination created by such romantic love relationships could, according to Giddens, be avoided by democratizing personal life. The result would be a love that promises intimacy as possible only between persons who have their own distinct personal boundaries, who are self autonomous (that is, free of compulsions), and who have self-respect.[27] I find this insight strikingly helpful.

The self we seek to nurture cannot merely be relegated to the private or domestic world. All too many families and tight communities are not the antidote for the self's poisons but rather the location of them. They can be, for lack of a sub- or hidden transcript, the most effective sites for domination fatal to the soul. What is instrumentally needed for nurturing the self are democratized family relations and civic society—a society that provides for the free association of persons for shared purposes.

Before moving on to a consideration of civic society as a general condition for the nurturing of selves, I wish to add a cautionary coda to Giddens's observations about the desirability of "confluent" or democratized love over romantic love. It is not easy. I know of an elderly couple, Hermann and Anna, who separated after fifty-eight years of marriage. As Anna's short-term memory began to fail, Hermann, eighty-four years old, started imprisoning her in their home. As her humor wore thin, eighty-year-old Anna began to pummel him with her fists. She claimed that he had taken her money. One night Hermann called 911 to send Anna away. Her arms were bruised from his restraining her. They never saw or spoke to one another again. What happened? Were they not listening to each other's story? Why would Hermann try to hide his wife in their house? He had his rational responses: "She never wanted to go out when I was ready." "She'd been out, but had just forgotten." "She didn't feel well enough to go out." Why would Anna hit her husband? She had her rational response: "He took my money." These were the accounts offered consistently, repeatedly.

What did not get told were the generative stories behind the rational reasons and irrational acts. Hermann's brother, who was four years his elder, had either been born "retarded," as said early in the twentieth century, or had became so from some crippling disease at age four. Whichever it was, the brother was severely taunted and beaten by other boys at school. As a young child, Hermann was afraid that he, too, would become "retarded," and participated fully in his family's sequestering of the disabled brother. Throughout his adult life, Hermann frequently boasted of his excellent memory, which he had. His boasting belied his old fear of becoming like his big brother. His irrational, but more accurate response, yet inaccessible to him, would have been that it only looked as if he were hiding Anna, whose short-term memory loss reminded him of his brother. In fact, he was hiding his long-dead brother. Similarly, as a child Anna had suffered, through sexual abuse, a literally unspeakable loss. The closest she could come to expressing that unacknowledged pain was to complain bitterly and at length about something that she rationally construed to be the loss of money. She was hitting not Hermann but her then-teenage brother, now dead for some years.

The message of this and countless other similarly tragic tales is that the self, at least in part a response to unspeakable cruelties, is partially constituted by demonic irrationalities that themselves are fully capable of generating evil. If nurturing the self of a child requires safe harbors for trusting others enough to let them be a part of one's being, so nurturing the self of an adult may require safe harbors for meeting and confronting one's demons. In either case, the trust needed surely strains human possibility. Given domination and violence born of cruelties inflicted seventy-five or eighty years ago, the prospects seem dim, but try we must.

Conditions for Nurturing the Self

Many have called attention to the importance of recognition, mutual respect, and trust as a basis for moral lives and democracy.[28] (More specifically, I would argue that respect and trust are constituents of both nurture and the social fabric that supports it.) Fewer are the number who have understood the problem of living morally when we live among strangers, or at least among those whom we do not know personally or broadly. Indeed, some would argue that we should limit the size of our institutions and associations (schools, neighborhoods, and the like) to "human scale"—the number whom we can know by first name or the number with whom we can interact in the course of, say, a month.[29] It is, so the argument goes, only within such associations that we can morally find ourselves and one another. Therefore, if we are to attend to the nurture of our selves and one another, we will need somehow to return to our extended families, small rural communities or distinct city neighborhoods, and churches. Therein, it is claimed, lies the hope of a rich civic society, of democracy, of nurture.

Some who see public institutions crowding out the home argue that we should either turn our public relationships into the "moral equivalents" of kinship relations (such as Jane Martin's school-homes[30]) or, on the publicly biased side of the aisle, that we should set aside nostalgic images of now-nonexistent families in favor of institutions beefed up by policies that will enable strangers to do the job we once thought could be accomplished in the context of intimate kinship relations, such as caring for children and the elderly.[31] The first of these views gives up hope for the moral utility of the public realm as we have known it. The second, observing conditions that no longer support the family, proposes abandoning the private realm in favor of public policy.

The observations employed on both sides are sadly accurate. Fewer adults are available for less time at home with children and aging parents. Given the isolating forces of contemporary society, ranging from the addictive uses of television and ever larger percentages of parents in the paid workforce to the decline of the community school and the socioeconomic segregation of shared activities, we seem to have increasing difficulty in feeling connected to one another. Ever more commonly, we find in our cities high percentages of single-person households. Ever more commonly, we know one another only indirectly and distantly, in ways that enable us to pretend not to notice when we see someone being mugged. As Mary Ann Glendon has noted, in this environment of disconnection, we use rights as clubs, impoverishing our political discourse.[32]

Some call for strengthening family and community, those "seedbeds of a civic virtue."[33] As seductive as these arguments are, they concern me. In passing, Rawls notes that a healthy family is necessary to underwrite a just society. In passing, Martin says that her "schoolhome" should not, of course, be the moral equivalent of a dysfunctional home. Glendon seems to assume that families and communities are, willy-nilly, the source of civility. Regarding nurture, families and communities are far too problematic to treat merely in passing. They simply cannot be assumed to be generally the sources of civility, of mutual regard and trust. I, too, am predisposed to feel the warmth of hearth and the vibrancy of the town square, but then I should warn you that I am all too inclined to stick with my fantasies, with how I wish the world were, rather than with social and psychological realities common to families and communities.

There may be reasons why at the same time we uncritically glorify family and community we also understand and honor Huck Finn's running away from home, Rip Van Winkle's abandoning his family, explorers having left their communities to strike out into the unknown, and families having packed their bags to leave close-knit European communities in the last century.[34] These leavings were motivated by all manner of domination within family and community. As noted more cursorily in an earlier section, family and community, seats of nurture, can provide rich opportunities for some to place others under their heel, accomplishing the opposite of nurture. Danger lurks in a failure to recognize the "Myth of the Ever-Nurturant Family and Community."

In the name of nurturing ourselves and one another, rather than trying to rededicate public resources to supporting just any families and communities, we should encourage whatever particular associations, including families and communities, bring specifically mutual respect and trust to human relationships. Generally, it is those traditionally based institutions—places that one cannot easily choose to leave—that are especially prone to the evils of domination. Almost never can the child choose to walk away. Hence, children are not uncommonly used as instruments for all sorts of adult purposes, which tend to destroy rather than nurture children. These range from pressing children to fulfill parental dreams from their own childhood to requiring children to comfort adults psychologically and sexually.

Some forms of such domination are less odious than others, but none is more nurturing than another. Likewise, the labels and stations of traditional, small towns too often ossify, casting community members in limiting roles built around not some notion of mutual nurture but around sustaining the traditions and power structure of the community. If the community is the source of one's livelihood, the place of one's friends, and a home to one's children, the costs of leaving may seem prohibitively high, especially if one cannot be sure of the alternatives. (I am reminded here of the phrase "born on the wrong side of the tracks," which literally doomed, by virtue of geography and poverty, some kids in the small Midwestern town where I spent most of my childhood.)

Just what is it that would distinguish a community that holds its members in moral regard from one that does not? Specifically, where would we more likely find a place for our own nurture and that of one another? In his book *Making Democracy Work: Civic Traditions in Modern Italy,* Robert Putnam suggests a possibility.[35] A twenty-year study of the evolution of regional governments in Italy, Putnam's work focuses on trying to understand the conditions that would create "strong, responsive, effective representative institutions."[36] Over the initial twenty years of existence of the regional governments, from 1970 to 1990, why did those in the north generally succeed, while those in the south did not? As he sifts through impressive, pertinent data to try to understand the differences in performance, Putnam develops the thesis that the prominence of specifically *civic* community in the north, as opposed to force and family in the south, may explain the difference.

Abbreviating Putnam's instructive discussion of the nature of specifically civic community far too much, I nevertheless mention four features:

1. *Civic engagement:* This is civic participation characterized by a dialogic notion of our selves, in which self-interest is "alive to" (to borrow Tocqueville's words) the interests of others.

2. *Political equality:* This is the binding together of a community
   by "horizontal relations of reciprocity and cooperation," with
   a clear appreciation that the absence of community power
   empowers those who would dominate on the basis of their
   personal power and, at the other extreme, that absolute individual power—against which horizontal relations protect—
   structurally empowers tyrants.
3. *Solidarity, trust, and tolerance:* Civic participation, which cannot
   be conflict free, relies heavily on a strong notion of civic virtue
   consisting of being helpful, respectful, and trustful toward one
   another, even when others differ on matters of substance.
4. *Dense networks of social cooperation:* These are rich congeries of
   voluntary associations through which people develop "habits
   of cooperation, solidarity, and public-spiritedness."[37]

Putnam finds that democracy takes root best in strongly civic
communities. Especially interesting for our purposes, Putnam also
finds that persons who live in more highly civic communities report
that they are much more satisfied with their lives than those who
live in the less-civic communities in which rule by family and force
prevails.[38] Could it be that people's lives are nurtured by their conditions? Could it be that we are fed by joining with others in quilt-
ing, in designing new software, in troubleshooting urban electrical
problems, in choral singing, in bird-watching, in bowling or playing on roque teams, in arranging for community festivals, in discussing books, in square dancing, in repairing low-income housing,
in collecting canned goods for food banks?

Images of Vivian Paley's classroom return to mind: children
directing their own stories, yet having to call on one another to
stage their plays; children voluntarily placing the metaphors and
persons of others' stories in their own in order to express their own
interests; Jason's being trusted with his helicopter, being allowed
to let his need to hide it run its course, providing the social space
needed for him to become curious about others and to figure out
a way to connect with them—these are the stuff of civic community.
These, according to Putnam, are the conditions that make democracy work. They also happen to be the conditions that feed the
soul. They are spaces for recognition, mutual respect, and trust.
These particular spaces have built-in protection: one can walk away,
if needed.

If we have collectively been deluded by the uncritical glorification of family and community, there is a second obfuscating myth that regards who is lacking and therefore needful of nurture. Let us call it "The Fable of the Needful Other." According to this fashionable fable, the poor, minority groups, and the dispossessed are the ones who are suffering from a failure of nurture. It is, unfortunately, a fable that tends to serve as the main engine of social policy. According to this myth, these groups are deprived, perhaps depraved.

Conservatives say it is the labeled persons' own fault and not "our" responsibility to fix "their" lives; liberals tend to say that it is the conditions in which "they" live that have caused the problem, that we are collectively responsible for those conditions, and that therefore we need to fix the problem. Those who would get on with the solution tend to define the children of the disadvantaged as "at risk." The point of their schooling, it follows, is to provide corrective measures that will reduce the risk factors. As Valerie Polakow points out in *Lives on the Edge: Single Mothers and Their Children in the Other America*, the pedagogy of the poor corrects for their chaotic lives by focusing on containment, order, and control.[39] It is a pedagogy in which there is no space for a self to grow. "Free play is neither free nor playful for the children,"[40] and "children's experiences of stories are vitiated and de-storied."[41]

In telling contrast to Vivian Paley's preschool classroom stands that of Mrs. Berry, as recounted by Valerie Polakow. There are three boys—Chris, Jeremiah, and Yasser—in the painting area at "choice time." "Yasser and Chris have pocketed small wooden cars from the block area and secretly sneak them over to the easel area. Jeremiah has painted 'a curvey road' with a series of arrows pointing in one direction and a stop sign in red. Chris and Yasser are trying to drive their cars on the road made by Jeremiah without touching the wet paint, saying, 'we going to Chicago—vroom.'" Mrs. Berry confiscates the cars and reminds the children that "we do not drive cars over the easel," that easels are for painting only, and that the three of them never pay attention.[42]

For these and other "disadvantaged" children, schooling is made a location for conforming to notions of external order, rather than for helping children make sense of and give meaning to their own lives. I see no choice here but to agree with Polakow that the central agenda, undertaken in the name of helping or "nurturing" the disadvantaged, is just the opposite: the imposition of yet another form of domination. Policies targeted to "at risk" populations are too commonly designed to correct lives rather than to nurture them.

The Fable of the Needful Other not only obstructs the nurture of persons who find themselves part of the labeled "population," but also blocks our seeing that the children of the "advantaged"— and, of course, advantaged adults as well—can and do suffer from flattened or undernourished selves. In Robert Coles's work on children of privilege, one is struck by how self-regarding, isolating, and flattening can be the experience of children reared by parents confused by their wealth.[43] The extraordinary persuasiveness of glass mirrors to reflect the physical self, "friends" carefully arranged by adults, and sometimes highly precise career or other expectations borne of parental wishes all can render it almost impossible for children to give credence to their own pains, yearnings, and comforts.

Caught in the ghetto of fantasies of particular adults' lives, many children of privilege risk regarding themselves as pretty packages carefully designed to serve purposes that can only have meaning in the context of stories acceptable to those adults on whom they rely. Mind you, this is not a universal story, but it is likely more common than ordinarily understood. Being born into a family of social and economic privilege can disadvantage the soul. Perhaps less obviously, but just as devastatingly, such confusions of materialism can impoverish an adult.

There is Grayson, the company vice president who always dines at the finest restaurants, stays in the most posh of hotels, attends the most gala of performances in the most progressive cities of the world, finds the most beautiful of mistresses, sends his children to the best of private schools, skis the most breathtaking slopes, all while hungering for a sustenance that none of this provides. In these matters, the central difference between the most "advantaged" and most "disadvantaged" persons is that the advantaged are, because of their wealth and lack of reliance on public institutions, better able to hide themselves from those who would seek to label and "solve" them.

I wish to mention a third and final myth that tends to confound us when we think of nurture: "The Myth of Nurture as Intervention for Targeted Populations." As best as I can discern, it goes something like this: the most potent public way we have of caring for one another is through the delivery of social services, including all of the services of all governmental agencies on any level. This includes public schooling, public health services, various housing referral services and providers, mental health clinics, community centers, numerous social work services, shelters for the homeless and abused, rehabilitation counseling centers, and so on. It may even include nonprofit charities that welcome referrals from public agencies. According to the language of this myth, populations are to be served rationally. (No one talks of nurturing persons, much less souls.) That is, knowledge of the sciences and social sciences is to be brought to bear in defining the problems to be addressed and the populations to be served and in identifying "interventions" or services to be provided.

The tests of service delivery are effectiveness and efficiency, for the point is not to waste public resources and to see that the specified interventions are made under the conditions outlined. According to today's most common rendering of this myth, the reason we fail to provide the needed social services and fail to do so efficiently is that we lack interagency coordination that could be provided if teachers, social workers, health care providers, counselors of various sorts, employment offices, housing providers, and so on could and would coordinate their information and services. With such coordination, so the story goes, populations could be better served. This is, presumably, how we can help one another (nay, the language is "targeted population") and be treated with decency and respect. According to this myth, we collectively seek to address the full array of our society's problems, ranging from its numerous forms of violence to unemployment and disease.

Now, it is unclear whether such activities can have much to do with the nurture of selves and meaning in lives, but many who study, plan, and staff such services sincerely believe that they do. That being so, I wish to deconstruct the myth in three ways. The first way has to do with the "solving" of populations. "They" are cast as problems, and agency actions are cast as solutions. This is how, for example, school districts and others institutionalize homelessness, rather than seeing the problems in their broader socioeconomic context. Once we avail homeless children of classroom time and other social services and once we avail homeless adults of shelter referrals and the like, we have solved the problem as best as a society bent on interventions aimed at targeted populations can. What remains unnoticed are the unfairness and pains of homelessness as persons with names experience it. Unnoticed are dignity and the self.

Second, I am reminded of a point that Robert Coles makes in *The Call of Stories*.[44] When doing his residency in psychiatry, Coles met regularly with his mentor, one older curmudgeon, Dr. Ludwig. Week after week, Coles reviewed one particular case through the various lenses of psychoanalytic theory, but did not seem to be coming to know or understand the patient any better. Finally, Ludwig asked if Coles would tell him some of the events in the patient's life, some of her story. In doing so, Ludwig gave Coles permission to see the patient as a particular person, not just as a case, and to do so with his full repertory built not just from particular theoretical perspectives, but also more richly and broadly from his experience as a human being. Suddenly, Coles could see the patient with far greater clarity.

What troubles me about setting our task as one not of nurturing individuals but of "caring" for populations or providing "interventions" in lives is that we deny ourselves the possibility of seeing another person as more than a case or a representative of an entitled category. Is it any wonder that housing projects undertaken as solutions to externally defined problems would be abused by the "solved" populations? And on the obverse side, is it any wonder that persons treated as if their experiences mattered and as if they are the ones who make meaning in and so define the problems of their lives would appreciate the choices they themselves make?

The fantasy of the Myth of Nurture as Intervention for Targeted Populations can be further brought to light with a distinction that Alan Wolfe makes in his book *Whose Keeper? Social Science and Moral Obligation*.[45] Wolfe notes that in modern societies (his specific examples are Scandinavia and the United States), the expansion of both the market and the state have eroded civic society. In skeletal form, Wolfe's argument, embellished for this context, runs roughly as follows: it is in civic society, in "families, communities, friendship networks, voluntary organizations, and social movements"[46] that persons "mature and develop as agents through their interaction with others."[47] It is through this agency that a life acquires a moral dimension. A market-oriented society, such as that in the United States, focuses mainly on procedures, on a "concern for property rights or the rule of law," with an emphasis on formalism and specificity regarding obligation. Welfare states, especially as have developed in Scandinavia, tend to accept as justifiable any morally attractive results that could be produced.[48]

Even if the best of a market society and the best of a welfare society were combined, they would lack a moral dimension if individual selves did not develop. That is, we can imagine a perfect market society, a perfect welfare society, or some combination of the two, that would constitute a world that no soul could inhabit. That is, selves take root in the soil of civic society. Following the rules of the market and being the target for interventions by the state cannot create lives of meaning and responsibility. In short, the market and the state cannot make life worth living. *Only civic society can nourish the soul.* Wolfe's point should at least give pause to those who live by the Myth of Nurture as Intervention for Targeted Populations.

The world that the thoughtful interventionist desires appears not to be in fact achievable through intervention in the lives of others. It may instead call for messy, labor-intensive work and require thoughtful listening by persons who are willing and able to be curious about the lives of others and to make the experiences of others an integral part of their own stories. What is needed is nurture that roots itself in the endangered realm of civic society.

What to Do?

I am confident that nurture requires a civic society. I am persuaded that having market corporations tinker around with our schools, our museums, the care of our sick and elderly, and the like will not enhance our prospects for nurturing one another. Likewise, I am persuaded that massive efforts to coordinate governmental policies and to render service delivery more effective will only distract us from our morally ultimate aim of nurturing ourselves and one another. By turning to the market and state to create our worlds, we generally become instruments in others' investment strategies and problems of others' definition, waiting for their solutions. From the position of neither the investor nor the problem solver can a self find nourishment.

Like those who would unleash corporate interests and those who would energize governmental agencies, I too am deeply concerned about our disturbing social problems. So what in the world would I propose to do? With our map barely begun, everything is premature, but that will not slow the cadences of the market and state. With a deep breath, let me get specific. But where to begin?

Let us first try this: we need to talk freely and openly about the moral meaning of nurture in its civic context. This will not be easy, inasmuch as it is hard to find a "public forum" that has not already been co-opted by the market. I am reminded of Herbert Schiller's book, *Culture, Inc.: The Corporate Takeover of Public Expression.*[49] With the airwaves and print almost entirely commercialized, and with our major retail markets, shopping malls, now privately owned and controlled solely for commercial purposes, where are our public forums for a free discussion of nurture and civic society? Are we left only with those churches not peddling moralities of angry gods and with whatever functioning community centers might remain? I am reminded also of John McDermott's *Corporate Society,* in which he argues that the substantial, highly trained, relatively well-paid professionals are vested in maintaining the power of the corporation.[50] Clearly, such talk of adjusting priorities out of deference to our needs to be nourished and to live in a civic society may seem threatening to some blinded by their own market interests and to some whose identities have become tied to careers vested in government programs.

I am not so sure about this first suggestion. With it, we seem to be thrown off course by casting the struggle for a more nurturing society as a call to an all-knowing David to slay modern Goliaths, those uncaring participants in the market and those dangerous busy-bodies of the state. It is likely plausible that certain facts about the strength of corporate interests and particular intransigencies of careerism in government, for example, may help perpetuate some confusions. However, in characterizing the prospects for developing a civic society through a sociopolitical clash of interest groups, we risk overlooking the very thing that would bind us together in civility. Part of our shared psychological heritage is that contexts of recognition, mutual respect, and trust—places of nourishment—feel good to all of us, regardless of where we are individually positioned in the market or in the state. It is there that our souls are fed.

Recall Grayson, the corporate executive who strives to have the "best" of everything, all the while hungering for something that is not fed by his consumption and exploits. Could it not be that Grayson, along with Jason, Vivian Paley, Hermann, Anna, Eva Hoffman, Richard Rodriguez, Huck Finn, and you and me, would find nourishment only in a civic society? And might it be that civic society is defined not by the demands of markets and states but by the play of participants as they recognize one another and respect one another and so create a place where they (we?) can trust themselves with one another? Perhaps pertinent for our considerations is not special interests and conflicting values, but the very power of the experience of being nurtured when one is touched by another, such as the moment "when Nietzsche wept"[51] and when Mill found himself in Coleridge. There is strong evidence that nourishment of the soul holds such power for us all, even though some, who as children experienced disabling cruelties, may be initially unable to bear the vulnerability that trust requires.

If setting out to do battle with representatives of the market and state obscures the power of our shared hunger for the nourishment of civic society, then perhaps we (many of whom are doubtless employed by either the market or the government) need to consider what we as persons acting outside the market and beyond our role as citizens could do to enhance civic society. Here, it would be important for us to consider ways to create voluntary associations to include persons who are culturally, economically, racially, or otherwise different from one another, lest we fail to address some of the politically harder cases of mutual recognition, respect, and trust. Maybe we, both insiders and outsiders, should review both corporate activities and governmental practices to ask which of these seem specifically to erode civic society. There would surely be great objections from some "bottom-liners" and policy pushers, so even raising the topic might take great courage. We, both as insiders and as outsiders, might consider reviewing corporate ledger sheets and governmental powers to determine what actions could be taken to enhance civic society. Maybe for purposes of reminding ourselves of our common hunger and our common need for nourishment, we could develop political and economic unions dedicated expressly to promoting conditions conducive to nurturing ourselves and one another. Maybe such associations could themselves give us a sense of solidarity needed to press for the abandonment of activities and policies erosive of civic society and for adoption of corporate and governmental plans to enhance civic society. Possibly we could do these things.

Meanwhile, lives must continue to be lived prior to even the development of such visions of great programs. (Here, you understand,

I am chary of any suggestion that might reduce nurture to a project that can be placed in a file folder or delegated to others. That was my old misunderstanding, from which this journey began.) That is, in the worlds of our daily lives, we need to recognize, mutually respect, and give each other reason to entrust our selves to one another. We need to create little civic societies. If Vivian Paley can help that happen with a small group of four-year-olds and herself, cannot my colleagues and I in the workplace do so as well? Cannot my students and I do so in the classroom? How many are the places where I dwell? In our civility, could we possibly provide the conditions for one another's nourishment (and, yes, still give what is required to the market or state)? My guess is that the hardest task for us, the participants, would not be to give up obvious forms of domination, though that might be cause for some struggles. The greater challenge would be for each of us to come to understand our selves well enough to distinguish between listening to one another and hearing the noise of our own demons. None of this could possibly be easy; but then, nothing could be so exciting. No other stakes could be so high.

Notes

1. John Rawls, *A Theory of Justice* (Cambridge, Mass.: Harvard University Press, 1971).
2. Alasdair MacIntyre, *After Virtue* (2nd ed.) (Notre Dame, Ind.: University of Notre Dame Press, 1984).
3. Rawls, *A Theory of Justice,* especially p. 301.
4. I borrow the idea for this case from Walker Percy's "Loss of Creature," in *Message in a Bottle* (New York: Farrar, Straus and Giroux, 1954), pp. 46–63.
5. For a thoughtful, clear essay critical of the use of the computer metaphor by cognitive scientists, see Jerome Bruner, *Acts of Meaning* (Cambridge, Mass.: Harvard University Press, 1990).
6. John Stuart Mill, *Autobiography of John Stuart Mill* (New York: Signet, 1964).
7. For consideration of instrumental thinking as a feature of modernity, see Charles Taylor, *The Ethics of Authenticity* (Cambridge, Mass.: Harvard University Press, 1992), and *Sources of the Self* (Cambridge, Mass.: Harvard University Press, 1989).
8. Eva Hoffman, *Lost in Translation* (New York: Penguin Books, 1989).
9. For an extensive exploration of the effect of clashes of cultures on the daily, intimate lives of people, I know of no finer work than

Ramon Gutierrez's book, *When Jesus Came, the Corn Mothers Went Away: Marriage, Sexuality, and Power in New Mexico, 1500–1846* (Stanford, Calif.: Stanford University Press, 1991).

10. Richard Rodriguez, *Hunger of Memory: The Education of Richard Rodriguez* (New York: Bantam Books, 1983).

11. James C. Scott, *Domination and the Arts of Resistance* (New Haven, Conn.: Yale University Press, 1990).

12. Scott, *Domination and the Arts of Resistance,* p. 120.

13. Scott, *Domination and the Arts of Resistance,* p. 122.

14. D. W. Winnicott, *Playing and Reality* (London: Routledge, 1989).

15. For a fine-grained, poignant collection of accounts of adults failing to recognize, much less to respect, children's experiences, see Jane Adan, *The Children in Our Lives* (Albany: State University of New York Press, 1991).

16. Vivian Gussin Paley, *The Boy Who Would Be a Helicopter: The Uses of Story-Telling in the Classroom* (Cambridge, Mass.: Harvard University Press, 1990).

17. Eli Sagan, *Freud, Women, and Morality* (New York: Basic Books, 1988). A work with strikingly parallel arguments is Nel Noddings's book, *Women and Evil* (Berkeley: University of California Press, 1989).

18. Michael M. Bakhtin, "The Epic and the Novel," in *The Dialogic Imagination: Four Essays* by M. M. Bakhtin, edited by M. Holquist, translated by C. Emerson and M. Holquist (Austin: University of Texas Press, 1981), pp. 3–40.

19. Alan Roland, *In Search of Self in India and Japan: Toward a Cross Cultural Psychology* (Princeton, N.J.: Princeton University Press, 1988).

20. Anthony Giddens, *The Transformation of Intimacy: Sexuality, Love, and Eroticism in Modern Societies* (Stanford, Calif.: Stanford University Press, 1992).

21. Bakhtin, "The Epic and the Novel," p. 34.

22. Bakhtin, "The Epic and the Novel," p. 39.

23. Roland, *In Search of Self in India and Japan,* p. 1.

24. Roland, *In Search of Self in India and Japan,* p. 12.

25. For a brief, clear summary of the psychopathologies deriving from culturally different sorts of intrapsychic imbalances, see Roland, *In Search of Self in India and Japan,* pp. 324–329.

26. Giddens, *The Transformation of Intimacy,* p. 46.

27. Giddens, *The Transformation of Intimacy,* p. 189.

28. For a particularly impressive, recent book that focally addresses questions regarding recognition, see Amy Gutmann (ed.), *Multiculturalism: Examining the Politics of Recognition* (Princeton, N.J.: Princeton University Press, 1994).

29. For an extended embellishment of the thesis that living beyond

"human scale" is inhumane and the source of social problems, see Kirkpatrick Sale, *Human Scale* (New York: Coward, McCann & Geoghegan, 1981).

30. Jane Roland Martin, *The Schoolhome: Rethinking Schools for Changing Families* (Cambridge, Mass.: Harvard University Press, 1992).

31. Jan E. Dizard and Howard Gadlin, *The Minimal Family* (Amherst: University of Massachusetts Press, 1990).

32. Mary Ann Glendon, *Rights Talk: The Impoverishment of Political Discourse* (New York: Free Press, 1991).

33. Glendon, *Rights Talk*, p. 109.

34. Martin, *The Schoolhome*, pp. 174–176, sees such cases in literature, along with Thoreau's *Walden* and Emerson's *Nature* and "Self Reliance," as "idealization of disconnection" and as expression of "domesticity repressed" in American life. I see such cases as evidence of our collective failure to nurture one another. The two interpretations are not so much in disagreement as they are reflective of different emphases, different rhetorical devices, and perhaps differing views about political strategies for attempting a more moral society.

35. Robert D. Putnam, *Making Democracy Work: Civic Traditions in Modern Italy* (Princeton, N.J.: Princeton University Press, 1993).

36. Putnam, *Making Democracy Work*, p. 6.

37. Putnam, *Making Democracy Work*, pp. 86–91.

38. Putnam, *Making Democracy Work*, p. 113.

39. Valerie Polakow, *Lives on the Edge: Single Mothers and Their Children in the Other America* (Chicago: University of Chicago Press, 1993).

40. Polakow, *Lives on the Edge*, p. 122.

41. Polakow, *Lives on the Edge*, p. 123.

42. Polakow, *Lives on the Edge*, p. 124.

43. Robert Coles, *Privileged Ones: The Well-Off and Rich in America,* Volume V of *Children of Crisis* (Boston: Little, Brown and Company, 1977).

44. Robert Coles, *The Call of Stories: Teaching and the Moral Imagination* (Boston: Houghton Mifflin, 1989), p. 189.

45. Alan Wolfe, *Whose Keeper? Social Science and Moral Obligation* (Berkeley: University of California Press, 1989).

46. Wolfe, *Whose Keeper?*, p. 233.

47. Wolfe, *Whose Keeper?*, p. 245.

48. Wolfe, *Whose Keeper?*, p. 245.

49. Herbert I. Schiller, *Culture, Inc.: The Corporate Takeover of Public Expression* (New York: Oxford University Press, 1991).

50. John McDermott, *Corporate Society: Class, Property and Contemporary Capitalism* (Boulder, Colo.: Westview Press, 1991).

51. Irvin D. Yalom, *When Nietzsche Wept* (New York: Basic Books, 1992).

Chapter Three

Democracy, Ecology, and Participation

Mary Catherine Bateson

A father is brushing his teeth, busily moving the brush up and down while water swirls into the sink and down the drain. His six-year-old son appears beside him and pulls at his sleeve, "Dad, you're not saving the earth," he says.

This is a scene played out in hundreds of households in different permutations. "Mom," my daughter said, "don't tell me you're still using paper napkins." My friend's daughter has multiplied the number of recycling bins in their home and examines every piece of packaging. When his mom pulls up to a fast-food restaurant, the little boy in the backseat says, "Ugh, not hamburgers. Don't you know they're ruining the rainforest?" And from another child we hear, "I don't care if you've had that fur coat for ten years, just don't wear it when you come to pick me up." Clearly, the last two decades have seen the accelerating creation of an ecological consciousness in children, both in schools and through television and other media. A number of organizations are focusing on ecological education, and materials and curricula are being widely developed.

Arguably, changes in human treatment of the biosphere, the slowing and reversing of existing patterns of degradation and exploitation, must be rooted in childhood learning. A new attitude toward the living world requires a new kind of common sense, new fundamental assumptions, changed expectations and aspirations.

A move to sustainability will require a rethinking of both education and the processes and institutions of democracy.

So far, the process is piecemeal. On the one hand, I suspect that few children are proposing canceling vacation trips because of the consumption of hydrocarbons. On the other hand, many of those who are working on the promotion of ecological consciousness through education manage to leave unacknowledged the fact that the changes involved are deep and profound, not only in patterns of consumption and travel but also in basic philosophy. For a long time, nature programming on television was regarded as essentially innocuous and noncontroversial (unlike, say, ethnographic programming), but this is changing and will change further. Today, every visit to the zoo is likely to include information about which species are threatened and why, which begins to open up the issues of competing interests. Kittens and puppies have always been used to teach gentleness and responsibility; today, whales and pandas are used to translate the infant's need for love in the immediate environment of the home into social concern. It is not possible to deal for very long with environmental issues without addressing fundamental questions of birth and death, ancient beliefs about the nature of the good life, about what human beings want and need and what our rights might be in a complexly interlocked biological system, and about how political systems must be structured to take these wants, needs, and rights into account.

Furthermore, I would argue that if ecological issues are to be addressed at any depth, they must be addressed in the *processes* of education as well as in the content. Many of the traditional habits of education are linked to assumptions that have been marked out as sources of environmental dissonance, including the assumption that knowledge can be separated from participation, the value of competition as a classroom tool, the ideal of objectivity, and the efficacy of rationality.

The ecological component in education is sure to become increasingly hotly contested, for it is by no means neutral. Elementary school children are emerging in this country as an earth lobby. It is entirely appropriate that they should do so, for ecological damage is slow and cumulative and they are the ones who will suffer tomorrow the consequences of today's short-sighted policies. Ecological education may be the front line of values education in this country, partly because of the implicit lessons it carries for thinking about other kinds of community, for identifying goals to strive for, and for critiquing business as usual among people as well as between humans and other species.

New ecological understandings demand genuine change. Sustainability is still a long way from being a shared value, from motherhood and apple pie, for Americans carry the memory of pioneers who could simply move on to new forests and grasslands rather than conserving what they had, and as a nation we have perhaps gone further than any other in our faith in technology. The conservation of natural beauty has been around as a rather specialized concern for some time, but it is not enshrined in our founding documents, and the scriptures of Judaism and Christianity have long been read to license human irresponsibility. Furthermore, even the tradition of conservation that we do have is conceptually different from the emerging emphasis on preserving the systemic integrity of the biosphere. We scramble to find ways to link environmental values with older frames of reference, such as in talk of stewardship. Activists search for constitutional arguments, but the Bill of Rights contains no protection for any life other than human. Still, I believe it may be possible to find a certain congruence between the traditions of democracy, if only we read them more inclusively, and the emerging themes of ecological concern. We may be moving toward an understanding of ecology that brings humanistic values—respect for the integrity of others above all— into the debate and ecological arguments into our attitudes toward human relations.

Ecology has three faces in the classroom. The debate about ecological education can be expected to shift between these different points of view.

The first face, *empirical ecology*, is the most obviously academic and practical, drawing on several fields of biology as well as on geography and meteorology to offer children a knowledge of the world they live in and the ways it is changing. It is worth noting that this is an area in which efforts to make education more concrete and experiential—such as field trips, tests of air and water, experiments with plants, and the keeping of aquariums—are likely to be successful. Ecology in the classroom builds upon earlier traditions of nature study that were more taxonomic. It is one thing to collect and identify different leaves, another thing to discuss the interrelations of the various species in a given biome. Bird-watching becomes ecological when watchers attend to the niches of different species rather than simply accumulating lists of sightings.

The second face of ecology in the classroom is *environmentalism*, which turns the discussion to the decision making and actions of human beings and is political, involving policies affecting a range of interest groups. The environmentalist side of ecology is often reflected in school projects: cleaning up a marsh or a wood, planting trees, organizing recycling drives. It seems possible that environmental action will educate a new generation for activism, as the generation of the sixties was educated through the civil rights movement. Projects like boycotting McDonald's for using styrofoam containers might function in the same way as picketing Woolworth's for segregating lunch counters did for young people long before they went south to register voters; but different fields of activism no doubt result in different kinds of participation. Action for the environment can be projected out to South American rain forests, but it also affects lifestyles and raises new questions about the cumulative effects of individual actions.

The third face of ecology is *systemic* and has to do with patterns of thought. A new understanding of the interdependence and diversity of natural systems will not be limited to the natural world, but rather will be folded back onto other kinds of issues. Learning to think ecologically goes beyond the development either of an attitude of loving wonder or of a practical concern with conserving resources. It involves a change in ways of knowing and thinking, attention to the characteristics of wholes rather than to their parts, changed models of causality and therefore of problem solving.[1] It is with these epistemological changes that this chapter will primarily be concerned.

Today, there is a significant backlash developing against environmentalism, which is already beginning to replace communism as the favorite target of the far right. Those who want to harvest old-growth forests, to graze cattle on federal lands, or to develop vulnerable stretches of real estate are gradually recognizing that their antagonist is not the spotted owl but a new way of thinking about the biosphere, and that in many cases this new way of thinking is religious, at least in tone. We can expect court cases protesting the use in schools of the photograph of earth from the moon, on the grounds that it is being used as a religious symbol.

Epistemological Change

The contemporary study of ecology is not the study of plants and animals—these are, after all, the concerns of botany and zoology—but of the relationships between them. These relationships involve exchanges of information as well as energy and materials in elegant and self-sustaining patterns linking large numbers of organisms, like the nitrogen cycle or the food chain. Increasingly we see the biosphere not as a sort of background for separate organisms but as itself a product of life processes that determine the characteristics of the atmosphere, the soil, and even the rocks and the weather. One of the primary shifts needed is a shift in gestalt from "I see a robin" and "Look at that pretty flower" to seeing robin and flower and child as part of a single interacting and interdependent whole—a system, many parts of which are invisible to the naked eye. A second shift makes it possible to see basic similarities in pattern among different systems, among robin and flower and child and the forest that contains them all, "a pattern which connects."[2] Such a recognition makes it possible to feel kinship and empathy not only with a dead robin but with a devastated forest or a broken community.

The discipline that studies such patterns of relationship and organization, including those of ecology, is *cybernetics,* or systems theory. Many people associate cybernetics with mechanistic ways of thinking, because of the engineering and computer science applications of the discipline, yet the most persuasive models for complex systems are biological, and the abstract study of systems opens up a whole new range of metaphorical recognitions. I like to express this potentiality of systems theory by saying that "cybernetics makes poets of us."[3] An awareness of the systemic relationships in the environment demands great discipline, for we have inherited many casual metaphors that deny biological processes or reduce organisms to commodities. Sometimes a return to mythology can be more accurate than simplified versions of science.

Alas, metaphor always carries the possibility of distortion as well as illumination and the poets in us may sometimes dilute the force of cybernetic arguments. Thus, James Lovelock used the name Gaia,[4] the goddess of earth in Greek mythology, to dramatize his argument, already metaphorical, about this planet as "a living organism"—a self-regulating system. The multiple layers of metaphor—cybernetic system, organism, person, goddess—made many people nervous, yet the metaphor allowed a certain swift comprehension. The earth as a living organism represents a very great advance, descriptively and intuitively, over Buckminster Fuller's metaphor of "spaceship earth."

Systemic thinking is often referred to as "holistic." Here, too, there are possibilities for confusion. Properly speaking, a holistic view of education includes an understanding of whole persons embedded in whole systems, a view that separates neither developing mind from body nor school from community. A holistic view of the forest is not limited to the growth of trees for potential human use, but includes the interactions of wind and rain and the bacteria of decay in the soil. By now, however, because the term holistic has been appropriated and applied to a congeries of antiestablishment movements in medicine, it often obscures more than it clarifies. Traditional establishment medicine has not been holistic, because it focuses on limited aspects of human health and well-being, failing to use the full healing potential of touch and imagination, of ritual and nutrition. Yet, practitioners who specialize in addressing one or another of these alternative areas often lose track themselves of an inclusive model in the pursuit of a specific use of herbs or form of massage. Systemic or holistic thinking about the human body or about the planet must imply inclusiveness: chemistry and poetry, meditation and technology, complex systems approached through multiple paths of knowing.

Central to the study of ecosystems is the study of circular processes of self-regulation and self-correction. If children grasp the concept of self-regulating systems, they can apply it to systems of all kinds, including the functioning of their own bodies or families, schools or neighborhoods. When an abstract pattern has been recognized in a single memorable example, the possibility of multiple analogy is created. In this sense, ecology offers tools for thinking about why it is unwise to experiment with addictive drugs, about the course of family quarrels, or about the damage done by racism.

Everywhere, cultural views of the world include metaphorical extensions of relations within one area of experience, as a given culture constructs it, onto another. Often, relations within the home are projected out onto a wider world, as in the ethical metaphor of the "brotherhood of man." New metaphors drawn from ecology are the modern version of a familiar process, but they may lead to new conclusions, perhaps to a realization that observation can never be separated from participation. Learning to think about how ecosystems function might provide analogies for respect for difference within a multicultural society, or for understanding the interactions between different players and interest groups in a democracy. Valuing ecological diversity might teach pluralism and the conviction that the goal of the political process is not specific solutions but the maintenance of conversation.

Years ago, I wrote about the experience of caring for an aquarium set up with my father as a way of introducing the concepts of cybernetics: circularity, feedback, self-correction, equilibrium, and the linking of systems. The aquarium that stands today in so many classrooms can teach the same lessons, but the risk is that the children will think of themselves as outside the system. An aquarium makes a good model for what has been called First Order Cybernetics, but I was always taught to include myself, outside the glass sides of the aquarium, as a participant in the process, and to see it as coupled with other systems, a point of view now referred to as Second Order Cybernetics.[5] To understand what an aquarium in the classroom can teach, and what can then be applied to neighborhood ponds and their surroundings, it seems worthwhile to quote my earlier writing:

> The tropical fish were the first living things for whose care I was responsible. The aquarium, both sheltered and exposed by its glass walls, had a certain elusive self-sufficiency. I sat beside it by the hour and brooded on the relationships between the fish and on the balances that would have to be maintained in order for them to live. Sometimes, indeed, I interfered in ways that disrupted the balance in the tank, adding too many fish, uprooting the plants to rearrange them, or dosing the aquarium with tonic. It was the community I learned to care for, self-contained to a degree, and yet dependent on me and on our household on Perry Street, so that the lives of those fish depended on the peace and continuity of our

lives, just as our own peace depended on a wider political peace in those early years of the Cold War. The aquarium was a world within a world, connected to these wider systems through my capacity to understand and respond to its needs.[6]

The aquarium was beautiful but frustrating. In a low-keyed way, it could be both demanding and recalcitrant. What is critical is that it could not educate me about ecology without also posing wider questions. Aquariums stand in the schoolrooms of thousands of children, alongside the cages of gerbils and guinea pigs, which also require care and teach the lessons of living and dying. Unlike much of what is done in a classroom, mistakes made in caring for an aquarium have real costs. Caring for living creatures requires action in uncertainty, for we can never ask the fish about their needs or fully know what is happening. The frustrations of keeping an aquarium or a garden are a reminder that human observers are not omniscient and that human actors often do harm. Seen through the lens of an aquarium, the world looks different.

Models of human relations may be projected onto the cosmos, and models of the functioning of the natural world spill over into societal arrangements. The great Chain of Being, ordering relations from God down to the most lowly of creations,[7] matched the hierarchical structure of medieval life, including that of the family. Thus, a change in understanding of any aspect of life is likely to carry over into other aspects.

In 1986, Christian fundamentalist parents in Tennessee brought a lawsuit against the school system, arguing that their children were being taught the "religion of humanism."[8] One exhibit showed an illustration from an elementary school reader in which a little boy is putting bread into a toaster while a little girl reads instructions. One can argue that the problem posed by this picture goes far beyond gender and the family, for traditional gender roles are based on the notion that there is an isomorphism among God's rule over creation, the rule of humankind over the rest of the natural world, and a man's rule over his wife and family—indeed, an isomorphism with all hierarchical systems in politics and business as well. In each of these systems, an emphasis on authority at the top tends to block awareness of circular paths of information and control. Similarly, the teaching of evolution not only undermines the role of God as creator and ruler, but also other social relations constructed on the same model.

The early appropriation of evolution by Darwin's contemporaries was also a source of error, for they extended its meaning in ways that ecological study has shown are not good biology. The discovery of natural selection as the mechanism of biological evolution offered a rationale—the survival of the fittest—for the exploitive practices of colonialism and the early industrial revolution, suggesting that the elimination of the weak was beneficial. Our society is still haunted by the notion that competition leads to improvement and that the strong should dominate the weak.

Essentially, the teaching of ecology offers the metaphor of interdependence and symbiosis to replace the metaphor of dominance. It represents a profound shift in thinking that goes far beyond nature study to imply changes in family life and in politics. Neo–Darwinian theory emphasizes populations rather than individuals, the resilience given to populations by genetic diversity, and the frequency of symbiosis. In effect, it suggests metaphors of cooperation rather than competition, the need of the individual for the collective rather than the viability of the autonomous individual.

Such metaphors are not automatically applied to all areas of experience, but spread out in ripples, just as it took a long time to understand that Enlightenment ideas of the rights of man might apply to all human beings. Systemic metaphors run counter to much of what is usually taught in economics and political science. They also pose to children the question of their place in the larger system, a possibility of contribution as well as subordination and dependency.

Ecology in the Conduct of Education

Within the larger structure of culture, different societies have different assumptions about where childhood and schooling fit in. When nature is seen as inchoate and threatening, and natural impulses as dangerous, classrooms are likely to be rigidly disciplined, but when the natural world is seen in terms of emergent patterns of self-organization, we begin to treasure spontaneity. Schools, like gardens, are planned and organized; they reflect the basic understandings of a society or of a community. Just as the gardens of France and Japan and England echo different attitudes toward nature and discipline and pattern, so do their classrooms. Even in democracies, however, schools have not traditionally been particularly democratic, and the day-to-day organization of lessons and classrooms has often been based on assumptions that are implicitly antiecological.[9] Much of contemporary education has replicated the patterns of agribusiness or industry rather than those of natural ecosystems. Thus, we divide up the educational enterprise among a series of time-slot subjects and specialists, who often fail to make connections between the subjects they teach, and we teach children in batches selected for various kinds of uniformity, particularly age, having segregated them from the life of the community. All too many classrooms are modeled on a hierarchical cosmos, with a teacher who must always be right and in control, because participation and diversity of opinion make for an unpredictable and sometimes noisy classroom.

Education occupies a slot in the life cycle that is variously conceived, sometimes as a model for the rest of life, sometimes as a necessary preliminary to be escaped as quickly as possible, but in either case, school is contrasted with "real life" and children are not seen as full participants in society. Some educators emphasize competitiveness, while others emphasize adaptability, two alternative evolutionary strategies that play different roles in ecology. In the same way, some systems value specialization while others value breadth, some value diversity while others value uniformity. We are living in a time of both creativity and concern about education, and the decisions that are made for the classroom will feed directly into the way graduates participate in society and the way they impact on the natural systems around them. The decision, for instance, to supply funds for the arts has one kind of implication, and the decision to supply funds for athletic teams has another.

We are only a few decades away from a period when schools were deliberately constructed so that classrooms were without windows. This was based on a rather narrow understanding of the kind of attention appropriate in school children and on a selected style of learning. Children were expected to be immobile and narrowly focused on the words of the teacher, achieving specified goals as uniformly as possible. If one takes a group of children on a walk through the woods, however, they will notice different things and bring back different memories, expressing a variety of different kinds of attention. We need those different kinds of attention in the population if we are to be ecologically sensitive.[10]

Both democracy and ecology argue for diversity. In the search for solutions, it is easy to become focused on a single definition of educational goals, to try to maximize some aspect of education, and to set fixed standards. Yet, perhaps any dogmatic adherence to a single strategy is antiecological. One of the great lessons of the end of the Cold War is that in a society in which decision making is highly centralized and disagreement not allowed, a society with narrowly defined goals, many important issues will be unexpressed. Concern for protecting the natural world was limited for years to a small and eccentric minority, who used to be described as "little old ladies in tennis shoes." These peripheral visionaries were not silenced, however, and their concerns have gradually become part of a shared agenda. There is thus a relationship between the development of a viable environmental movement and democratic institutions. If a classroom is to function as an actual model for either democratic participation or ecological understanding (rather than a source of unilateral authority), schools will have to change.

Children in the Democratic Process

Schools are part of the larger social ecology, affecting the place of children in the democratic process. Within an understanding of circular systems, children can learn to see themselves as teachers as well as learners.

Children carry home to their families what they learn, thus influencing the participation and decision making of their families. Children have played a number of different roles in the education of their parents in the history of this country. The children of immigrants have often coached their parents in how to live here, mediating their contacts with outsiders and forging ahead in language skills. Within native-born populations, higher levels of education in succeeding generations have often been the norm, and this continues to be true even in this era of criticism of public education. Children are often exposed to new technologies, like computers, or to new consumer trends in which they are diligently propagandized by marketers, or to new ethical issues, before their parents.

This education in reverse is not always welcome. It is not new for children to say, in effect, "Walk your talk." The "generation gap" of the sixties was interpreted by some social scientists[11] as a process in which adolescents turned the claims of the older generation back against it, demanding for instance that equality and democracy be made into realities rather than slogans. Some young women are able to rebuke their fathers'—and mothers'—assumptions about gender roles. Some of the anger about "political correctness" may originate in parental irritation at domestic debate about derogatory terms still used "All in the Family." Young children often dislike cigarette smoke, and today they have the ammunition to complain. Some of these patterns of speaking out are probably limited to middle-class households, but others are more widespread.

Schools today face new demands for the teaching of "traditional values," those values that parents—or small activist groups of parents—want to see taught. But changing times demand new emphases and recognitions, a new appreciation of cultural diversity, responsible sexuality replacing chastity, lifelong learning replacing early commitment and security. The teaching of ecology represents a major frontier of values change that may often prove as unwelcome to parents as sex education. How should we understand the propriety of teaching values to children when it leads to their criticizing their parents' behavior, and who has the right to make these decisions?

Furthermore, the particular value changes involved in the teaching of ecology suggest major shifts in intergenerational relationships. Children constitute an interest group, one whose interests may not coincide with those of their parents, but which remains disenfranchised.[12]

Democracy has always had a limited franchise, and our understanding even of human rights has had to be broadened time and again. Decisions about suffrage are always ambiguously poised between the issue of competence and the issue of standing, the right to participate in a decision by which one is affected. At one time, only mature white males who owned property were considered qualified to vote, and the struggle for voting rights (both theoretical and actual) for African Americans and for women's suffrage revolved around both competence and standing. Until the

Vietnam War, males between the ages of eighteen and twenty-one were considered old enough to be drafted and sent to die on the battlefield, but not old enough to vote.

Today, several groups of people making their homes in the United States and affected by political decisions are not fully enfranchised, including residents of the District of Columbia and Puerto Rico, native Americans, and, of course, permanent residents of this country who are not yet citizens. Beyond these specific groups, we make decisions affecting the lives of others—citizens of other countries and of the future, and above all, children under eighteen. Children are clearly the outstanding stakeholders in the future, the ones most obviously subject to injury by bad environmental policy.

Some environmentalists would argue that forests and wetlands and threatened species themselves have rights, but that is a position that is not yet politically viable. We are moving, however, toward a situation in which children may become effective as the principal advocates of threatened species and ecosystems, and may have the clearest understanding of and identification with their needs.

As surely as the court of King George putting a tax on tea drunk in the distant American colonies was taxation without representation, when the federal government borrows money to be repaid in the future, it is engaged in setting tax rates and commitments for those still too young to vote; the same is true of the creation of new entitlements, which will affect those who are under eighteen, who are given no voice in the matter. Similarly, when policies are enacted that will reduce available resources or make the environment less salubrious twenty years from now, those who are now underage or still to be born have the greatest stake in opposing shortsighted decisions. The situation is summed up in a bumper sticker I saw recently on a shiny camper far from its home state: "We're spending our children's inheritance."

There are a variety of reasons why parents can no longer be regarded as adequate spokespersons for their children's future interests, if indeed they ever were, which I will not explore here, including the credit-based economy and the emphasis on consumption. Perhaps the most important reasons come from increased longevity leading to new anxiety about economic security in old age and changed patterns of generational overlap. Today, most parents die well past the maturity of their children, passing on property and encountering grandchildren at a different stage in the life cycle, and we live in a society that is in many ways segregated by age.

The environmental awareness of children is increasing and being fostered in the schools in the context of a society in which children do not have a political voice and have few mechanisms to defend their long-term interests. The evolution of a childhood earth lobby is bound to lead to an increasing consciousness on the part of children and young people that an injustice is being done to them—and to their children and grandchildren. As a society, we are often preoccupied by issues of equity in the present or reparations for past damages, but we have few tools for thinking about equity across generations. Environmental issues pose a whole new area of social justice, expressed in a widely used slogan: "We do not inherit the earth from our parents; we borrow it from our children."

The issue of intergenerational equity and its relationship to environmental issues is being taken up in many places. In Boulder, Colorado, in the summer of 1993, a mock hearing on whether it would be possible to sue on behalf of future generations was used as part of the inauguration of the new Walter Orr Roberts Institute at the University of Colorado's National Center for Atmospheric Research (NCAR).[13] At the same time, extending over several days, there was an intergenerational conference at NCAR on the theme "Inherit the Earth." To make sure the conference was intergenerational, local young people were recruited, as were the residents of a local retirement community. The lead-up to the on-site conference was a computer conference in which all participants were anonymous, individual voices not labeled as "youth" or "age" or, among the middle-aged contingent, "scientific expert." At the end, one of the key proposals was that a forum be created for intergenerational discussion of environmental policies that would be sufficiently broadly based to be quoted by the media, offering a voice through an alternative channel.

Central to the message of the younger participants in the Boulder conference was the awareness that it is their lives and their children's lives that are being bartered away. Many of the older people also seemed to be saying that senior citizens' lobbies such as the American Association for Retired Persons misstate the profound interest of the old in a sense of ongoing continuity with the lives of future generations: it is their immortality that is being bartered away. It seems probable, therefore, that the study of ecology in the educational system will change our understanding of the kind of voice children can and should have, whether through formal voting or through some other mechanism of opinion, as children become more aware of the legitimacy of their interests.

In any debate about extending the franchise, the question of competence carries over into questions about whether a given group speaks for itself or simply parrots the views of some other group. Women, it was said, would simply vote as instructed by their husbands. Blacks, it was said, would be manipulated by unscrupulous outsiders—and for many years, demands for improvement by African Americans were attributed to communist agitators. If the rising wave of environmental concern among children begins to have a real effect on policy, whether through developing and expressing opinions or through boycotts and lobbying, far short of actually gaining the vote, the sinister manipulators blamed for using children like ventriloquist's dummies may be teachers and other educators.

Conclusions

Although the models of organization offered by ecology suggest new ways of teaching about society and about family life that are congruent with democracy, the connection is not automatic. One cannot assume that all environmentalists are "ecological" in their social and political behavior, and one cannot assume that "nature studies" are ecologically sound, for all too often the pictures of natural systems leave out vital elements. Thus, saving the whales is irrelevant without a concern for plankton, and forest ecology requires a recognition of the role of fires. Whales or spotted owls, discussed out of their systemic contexts, are just as misleading as an exclusive focus on any other species, including our own. Children respond most easily and directly to the young of other mammals, warm and fuzzy, but that can be no more than a starting point. Baby seals are easy for children to identify with and defend, even within the context of old systems of values, but activism on behalf of seals is rarely extended to the seals' cold-blooded neighbors. One test of whether the teaching of ecology is systemic is whether the necessity of death is included, for the denial of death distorts understanding of wider natural processes. Teaching about nature that does not embrace death, predation, and decay is no more than a form of sentimentality.

Environmentalists are like the rest of us in their willingness to believe that they are right and others are wrong and in using whatever tools come to hand to achieve a defined goal or to get a job done, and this sometimes leads to actions that distort ecological understanding or disrupt the ecologies of human communication. For instance, environmentalists have used the spotted owls as a political lever for the protection of old-growth forest—a single threatened species as the rationale for preserving a total system. Similarly, we have heard much about the possibility that ancient ecosystems might include species like the Pacific yew, invaluable for medicine. Yet, arguments based on a single species or the meeting of a single human need obscure the fact that the struggle is really about preserving the integrity of whole systems that can never be replicated—and about the principle that whole systems are really worth preserving. In the same way, no charity is raising funds for a particular poster child, but for a population of the sick and disabled, and for the principle that a society should be concerned about its most vulnerable members. Lawsuits on behalf of the spotted owl may be useful tactics (and critical to halt plans for immediate cutting), but they run the risk of obscuring what is really at stake—and making environmentalists vulnerable to attack and caricature.

Typically, environmentalists approach debate with a sense that the compromises and delays of the democratic process will offer too little too late, and with the willingness to demonize opponents. Competing with other interests, environmentalists have gotten into the position of seeming to deny other kinds of needs, instead of exploring the place of those needs in a larger system. Concerned with correcting flaws in value systems, environmentalists have tried to *add* environmental values to the national agenda, or argued for the need to set environmental values in place of anthropocentrism, without offering an acceptable context for humanistic values, letting these be someone else's business.

Just as a holistic concept of human well-being must include both meditation and chemistry, a holistic concept of the biosphere must acknowledge the place of human beings. Thinking of the natural world as if human beings were not part of it is just as likely to lead to error as is putting human beings at the center and regarding all other forms of life as expendable. Similarly, it is a source of confusion to regard some vegetables as more organic than others, or to regard some human behaviors as "unnatural" or outside of nature. There is a new kind of anthropocentrism emerging that starts from valuing humankind, but that emphasizes that humankind is part of and dependent on a larger system—that the unit of survival is *the species in its environment,* and that the species that destroys its environment destroys itself. Within the context of this new anthropocentrism, it is possible to juxtapose compassion for starving children with concern about desertification and soil depletion, and to emphasize the need for population control within a sustainable model for human quality of life.

It seems important for environmental activism and ecological education that the rhetoric used reflect the real complexity of the situation, including the ecology of political change. The political process in this country, however we phrase democratic ideals, is still based on vertical hierarchy and modeled on crude forms of competition and win-lose games. In the past, after all, the lessons of domination and competition were taught in church and in the home as well as in school. The much more systemic notions of pluralism and the balance of powers built into the Constitution have been at odds with other habits of thought, creating an ambiguity that has been uncomfortable but no doubt productive. It is not surprising that environmentalists approach political conflict with the conviction of having the truth and the determination to win, for this is the American way. It is in fact extraordinarily difficult to shift the vast momentum of a society like our own toward a higher level of responsibility, and it is understandable that those who see a need for change might get trapped into action through adversarial institutions and wish secretly that they could bring it about by fiat. But change by fiat belongs to the old model.

Teaching ecology in the schools—teaching children to think systemically—carries with it the lesson that even as each species goes about surviving in its distinctive way, the other species are also necessary. The effort to affect systemic outcomes takes place from within rather than from without—second order rather than first order cybernetics. This is a lesson to be carried over into the process of political debate, recognizing that the normal sequence of change is not one in which one side wins and the other loses, but a long slow process of compromise. Ecology carries with it a set of ideas about what it is to be part of a larger system.

Notes

1. Gregory Bateson, *Mind and Nature: A Necessary Unity* (New York: Dutton, 1979).
2. Mary Catherine Bateson, "Into the Trees," in *Sacred Trusts*, edited by M. Katekis (San Francisco: Mercury House, 1993).
3. Mary Catherine Bateson, *With a Daughter's Eye* (2nd ed.) (New York: Harper, 1993).
4. James E. Lovelock, *Gaia: A New Look at Life on Earth* (Oxford: Oxford University Press, 1979).
5. Heinz von Foerster, *Observing Systems* (Salinas, Calif.: Intersystems, 1982).
6. Mary Catherine Bateson, *Our Own Metaphor* (Washington, D.C.: Smithsonian Institution Press, 1991), pp. 6–7.
7. Arthur O. Lovejoy, *The Great Chain of Being: A Study of the History of an Idea* (Cambridge, Mass.: Harvard University Press, 1936).
8. Alan Sanford, "Tilting at 'Secular Humanism,'" *Time Magazine*, July 28, 1986, p. 68.
9. C. A. Bowers, *Education, Cultural Myths, and the Ecological Crisis: Toward Deep Changes* (Albany: State University of New York Press, 1993).
10. Mary Catherine Bateson, *Peripheral Visions: Learning Along the Way* (New York: HarperCollins, 1994).
11. Ken Keniston, *Youth and Dissent: The Rise of a New Opposition* (New York: Harcourt, Brace, Jovanovich, 1971).
12. Richard Farson, *Birthrights* (New York: Macmillan, 1974).
13. National Center for Atmospheric Research, *Inherit the Earth: An Intergenerational Symposium on the Environment*, Boulder, Colorado, July 14–17, 1993.

| Chapter Four |

Democracy, Education, and Community

John I. Goodlad

The four central themes of this chapter are embedded in the following quote:

> If America can commit itself to this next task—educating all children well—the historic promise of free public schooling will be fulfilled. It doesn't require a nationalized curriculum backed by a high-stakes testing program that falsely promises order and control; or a privatized market-driven system offering the illusion of freedom and individuality. What it requires is tough but doable: generous resources, thoughtful and steady work, respect for the diverse perspectives of the people who work in and attend our schools and, finally, sustained public interest in and tolerance for the process of re-invention. Nothing else will do it.[1]

Two of these themes are concerned with the meaning of "educating all children well." First, a context invariably shapes the educational process. The shaping that takes place in a fascist or communist regime is quite different from that which takes place in a democracy. Second, there is education itself. Is it a mere instrument to be fought over and then used to serve the dominant interests of the context? Two more themes arise out of issues surrounding the nature of freedom and the public interest and the relationship between them. The balance in this relationship determines the quality of community life and, indeed, whether there exists anything warranting the description "community."

The tension in the provision of education and schooling in a democracy is a reflection of the tension within democracy itself—between the rights and responsibilities of the individual and the polity. Maintaining an appropriate balance strains a democratic government. This balance is a condition to be sought continually; it is not the norm. Benjamin Barber has stated the challenge well: "Democracy is anything but a 'natural' form of association. It is an extraordinary and rare contrivance of cultivated imagination."[2]

The shadow hanging over Convention Hall was the question of whether the American people could govern themselves, in the sense of balancing the individual and the commonweal. Education came to be seen as the essential condition to be in place. Yet, the founding fathers left it out of the Constitution. Were they so prescient as to realize that education is both so pervasive and so powerful that it must always be protected and promoted but never used as an instrument of government?

This chapter seeks to link concepts of democracy to concepts of self and *civitas*—a body of people constituting a politically organized community—in part through developing an understanding of what education is and what schools are for. Chapter Five will pick up where this one leaves off, exploring a deep understanding of the role of schools in a democratic society.

Beyond Political Democracy

Preceding chapters have provided perspectives on the meaning of democracy; there are more perspectives to come. The propositions of this chapter require distinctions among political democracy, social democracy, and democracy of the human spirit. Making *political democracy* work is a complex, delicate process. Even more complex and precarious is *social democracy*: the living together of people endeavoring to follow democratic principles. People who run away from the bureaucracies that characterize all genres of democracy and, indeed, government are staggered by the interpersonal difficulties encountered in seeking to establish small communes characterized by the utopian principles they envisioned. They soon come to realize how necessary and difficult it is to expand the few values shared to a much larger common core. When the concept of social democracy is broadened to include all people in a democracy that embraces humankind and the human condition, the problems of resolving religious, ethnic, and racial differences appear overwhelming. Yet, that spark of hope never dies out. Beyond divisiveness there is the *democracy of the human spirit* that transcends all individuality and binds humankind—somewhere a place for all of us, together.

Political democracy depends heavily on traditions, customs, and laws. Social democracy depends heavily on the exercise of civility and *civitas*.[3] Citizens are not born with the necessary traits; they are acquired through education. The role of education in developing these traits is not at all free from disputation, but disagreement heightens to a level of violence when the route to a democracy of the human spirit is the subject at hand. How are the differences within, let alone between, secular and sectarian belief and dogma to be pushed aside sufficiently to permit the emergence of a common center?

Even to suggest common ground where two such differing paths to truth join in a sense of the sacred sufficient to provide a moral grounding for democracy—political, social, and of the human spirit—is to bring down on each a pox from the other. Yet, the future of civilization depends on there being widespread agreement on "the sense of interconnections among the individual, the collectivity, and ultimate purpose and meaning of human existence."[4] No such agreement is possible if there are not in the culture educational contingencies that subject all belief to intense scrutiny. The essence of democracy is freedom to engage in this scrutiny with impunity. This means that the very principles on which democracy rests are not immune from inquiry.

A political democracy requires for its sustenance the reiteration of truths and widespread allegiance to them. The more comprehensive these truths and the more commonly they are shared, the more sustaining the democracy ascribing to them will be. In this, the American democracy is widely regarded as a model, a haven for the oppressed and dissident seeking amnesty. First, we have the "self-evident" truths and unalienable rights of the Declaration of Independence: "that all men are created equal; that they are endowed by their Creator with certain unalienable rights; that among these are life, liberty, and the pursuit of happiness." Then, we have the Constitution to secure them; then the amendments (the first ten of which are known as the Bill of Rights) that assist interpretation and implementation;[5] and to guide the process of ratification for the years that followed, there is that lasting monument to Alexander Hamilton, James Madison, and John Jay, their incredible analysis of every part of the Constitution, *The Federalist*.[6] To make it all more human, we continue to commemorate the Founding Fathers, particularly John Adams, Benjamin Franklin, Alexander Hamilton, Thomas Jefferson, James Madison, and George Washington. We are blessed, indeed, with a comprehensive picture of the good work to be carried out by the citizens, the elected representatives of these citizens, and their agencies in sustaining the American democracy.

It is appropriate for a government to sustain a system of education to ensure among the citizens both understanding of and belief in this comprehensive picture. Many years before the American republic was forged, the householders of the early towns taxed themselves for schools in which all the young would be taught "the laws of the land, and the principles of religion." Since they did not need schools for their own children (they could afford tutors and the luxury of sending their children abroad or, eventually, to private academies at home), this self-taxing would appear to be an act of considerable magnanimity. However, it was as much or more motivated by self-interest.[7] These comparatively prosperous settlers did not want the religion and the ideals of self-government they had brought with them to be endangered by the ignorance of growing members of newcomers lacking access to schooling.

These early schools—and those of many decades to follow—had a comparatively easy time of it with respect to mission. The Christian faith and the laws of community living were seen virtually as one. Home, school, and church worked together in a common sense of what it means to be human in the image of Jesus Christ, the Son of God, and to have liberty under God, but the siren call of freedom was to attract to this land those of other faiths, no faiths, other beliefs, and even other gods. The mix was, in time, to sorely test and strain the great democratic experiment.

The resiliency of democracy was further strained and the role of schools muddied by the inexorable rise of "the human individual in his own idiom,"[8] driven by the intrusion of rationalism into all aspects of political, social, and personal life. "The conduct of affairs, for the Rationalist, is a matter of solving problems, and in this no man can hope to be successful whose reason has become inflexible by surrender to habit or is clouded by the fumes of tradition."[9] The moral theory pervading the pursuit of individuality embraced the individual's relationship with the self and with others. "But as a rational human being he will recognize in his conduct the universal conditions of autonomous personality; and the chief of these conditions is to use humanity, as well in himself as in others, as an end and never as a means."[10]

There appears to be little resolution between the concept of the human being as the creature of God and the concept of self-realization through a process of independent choice. How are both to be served equitably in a modern system of representative government? And what rights of the citizen and duty to government is that government to protect and promote? The laws that come down from the legislative bodies favor individual freedom, including the freedom of religious belief and observance.

Political democracy can never resolve dissonance in the fundamental beliefs of its citizens, nor should it. Nor should these citizens expect such resolution. The best a democratic regime can do in this domain is to recognize freedom and support the conditions that sustain it. The end purpose of this freedom goes beyond unabating celebration of the democratic state. The ideal of freedom and of democracy is the autonomous individual who transcends narcissism in the internalization of oughts and shoulds that lead to moral action in the moral community.[11]

The internalization of oughts and shoulds that lead to moral action in the moral community requires a conception of what society should be. "The vision explicitly rules out individualism as an *exclusive* basis for judging proposals for action. The thrust of the vision is that . . . the bond to be forged will contribute more to societal well being than either a riveting on individual rights or on a suffocating conformity to a collectivity."[12] The current problem of the American democracy is that of coping with a virtual explosion of individuals and collectives seeking to define their identity for themselves in the face of the realization that those in power over the years have been defining it for them. This drive for long-overdue recognition and a secure place in the culture (for minorities, women, gay people, disabled people, religious groups, and the like) has been accompanied also by a narcissistic obsession with self that has both hurt just causes and strained community. With the public interest being constantly redefined to accommodate diversity, the core of common vision shrinks.

It is appropriate to keep education always in view as the long-term hope for simultaneously sustaining a common core of beliefs and accommodating diversity, but the creation of high value and high visibility for education fuels the desire of diverse interest groups to make it work for them. This makes it very difficult for education to serve the commonweal. The problem is exacerbated when education is equated with schooling, as is largely the case in the United States. The schools become so instrumental in the cacophony of purpose attached to them that it is exceedingly difficult for them to know, let alone serve, the public purpose of education.

For education to undergird the renewal of both political and social democracy, it must transcend the divisions in philosophical and religious persuasion that exist in a diverse population and reach for some higher and more universal meaning of human existence. That there will be agreement on a common set of values and moral principles is unrealistic, if only because such a notion is secular and eschews the concept of divine law embedded in religious belief. However, we do know that the study of religions leads to an understanding of their commonalities and respect for their differences. Similarly, we know that the study of humankind leads to an understanding of the principles of civility, personal decency, interindividual and intergroup respect, as well as the caring necessary to community. We also learn of the human misery that accompanies the absence of these principles. Although we may not be able to come together in a common vision, the opportunity to pursue one's own vision depends on a significant proportion of the population being sufficiently educated to understand and appreciate what is required for the survival and advancement of civilization. So far, human ingenuity appears not to have created a better instrumentality for the cultivation and use of intelligence than a robust political and social democracy.

Education

The dilemma for education as the hope for sustaining a balance between individuality and *civicism* (devotion to civic interests and causes) is its very nature. Education is of and by the self. It cannot be given or taken away by another or performed for one's self by another. There can be no delegation to surrogates. Yet, education is not a private matter. As I have said, there is always a cultural context. There can be no definition and development of self apart from culture. The broader the context of enculturation, the better the prospects for education and for a self capable of participating comprehensively in the human conversation.

Beyond Training

The narcissism of the young child is exhaustively documented and abundantly clear. The process of transcendence from self-preoccupation to self-identification to multiple contextual connections and cultural identification cannot be taken for granted.[13] Unfortunately, there is precious little parental preparation for arranging the necessary educational contingencies, a situation that steadily grows worse. The nature of these contingencies during the months of infancy and the years of early childhood is particularly crucial.[14] This formative stage is very short, often proving to be a kind of parental internship in childrearing that parents hope will serve them well the next time around.

Erik Erikson provides us with both a disturbing and a challenging portrait of the tensions between positive and negative tendencies in his "eight stages of man," through which he says we pass in the life cycle. He stresses the "ritual practice" in the community—the common faith—that supports the development of trustworthiness, autonomy, initiative, industry, identity, intimacy, generativity, and ego integrity that are the characteristics of wholesome individuality, the indices of healthy self-transcendence. Similarly, he notes the significance of what must be ritually eschewed or even proclaimed evil in the community, such as individual mistrust.[15] Although the educating and the paths pursued are of the self, the shaping of that self in family, school, and community is powerful and relentless, and clearly, the educative agencies are multiple.

The message is clear: "There will be no liberty, no equality, no social justice without democracy, and there will be no democracy without citizens and the schools that forge civic identity and democratic responsibility."[16] If education were merely some kind of training—such as to paddle a canoe, ride a bicycle, or even add numbers—we could afford to be somewhat relaxed about its context. Yet even under such circumstances, we cannot afford not to address the question of ultimate use. My incarcerated students in the industrial school for (delinquent) boys frequently offered to teach me the craft of lock picking. They offered no accompanying manual or lessons regarding the moral circumstances under which use of my new skill would be legitimate.

One begins to understand the motivation among some people to require a system of schooling to be scrupulously devoid of moral teaching or scrupulously attentive to the ideological mandates of those in control. Pedagogy designed to develop critical thinking abilities is ruled out in both instances. In the first instance, parents can be reasonably comfortable with their expectation that what has been carefully taught at home will not confront alternatives at school. In the second, authoritarian officials can be reasonably comfortable that few of the seeds that grow into questioning and revolt will be planted. In both instances, not only is there no need for a liberally educated teaching force, there is disinterest in such—and certainly no interest in the professional education of teachers, especially that education designed to prepare teachers for the moral stewardship of our schools. The mentoring of new teachers into the well-established, noncontroversial ways of the old suffices; the salaries of teachers and the costs of teaching are kept low. Citizens with no desire to keep critical enculturation out of the schools, who simply have not thought about the connection between education and democracy, are pleased with taxes kept low.

The 1986 slogan of the National Governors' Association, "better schools mean better jobs"[17]—repeated over and over into the 1990s—sells better politically than "education for democracy." When, in the fall of 1993, one very thoughtful governor—Roy Romer of Colorado—managed to inject Jeffersonian concepts into a meandering discussion of schooling on the program *This Week with David Brinkley*, William Bennett (presumably an aspirant for a run at the presidency) waved him aside as if Jefferson had engaged in idle dreaming—this from a former secretary of education.

Increasing attempts from a wide array of special interest groups—strange bedfellows who will divide and quarrel bitterly once they succeed in enfeebling the educative function of our public schools and creating a unique model of private schools sustained by the public purse—both wittingly and unwittingly threaten all three of the democracies defined at the beginning of this chapter. What appears to drive most of these groups is a kind of individualism that eschews self-transcendence and the making of a democratic polity. They are endowed by their creator with unalienable rights: my life, my liberty, and my pursuit of happiness. The words triggering their attack on the public schools include equity, cooperative learning, global education, heterogeneous grouping, and critical thinking—and any others that speak to social democracy—and any concepts that appear to challenge a given group's aspirations for hegemony. After expressing his alarm, Barber reaffirms the imperative:

> Education in vocationalism, pre-professional training, what were once called the "servile arts" . . . may be private. But public education is general, common, and thus in the original sense "liberal." This means that public education is education for citizenship. . . . The autonomy and the dignity no less than the rights and freedoms of all Americans depend on the survival of democracy: not just democratic government, but a democratic civil society and a democratic civic culture. There is only one road to democracy: education. And in a democracy, there is only one essential task for the educator: teaching liberty.[18]

What Education Is

Liberty is a contextual concept. It conveys a sense of being unfettered: doors that open to the touch, no fences, no burdensome restraints, no regulations. The more we add words that picture unbridled freedom, the more troublesome the concept becomes. It leads to what Barry Bull calls "an embarrassment of riches" that must be overcome if the individual pursuit of liberty is not to be self-defeating.[19]

Bull argues that freedom must be limited when its exercise would unreasonably interfere with the freedom of others. The freedom to buy and sell other people, for example, must be restricted, whereas the freedom to hold religious beliefs must not. The necessary distinctions are not always this easily made, however. It is somewhat easier to identify self-defeating freedoms—the equal exercise of which by all members of society frustrates the very purpose of the freedoms themselves—than it is to distinguish risk-laden freedoms—those that impede the freedoms of others only under certain circumstances.[20] It is easy to see that the freedom to operate an automobile without license or restraint is self-defeating. It is much more difficult to argue that home schooling throughout the whole of childhood and adolescence is risk-laden for the family. It is even more difficult to argue that widespread home schooling is dangerous to the well-being of a democratic society. One can only make the argument convincing when there is common recognition that the aim of education is twofold: preparation for duties of citizenship and preparation to lead a good life.

Because those who seek to define the educative process usually have an implicit understanding of its personal, individual nature, most definitions stress the second of the two aims, sometimes to complete omission of the first. Also, because this awareness usually is accompanied by keen sensitivity to the corrupting of education through making it instrumental to all manner of political, economic, and social purposes, care usually is taken to close the door to such abuses.

There is, for example, very little room for contextual intrusions into Israel Scheffler's definition: "the formation of habits of judgment and the development of character, the elevation of standards, the facilitation of understanding, the development of taste and discrimination, the stimulation of curiosity and wondering, the fostering of style and a sense of beauty, the growth of a thirst for new ideas and visions of the yet unknown."[21] Yet, mostly because of its omission of education as instrument to jobs, Scheffler's definition is regarded in some quarters as elitist and out of sight for many. Mortimer Adler, on the other hand, simply yields to popular perception and adds preparation for earning a living to the dual aim of citizenship and self-realization.[22] Scheffler's "visions of the yet unknown" evokes images of cultivating the imagination and of provoking the wrath of those who interpret this to mean the elevation of human reasoning over divine will. This objection then leads to further argumentation over whose god or whose interpretation of god shall prevail.

The sobering reality, already sharply put forward in the quotes from Barber, is that education and democracy are inextricably woven together. If there is an instrumentality here, it lies in the fact that each is instrumental to the other. Education must ritually take place in a democratic context; democracy must ritually resort to educational processes. Ends alone must never be used to justify means; all means must be justified in their own right, with moral principles outweighing all others. This is a perspective that counterbalances the unbridled pursuit of individual freedom. It is a perspective that currently runs counter to many of the most popular contingencies of American life. The issue is whether there can be some common center—some *unum*—where rational, moral concepts of freedom and responsibility, the essence of democracy, join divine law, the essence of religion, where the rough edges of secular and sectarian dogma fade into the shadows. What is the role of education in creating and expanding that center?

Clearly, the role is a moral one that has little to do with behavioral doctrines and much to do with the circumstances of liberty.[23] The distinctions among political and social democracy and a democracy of humankind generate distinctions in the morality called for. Oakeshott denotes three idioms of moral condition: the morality of individuality, the morality of community ties, and the morality of the common good:

> In the morality of individuality, human beings are recognized . . . as separate and sovereign individuals. . . . Morality is the art of mutual accommodation. . . . In the morality of communal ties, human beings are recognized solely as members of a community and all activity whatsoever is understood to be communal activity. . . . This is an idiom of *moral* conduct, because the manner of this communal activity is, in fact, art and not nature. . . . The morality of the common good springs from . . . the emergence of a different idiom of human character. Human beings are recognized as independent centers of activity, but approval attaches itself to conduct in which this individuality is suppressed whenever it conflicts, not with the individuality of others, but with the interest of a "society" understood to be composed of such human beings. All are engaged in a single, common enterprise . . . and morality is the art in which this condition is achieved and maintained.[24]

The arts of mutual accommodation, of communal ties, and the common good are teachable. These are the liberal arts of Barber's educational imperative. They define a large part of what education is: a deliberate, systematic, and sustained effort to develop and refine human sensibilities and sensitivities.[25] Without it, democracy cannot be sustained.

Individual Freedom and the Common Good

The single-minded pursuit of individualism, whether in the human idiom or in the canons of religious doctrine seeking salvation of the individual soul, is the obverse of *communitas*—the cultivation of a spirit of community-mindedness. Mecca is a ghetto of one; association is of choice, not a moral ethic calling for moral art. At most, for the former, community is a collection of semi-isolated individuals who respect each other's isolation coming together to validate life's chase; for those espousing the religious idiom, it is an encampment of like-minded believers together sustaining faith. Personal comfort and assurance depend on the absence of dissonance; one seeks like-mindedness in neighbors. Given the dissolution of many communal arrangements through the exercise of such individualism over the centuries, what hope is there for democracy? And what might we expect from education, given the fact that it can be so readily interpreted as a celebration of the self?

This is not the place for elaborate documentation of education's triumphs. The evidence is all around us: in the courts' upholding of equity, in the contribution of the health sciences to human welfare, in the surge of learning to take care of our own bodies, in the steady march toward recognizing the rights of women and minorities, in adult testimony to primary grade teachers who fanned the sparks of their careers in human services, in deeds of sacrifice reported daily in the media. Anyone who has participated deeply over time in the conversation of adult seminars knows that profound changes in personality and world view are not the prerogative solely of the young. When education fails, it probably is falsely labeled.

Nonetheless, there is abundant, sobering evidence to the effect that immersion in circumstances designed to be educational provides no assurance that the desired results will occur. The record is replete with incidents of bright, much-schooled individuals who lie, cheat, steal, and kill. Some do so even after election to high office and commitments to be the nation's stewards. Graduates of our most prestigious schools and universities have brought their corporations to the brink of disaster and then blamed the public schools for economic malaise. We stand in awe of the incredible triumph of technology in transforming primitive dependence on natural forces into a large measure of control in just a few generations, but we are sickened by the human savagery and inhumanity that still abounds. Those who fear what education unleashes should fear more what education has not yet reached.

The canons of rationalism and rational government and the canons of religious doctrine and theocracy are couched in the language of peace and justice for all. Both denote a universality that embraces all people and a place for everyone. In the words of Philip Phenix, "the rationalist faith is that there is one standpoint—that of disciplined reason—which comprehends all the others, making it possible to escape the relativities of time and culture and the illusions of provincialism. This is the peculiar property of reason, that it enables man to achieve a degree of universality, to rise to some extent above the limitations of circumstance and history."[26] And in the words of Warren Wagar:

> Each of the higher religions sees divinity from its own special point of view, but . . . all agree that man is not the greatest spiritual presence in the universe, and needs contact and union with the higher spiritual reality beyond the phenomena of sense experience or physical theory. They differ in their holy places, rituals, taboos, social conventions, myths, and theological systems, but the openhearted behavior, by disengaging the nonessentials from the essentials in mankind's religious heritage, can find a common core of truth in all the positive religions.[27]

Wagar also states that, "in true religion the ultimate reality is a transcendental being, power, or principle. But . . . the same search for final meaning can be pursued in much the same way by secular religions, or ideologies. . . . The nation, or a given social order, or a type of humanity, is divinized.[28]

At the level of ideal, then, there is a center where the two major themes that have driven human existence come together, where the secular and the divine merge; but the rhetoric is of exhortation toward the ideal—of the "ought to do" to which reason or faith ultimately should lead. An unusually stimulating lecture on leadership or sermon on brotherhood may stir brief visions of self-transcendence in the minds of those consumed by narcissistic individualism, but the contingencies of marketplace and ghetto soon push these aside. Even for the young, not yet thus consumed, "society undoes each workday what the school tries to do each school day. . . . We honor ambition, we reward greed, we celebrate materialism, we worship acquisitiveness, we cherish success, and we commercialize the classroom—and then we bark at the young about the gentle art of the spirit."[29]

It is necessary to repeat here the proposition that the three democracies—of government, community, and the human spirit—require constant attention to all existing and potentially educative contingencies, the scope of which must extend far beyond schools. For a long time, I naively believed that changes in human behavior are motivated by *prior* changes in attitudes and beliefs effected largely through education, and that advances in human well-being, such as in the functioning of democracy, awaited this educating. This is part nonsense, of course. Education shapes civilization over time; it is almost always corrupted when called upon to deliver over the short haul. Meanwhile, impulses likely to be detrimental to the commonweal must be checked, in the much-debated view of Thomas Hobbes, by the laws of civitas.[30] These laws are obligatory, not because they are laws of nature or laid down by God, but because they have been made, promulgated, and interpreted (for example, by a democratic government) to keep the peace—in the vein of Hobbes, they are civil laws. Immediate improvement of the human condition depends on widespread recognition of and adherence to these laws, the making of public policy, social engineering to implement policies, and continuing attention to the material elements of the community infrastructure.

Realization of the degree to which some people have no access to education as defined earlier and of how others manage to elude the moral enculturation it promises readily produces commitment to varying degrees of behavior modification as the necessary solution—from "let the punishment fit the crime" to more benign arrangements. B. F. Skinner's *Walden Two*[31] designs the contingencies of pastoral-like community life that ritualize and massage the traits of mutual accommodation, community ties and activity, and the common good. These contingencies train one in traits that are rewarded through the resulting approval and comfort; the contingencies and their concomitants provide a kind of "moral" framework. (In recent years, we have witnessed the effort to turn the pursuit of wealth into a moral good.) Following this theory, we need not be moral artists in our chosen Waldens, but only to possess the limited skill of painting by numbers. "What these literary utopias have in common is that they were brought into existence by an act of controlled fantasy, and they avoid the evils of creation by a process analogous to the belief in virginal birth."[32]

All societies depend to considerable degree on the creation of utopian images—the American Dream has been the stuff of speeches at innumerable graduation ceremonies—and a degree of myopia in regard to current blemishes. The danger lies in obscuring the line between reality and fiction in the romantic illusion that the blemishes do not exist. As a people, we need to be constantly alert to the fact that there will always be tension between individual freedom and the common good, that there will always be individuals who push self-fulfillment until self-defeat pulls down many others with it. We need to be fully aware of the degree to which "the best and the brightest" and the seemingly most saintly frequently are among those who bring us to the brink and beyond.

More than six decades ago, the British philosopher Olaf Stapledon has his chronicler of humankind through billions of years into the future say the following about First Men (us):

The first, and some would say the greatest, achievement of your own "Western" culture was the conceiving of two ideals of conduct, both essential to the spirit's well being. Socrates, delighting in the truth for its own sake and not merely for practical ends, glorified unbiased thinking, honest of mind and speech. Jesus, delighting in the actual human persons around him, and in that flavour of divinity which, for him, pervaded the world, stood for unselfish love of neighbours and of God. Socrates woke to the ideal of dispassionate intelligence, Jesus to the ideal of passionate yet self-oblivious worship. Socrates urged intellectual integrity, Jesus integrity of will. Each, of course, though starting with a different emphasis, involved the other.

Unfortunately, both of these ideals demanded of the human brain a degree of vitality and coherence of which the nervous system of the First Men was never really capable. For many centuries these twin stars enticed the more precociously human of human animals, in vain. And the failure to put these ideals in practice helped to engender in the race a cynical lassitude which was one cause of its decay.[33]

Part of Stapledon's projection into the future depicts a struggle between the best and the worst in the United States of America: the creative contributions of the best minds, "with a fresh innocence and courage . . . in a huge wilderness of opinionated self-deceivers, in whom surprisingly, an outworn religious dogma was championed with the intolerant optimism of youth. For this was essentially a race of bright, but arrested adolescents. Something lacked which should have enabled them to grow up."[34] Decades after Stapledon's scenario of the decline and fall of First Men, Paul Kennedy projects a scenario that transcends the United States, one of worldwide, self-aggrandizing multinational corporations operating outside of the control of any nation, democratic or not.[35]

The canons of both rationalism and religion speak to quite different scenarios:

> This much, at least, is clear: if we descend from the mountain peaks of theology to the plateau of ethics, all the formulas for the spiritual unification of man converge in perfect harmony. The prophets of world order seldom try to anticipate the ethical context of the world faith, but in the whole body of their writings, most of them do take personal stands on the great moral issues, and they almost invariably uphold the same supreme values. They all affirm and reverence life; they all believe in the freedom and integrity of the person; they all urge the existential self to seek self-transcendence in organic union with mankind and with mystical or divine ground of the cosmos; and they all discover the spiritual resources for human effort in the power of unconditional love. About these four final values—life, personality, transcendence, and love—there is no disagreement whatever in nearly the whole range of contemporary prophetic literature.[36]

Equally clear, however, is the fact that these utopian affirmations, even if translated into contemporary understandings, are not readily converted to belief and action. Both the intellectual and the reverent still cheat and steal and kill as they did a thousand years ago, and thousands of years before that.[37] What, then, are the prospects for civicism and civitas? What are to be the moral arts that balance individual freedom and the common good, and how are these to be acquired? What is to be the meaning of "community," writ both large and small?

Community

The task of addressing these questions requires revisitation of the three concepts of democracy introduced at the outset: political, social, and of the human spirit. What are some of the conditions that appear to serve well the simultaneous protection and cultivation of individuality and the common good? What are some of the correlates that appear to both result from and sustain these presumably democratic conditions? What might be some of the educational circumstances that interact productively with these conditions and their correlates, not just to sustain them in their present form but to refine and deepen them through increased citizen participation in the moral arts that undergird the transcendent process through which democratic political conditions, democratic social correlates, and democratic education are established and fostered?

The Human Conversation

Since it is the democratic process that binds and connects these three sets of concepts, it might be productive to address the last question first. The essence of democracy is a multiplicity of occupations and preoccupations existing comfortably side-by-side, none dominant, with a multiplicity of horizontal connections and relationships among them— "in my house there are many mansions." In order for individuals to pursue their particular interests, it is essential that there be in place an array of mechanisms that function smoothly and efficiently to meet basic human needs for health, transportation, safety, and the like. When the infrastructure of services breaks down, liberty is impaired. One must now engage in tasks for which one is ill-prepared and probably disinterested. The pursuit of freedom requires individual investment in this infrastructure, be it approval and payment of taxes, participation and care in the selection of those who will perform the services, or the exercise of self-discipline in observing the civil laws.

Nonetheless, the more "procedures" take over, the less time is required for engagement in civic duties, leaving more time for individual pursuits. One becomes less encumbered, more superficially involved with neighbors, less driven by a sense of civic duty and responsibility. There is little need to cultivate the democratic moral arts. The valued contingencies become those that sustain one's rights, not those most likely to sustain the good society. These are the contingencies that tend to keep people apart, that discourage the horizontal human connections democracy requires.[38] Social capital is depleted.

The sustenance and renewal of socially democratic communities requires the existence or creation of a considerable amount of social capital in their citizens. James Coleman has presented a fascinating picture of decline in social capital in the transition of the United States from a highly agrarian society to a predominantly urban, corporate, global economic power.[39] This has not been only a change from one way of earning a living to another. It has also been accompanied by a profound shift in virtually every aspect of life—from an ethos of horizontal relationships to one of vertical relationships, from social capital invested in and derived from family and neighbor to financial capital independent of "family," from education in personal and civic virtue to schooling (and its credentials) as economic instrument. In sum, this transition has been accompanied by the loss of some moral center against which to check the validity of one's independent trajectory, and, too frequently, the substitution of "my right to liberty" as the guiding criterion.

From the perspective of the democratic community, at least four unfortunate correlates accompanied the shift from social to financial capital described by Coleman. First, there was a strong decline in the *practical* knowledge capital that is essential to the infrastructure of a democratic community (which rejects servitude on principle). Second, this decline was accompanied by a devaluing of the experience from which practical knowledge, in contrast to academic or technical knowledge, is derived.[40] Third, bureaucratized procedures increasingly took over most aspects of community life, largely eliminating the process of citizens coming together to solve their problems. The town hall meeting and the conversation that went with it became an anachronism in a procedural republic.[41] Fourth, there has been a decline of the *e pluribus* in *e pluribus unum* (from many, one) that now appears to be slowing extension of the tools and benefits of democracy to those most disadvantaged in the pursuit of financial capital. Worse, a significant portion of the nation's political leadership appears to be oblivious to or unconcerned about these developments and the urgent need to shore up our democratic way of life on all fronts.

How do we proceed? We talk. We need to talk *across* all levels of government and all walks of life. We need to talk *within* all levels of government and walks of life: in homes, on the job, in schools, in all manner of public forums. Do we know how? Wives and husbands talk with one another and their children very little, and much of this talk is argument, not conversation. Management theory encourages talk, but managers usually do not. A major objective of schools is language development, but talk is not encouraged. The measures used to judge the educational performance of students eschew talk. Television and other technological developments render talk virtually unnecessary.

It is said that the young are resorting more and more to violence because they do not know how to settle their differences otherwise, and much of the adult talk they hear is arguing for purposes of winning. We are not born knowing the art of conversation that is central to the moral art of democracy. What we learn in the cultural context of growing up are primarily certainties that hamper the search for alternatives and possibilities. One would think that participation in the conversation Oakeshott describes would be the daily reward of all who live in a democracy, but instead, it is a rarer treat than affluence:

> In conversation, "facts" appear only to be resolved once more into the possibilities from which they were made; "certainties" are shown to be combustible, not by being brought in contact with other "certainties" or with doubt, but by being kindled by the presence of ideas of another order; approximations are revealed between notions normally remote from one another. Thoughts of different species take wing and play round one another, responding to each other's movements and provoking one another to fresh exertions. . . . Conversation is not an enterprise designed to yield

an extrinsic profit, a contest where a winner gets a prize, nor is it an activity of exegesis; it is an unrehearsed intellectual adventure. . . . Properly speaking, it is impossible in the absence of a diversity of voices.[42]

There is no reason, however, to eschew the designation and rhetorical definition of the topics that are central to conversations about the meaning of democracy. In this, our government has been negligent—indeed, delinquent. Clearly, the process described by Oakeshott is an educational one, the mirror image of the democratic one, but neither the nature of education nor the meaning of democracy has been framed for conversation by our policymakers. Gary Fenstermacher pinpoints the double omission:

We hear a great deal about readying the next generation of workers for global competition, about being first in the world in such high status subjects as math and science, and about having world class standards for what is learned in school. We hear almost nothing about civic participation or building and maintaining democratic communities, whether these be neighborhoods or governments at the local, state or federal level. . . . Not only does the current national reform movement in the United States pay too little attention to the ideas and ideals of democracy, it pays far too little attention to the ideas and ideals of education.[43]

Surely it is not asking too much of a democratically elected government to request that it frame for the nation's people the conversation most essential to their well-being, and then promote and protect the integrity of that conversation throughout the land. It is then not asking too much of the people to expect their participation in that conversation, a metaphor for the whole of human engagement, to be to the utmost of their ability. "The informal structure of American political life that commentators from Tocqueville on have seen as the foundation of our democracy has collapsed. This foundation must be restored. Before we can reinvent government, we must recreate a public philosophy that values the art of governance. The first step in this difficult process is to elevate public discourse. . . . History demonstrates this can happen. History also clearly defines the commitment such a noble task requires."[44]

Political and Social Democracy

Participation in the human conversation requires face-to-face relationships and considerable willingness to subject one's views to a cacophony of voices. Remote government and procedures blind to differences and special circumstances remove the need and, indeed, the incentive for both. Why acquire the moral arts of democracy if government prescribes their nature and bureaucratic procedures prescribe their exercise? Regulation to protect people from the risks of self-defeating freedoms easily becomes the enemy of individual sensitivity to the common good. Regulation for this purpose readily becomes the enemy, too, of the pursuit of individual freedom, and yet, there must be regulation of some sort if the common good and individual freedom are to be kept in democratic balance.

Herein lie two quite different motivations for the civicness democracy requires. The pursuit of individualism that pursues financial capital is frustrated by the tendency of remote government regulation to be indifferent to special needs and wants. Affluence often provides routes around such indifference—but to no avail if the stable provision of specialized services declines and disappears. What price success if the amenities for its enjoyment are nonexistent? One answer for people thus frustrated is increased attention to and even participation in the processes of creating citizen-friendly community infrastructures. Democracy requires a symbiosis of the common good and self-interest. Self-interest can be a powerful catalyst for this symbiosis. Those citizens motivated by the common good must recognize this participation as an opportunity for those who have profited from the system to give back to it and, consequently, must massage it carefully so that this giving back becomes a community contingency.

The pursuit of individualism by those who connect liberty and the free exercise of human judgment is frustrated by excessive government regulation to protect them and everyone else from the risks of self-defeating freedoms. They often view this regulation as a kind of patronizing distrust in the ability of citizens to behave in mature ways. There is little here to foster cultivated imagination and challenge the human spirit. Why become educated in the moral arts of democracy if government removes the need for their exercise? An answer, for some people whose intelligence has been insulted, lies in cultivating local government and local procedures as an antidote to remote government regulation geared to the curtailment of lowest-common-denominator abuses.

These two sets of motivations often bring together strange bedfellows of quite different philosophic persuasions. Also, they bring into the business of community making some individuals whose previous preoccupations were essentially independent of family and community—in effect, nonproductive of social capital. The major difficulty in this process of community participation is the combination of the new learnings required and the frustration of discovering that many of the skills acquired in the pursuit of individual advancement and autonomy are handicaps.

Active participation in the horizontal relationships required for community building makes it abundantly clear that there are irreconcilable differences in viewpoint among individuals and groups of players. For example, there is a vast difference between individualism as salvation of the individual soul and individualism as the fruit of rational inquiry. There is a vast difference between those who believe that ownership of land brings with it freedom to do with the land as one wishes and those who believe that it brings responsibility to join with others in determining the limitations on this freedom. These differences are unlikely to be resolved simply by exercising freedom of speech. Discourse must be accompanied by a willingness to give ground, by the realization that impasses serve the commonweal poorly, and by an awareness that recourse to the courts is as likely to exacerbate moral tensions as to relieve them. These are the traits of a moral individualism that guides civic association and action in a moral community.

In many ways, informal relationships and networks are the flesh and institutions are the bones of community. It simply is more convenient and, in modern societies, essential for many aspects of daily life to be stable and ordered through institutions. It is also common to look to state and federal government for the creation and management of these institutions. A democratic government must seek to maintain a delicate balance between civicness and institution building so that social engineering "for the common good" does not run too far ahead of local initiative. The question arises as to how far and how fast a political democracy can proceed toward the creation of socially democratic communities when little civicness exists.

The inquiry conducted by Robert Putnam and his colleagues over two decades of the Italian experiment in regional representative government inaugurated in 1970 provides unusual and very rich documentation of connections between political and social democracies. Putnam compares the histories of north and south and their differing legacies of citizen participation in government and civic affairs. Over the centuries, southern Italy was dominated hierarchically by a landed aristocracy with feudal powers, the church, and the Mafia. In contrast, by the fourteenth century a "fertile communal republicanism" was taking shape in the north.[45] These contrary traditions profoundly differentiated the conduct of government and civic engagement in the regions and towns of the north from those of the south following the 1970 provision for creation of local governments. Putnam's research team found correlations between citizens' engagement in politics and their involvement in a wide variety of civic affairs that rather sharply contrasted regions in the north such as Emilia-Romagna, which scored high, with regions in the south such as Calabria, which scored lower, on their criteria of civicness:

> In the most civic regions, such as Emilia-Romagna, citizens are involved in all sorts of local associations—literary guilds, local banks, hunting clubs, cooperatives and so on. They follow civic affairs avidly in the local press, and they engage in politics out of programmatic conviction. By contrast, in the least civic regions, such as Calabria, voters are brought to the polls not by issues, but by hierarchical patron-client networks. An absence of civic associations and a paucity of local media in these latter regions mean that citizens there are rarely drawn into community affairs.[46]

Part of Putnam's analysis is of the effectiveness of government institutions. Beginning with the assumption that a good democratic government is both responsive to and effective in acting on the demands of its citizenry, he developed rigorous criteria for evaluating institutional performance. Putnam was able to establish high internal consistency among his twelve diverse indicators of institutional performance: "Regions that have stable cabinets, adopt their budgets on time, spend their appropriations as planned, and pioneer new legislation are, for the most part, the same regions that provide day care centers and family clinics, develop comprehensive urban planning, make loans to farmers, and answer their mail promptly."[47] These were also, for the most part, the regions with a legacy of civic-mindedness and civic participation.

Putnam observes that, in a civic community, citizens regard the public domain as something other than a battleground for pursuing personal interests, but he warns against ignoring the powerful motivation of self-interest. As stated earlier, the challenge is to bring about a symbiotic relationship between self-interest and community need. In today's world, this is not easy. Even when civic-mindedness is present, self-interest creates different images of the community to be sustained. At one extreme is the nostalgic ideal that blends God, family, neighborhood, town, and country in some modern reincarnation of a sacred core of regained meaning. At another extreme is a cosmopolitan view of one's own city linked to cities worldwide in a community of technological innovation and economic competition.

The coexistence of these extremes adds to the burdens of civic-mindedness. Putnam's descriptions of the functioning community appear to accommodate quite comfortably the first of these two visions, but it is the second vision that now seems to be growing in the civic-minded north he describes, especially among the young leadership that views itself as more commercially entrepreneurial than political. The increasingly powerful Northern League views the south as Italy's cumbersome baggage and Milan as their capital, with that city joined with other city states, such as Paris, London, New York, Los Angeles, and Tokyo, engaged in global commerce that transcends nationhood.[48] What is the meaning of and the potential for civicness and the moral arts of democracy under these circumstances?

Is the social glue that holds people together the same for nations, city states, and small communities? Wallace Loh argues that it is:

> What holds us together is a commitment to certain core values that define our national identity and undergird our common purpose. These values include liberties of the mind, the freedom of inquiry

and expression essential to an open society; tolerance for intellectual and human differences; respect for individual dignity; fair
process and equal treatment; mutual caring, a sense of responsibility for the common good. Some of the values are found in the Constitution precisely because its framers recognized that they are
fundamental civic virtues that make possible cooperative living in
an interdependent society. These values are learned.[49]

Democratic Education

"These values are learned." One more time, education is viewed as
the alternative to all of humankind's other ways for settling differences and disagreements and for advancing civilization—not the
instrument, but the alternative. In the second of Laurens van der
Post's pair of novels about a period of tumultuous change from the
Africa he had known as a child, the young hero, François Joubert,
hears the voice of his dead father:

> It was only by education and re-education and patient exhortation
> and evocation and change of heart and imagination that men
> could be permanently changed. You could not punish men into
> being better; you could not punish societies into being more; you
> could not change the world by violence and by frightening people
> into virtue by killing off their inadequate establishments. The
> moment was upon us when we had to accept without reserve that
> the longest way round in the human spirit was always the shortest
> way there.[50]

What François heard his father reject remains both cause and
effect in humankind's repertoire of ways to settle differences. How
is the educational alternative to prevail? Becoming a nation much-
schooled is, sadly, not sufficient. In the United States, we have compulsory schooling to the age of sixteen, one of the highest
secondary school graduation rates in the world, and a comprehensive system of higher education that is the envy of most other
nations. Yet, statistics regarding violence are shocking, and cults
espousing racial intolerance find ardent recruits among graduates
of our most elite universities. Good marks in school predict good
marks in school but not, it seems, later performance of the democratic moral arts.

Fenstermacher has pointed both to silence in regard to connecting education and democracy and myopia in regard to the ideals of education in the rhetoric of school reform. Barber, in turn, cites a social context that defeats daily the best that schools do to civilize the young. It should not be necessary to cry out for "democratic" education. "Education" should suffice; the addition of "democratic" is a redundancy. Yet, it seems that we must constantly remind ourselves that any straying from democratic means in seeking to justify or attain educational ends corrupts both education and democracy. Consequently, it becomes useful to employ the redundancy in discussing schools that fail to democratize and communities that count too much on schools as virtually their sole source of educational enlightenment.

What Schools Are For

The twentieth-century annals of schooling in the United States are replete with hundreds upon hundreds of reports articulating approximately the same comprehensive set of goals for our schools. This is part of the problem. Central purpose is lost in rhetorical overkill. The mission of schooling comes down to two related kinds of enculturation; no other institution is so charged. The first is for political and social responsibility as a citizen. The second is for maximum individual development, for full participation in the human conversation (with the concept of conversation expanded into a metaphor for the whole of daily living). (This mission and the dangers to it are discussed in considerable depth in Chapter Five.)

While the above is the time-honored mission of schooling, the prime function of schools, performed day after day throughout the land, is a custodial one. The democratic requirement is that this function be performed so as to ensure each child or youth physical, mental, and emotional safety in the school setting; status as a worthy person with rights and privileges no less or greater than those of any other; access to knowledge that is in no way impeded because of attributes irrelevant to learning such as color, religion, ethnicity, or financial capital; the pursuit of an individualism that represents the restraints imposed by the physical environment and the rights of others; and respect for those to whom the community has given the risk-laden responsibility of teaching. Unless these re-ciprocal conditions are in place, the schools fail to perform their custodial function according to the tenets of democracy. All sorts of coercive measures come into play to enforce the compulsory requirement. The less a community does to ensure that these democratic conditions are in place, the less able its schools will be to fulfill their educational mission.

The fulfillment of educational mission depends primarily on the ability of teachers to cultivate this democratic setting (moral stewardship) and to create learning opportunities that embrace all of their students (caring pedagogy). These are the abilities to be honed in professional education programs. Fulfillment of educa-tional mission, beyond the custodial one, also depends on the degree to which these teachers are steeped in and committed to the canons of democracy and humankind's domains of disciplined knowledge (liberal education). The less a community does to ensure such teachers for its young people, the less the schools will serve their public purpose—the teaching of liberty.

The maintenance and refinement of a system of public school-ing to serve this public purpose is more important than the main-tenance of a system of public roads and parks. We do not excuse citizens from paying taxes for the latter whether or not they use them, nor do we permit their claiming these public facilities for their private use. We take these stands in recognition of the pub-lic "good" over the private "right." We vacillate, however, in the much more critical domain of public schooling. Policymakers at the highest levels of government have endorsed or have not opposed the use of public money for essentially private schools—as one might direct public money to the creation of parks for private use. School boards and superintendents eschew questions regard-ing the public purpose of schooling when they consign the man-agement of the people's schools to for-profit corporations.

Perhaps the time has come to rethink the matter of compul-sory school attendance as distinct from the matter of a compulsory system of public schooling. The latter is essential to a democracy; it serves democracy's public purpose. It is a responsibility of citi-zenship to provide the necessary support, just as citizens are called upon to support other public facilities. But is it necessary for citi-zens to use these public facilities or for the state to insist that they do? Should citizens be any less obligated to refrain from abusing the schools than they are from abusing roads and parks? Do they have a moral obligation to ensure equal access to schools and the enculturation that is the mission of schools? The requirements of political and social democracy call for "no" answers to the first two questions and a strong "yes" to the third.

Would cultivation of the moral arts of democracy be in any greater danger than it currently is if school attendance were not compulsory? I doubt it. In spite of much exhortation for better public school retention, the graduation rate nationwide has remained quite stable for decades. The drive to keep school-age children and youths in school has contributed significantly to a punitive ambience surrounding schools that is reflected in a police-like truancy corps, a prison-like physical appearance of schools, and a plethora of custodial rules and regulations. The custodial demands on teachers, in turn, intrude significantly into the educational mission teachers are called upon to advance. One of the most insidious of these intrusions is the degree to which teachers feel compelled to stick with narrowly didactic instructional practices in order to retain control of their classrooms.

Not only have the bonds of mutual support between home and school weakened, home and family in many instances are scarcely there. Some families have decreed the facts and certainties to which teaching in school is to be confined and the diversity of voices to be tolerated. Political leaders who restate the mission of schools as the creation of better jobs in essence give schools permission to emphasize the "servile arts" and parents permission to request nothing more.

A proposition quite divergent from the one now undergirding public schooling in the United States is worth serious consideration: a compulsory system of schooling accompanied by voluntary attendance. As a citizen, one must provide the support required of all citizens. I have argued above that factors associated with compulsory attendance have endangered both the exercise of the moral arts of democracy and education in them. We must remember that these are much more than the arts of political responsibility: they embrace the morality of individuality, of community ties, and of the common good. They must not be abused either through the imposition of school regularities in the name of the common good that, blind to differences, hobble individuality, or through the intrusion of private interests that, blind to public interest, endanger the common good. This is a condition we accept as a matter of course with regard to our roads, parks, and many other public facilities. It is a condition that has eroded badly with respect to our schools.

For schools to fulfill their public purpose, then, there must be both conditions of use and the provision of education—a social compact entered into by the citizen, on the one hand, and the state, on the other. In choosing one's school, one accepts the public purpose the school is obliged to discharge and the democratic regularities that go with it (see Chapter Six). In providing schools, the state must bring to bear all those provisions of licensing, certifying, and accrediting that have been found useful in seeking for its citizens the best of care by such risk-laden professions as medicine, law, and dentistry. Regarding schools, however, the education of teachers in the moral arts of democracy requires very special attention, because both the lives of our children and our valued ways of life are at stake (see Chapter Nine).

It is of interest to note that this proposition regarding compulsory schooling but voluntary attendance offers to shift markedly at least two major and rarely questioned conventions. The first pertains to the relationship between private and public schools, the second to one's right to the latter. It is commonly assumed that the private school is the school of choice; the public school is always there to fall back on. There is two-way choice in the private school: both sides have the option of withdrawing. This must be the condition of all schools of choice, otherwise one side is at the mercy of the other.

It is worth noting, also, that the proposal leaves undisturbed the private school as we have known it. One major, ill-disguised motivation for schools of choice involving private use of the public purse is to gain control over tax dollars for personal ends. The idea of making private schools available to the poor is a cruel public relations hoax. What some canny patrons and stewards of private schools are coming to realize is that self-serving calls for the privatization of public schools, if implemented, would destroy much of what their schools now claim to offer: considerable freedom from public control. Once public money came to them, however, public control most assuredly would follow.

In the proposition I have just put forward, all schools are

schools of choice. The public school is an obvious option; I must help pay for it whether or not I use it. It offers the best that the present condition of our democracy has made possible. I may choose it, abide by its democratic rules (or be subject to rejection as in all other schools of choice), and join with my neighbors and the school's professional staff in seeking to improve it; or I may choose a private school that appears to be in harmony with my "private" interests, abide by its rules, and seek to improve it; or I may opt out of both options and take on personally the risk-laden responsibility of educating my own children for citizenship and self-fulfillment.

Fleshing out the nature of the compact proposed above is an undertaking beyond the restraints of one chapter in a book and beyond any one individual. Much that is required in the domain of policy and control is glossed over in my reference to state responsibility for the provision of schools. An important caveat is contained in what may have been the last interview of the very wise Ralph Tyler. He was asked: What do you consider to be some serious national educational concerns? Without hesitation or equivocation, he replied: Educational problems are local, not national.[51]

Toward Educative Communities

This chapter has shown, as will the next one, the degree to which schools are curtailed and fall short in their public purpose. There is widespread and growing awareness of what is being referred to as a struggle for the soul of the American public school. Many of the conditions necessary to the educational mission of schools are missing.

This is a serious situation in the United States, because of the degree to which education and schooling are equated and to which schooling, in turn, is made instrumental to whatever ends and means sell well on the political campaign trail. What miserable shape we would be in as a nation if the condition of our schools— good or bad—were seriously assumed to be the near-single cause of our prosperity and global economic competitiveness. A beacon our schools have been, an instrument of economic and military power they have not. The scathing criticism of the schools for a period of decline has not been followed by ringing praise for the succeeding period of rising productivity and shrinking unemployment. As Larry Cuban observes, the American people are the victims of a skillfully concocted scam that diminishes public confidence in schools.[52]

The consequences are serious for democracy. First, diminishing public confidence in schools (for not doing what they cannot do) diminishes the material and moral support they need for the democratic mission strong schools are able to fulfill. The vision of a system of public schooling as "the bright and shining beacon . . . the source of our enlightenment"[53] is tarnished. Justification for turning the public school system to the service of personal ends, since it presumably serves public ends poorly, is enhanced. Second, public attention is diverted from the fractures in the community infrastructure that result from emphasizing financial capital over social capital and frustrate the school's ability to educate. The school is increasingly called upon to compensate for deficiencies in the ecosystem that once embraced home, church, and school as allies in educating the young. Its unique educative role is further compromised.

This nation is faced with three imperatives on which the school's ability to fulfill its educational mission depends, but which go beyond schools in their implications for democracy, education, and community. The first is extensively discussed in this chapter and several others in this book: the need to address education in its own right, instrumental to democracy as democracy is instrumental to education, but to no lesser end. The second is the urgent need to shore up all of our health and human services agencies, not only to the end of extending them to everyone but also to the end of righting the inequities in regard to the readiness of all children to participate in the educational process and the human conversation.[54] Ensuring that all children are ready to learn is one politically initiated goal that has a solid moral base—but, as yet, only a halting, fragmented implementation strategy. The third imperative is that these agencies become self-consciously educative, adding to the school's essentially academic approach opportunities to acquire the practical, experiential knowledge on which the community infrastructure depends so heavily.

The proposal that all of our young people engage for an extended period of time in some kind of community service is neither new nor radical. Alongside of this one, and growing in its advocacy, is the proposal for apprenticeships in job training, but rarely are these posed as further educational insurance (beyond that provided by schools) that the democratic moral arts will be acquired and refined. The first proposal is often viewed simply as a way to get the young off the streets and out of trouble. The second is commonly viewed as compensatory for those who take to academic learning slowly or poorly; vocational education always has suffered considerably from this "second chance" and "second best" stigma. It is time to elevate a combination of the two to the status and support that is becoming increasingly necessary. Given the degree to which schools are muzzled in their freedom and ability to teach how and what a robust democracy requires, the need for this additional insurance is urgent.

Two major but not insurmountable obstacles to these proposals are cost and the degree to which our educational system encompasses the years of childhood, adolescence, and early adulthood in a tightly interlocking series of academic entities. These years provide a kind of half-education in what each successive entity requires of the other highly valued credentials that correlate poorly with the virtues and verities commonly associated rhetorically with the educational enterprise. Although this system appears to forget all those in the sixteen to twenty-two age bracket not encompassed by it,[55] it resists mightily the rise of alternatives likely to compete for public funds. The second of the two obstacles is the more formidable.

Resolution will require bold, creative measures. One answer to both problems is a radical restructuring of the N-12 (nursery through grade twelve) system of the kind I proposed years ago. Essentially it involves a downward extension of voluntary access to early childhood schooling to the age of four, just as it was extended downward to kindergarten and age five decades ago, and normal termination of secondary school at the age of sixteen. This restructured, 4-4-4 plan of schooling would embrace the cohort of four- through seven-year-olds in the first unit, eight- through eleven-year-olds in the second, and twelve- through fifteen-year-olds in the third.[56] We should be encouraged in this proposal by the experiences of the Swiss in emphasizing the educational importance of the early childhood years and the comparable earlier completion of secondary school.[57] Only the exploitation of adolescents in school for the athletic entertainment of adults would suffer—a bonus for both schooling and society. The money saved by shortening our system of schooling by one year would pay a good deal of the costs for the period of community service, teaching, and experiential learning described next.

The bulk of the interns would be, then, in the sixteen to eighteen age bracket, but one can envision the participation of older citizens attracted by serving in specific teaching roles and, of course, immigrants seeking naturalization. Some in each cohort would go on into extended residencies in various human service agencies and businesses, just as large numbers would enter colleges and universities. Older citizens presumably would take sabbatical leaves for experiences that had not been available to them in early adulthood. Some, refreshed by the experience, would change their careers. Social policy to ensure the opportunity to return to previous jobs and the continuation of health care and other benefits would be essential.

Each intern would become a participant in the local, state, or national infrastructure through planned, guided immersion in essential elements of it: the functioning of health and other human services (child care, aid to the disabled and elderly, and so forth), the ecology of open space and human habitation, the ecology of human enterprise (such as good work for employees and profit for the company) and the preservation of natural resources, the structure and conduct of government, the formal organization of political life, technology and communication, domestic and global commerce, and more. Internships would be accompanied by reflective seminars led by persons regarded as very competent in their fields of endeavor. A nonlinear, nondidactic kind of instruction would connect hands-on experiences, relevant reading, and individual internalization of the whole through disciplined conversation. Interns, modestly paid, would add to, not replace, persons engaged full time as employees in the infrastructure. However, their participation would, in many cases, make it unnecessary to replace workers on sabbatical leave enjoying internships in some other part of the infrastructure. The movement of interns through the system and their contribution to it would help to balance out some of the costs.

If the proposed internship-apprenticeship program is to function effectively, many people who view their present work responsibility only as getting the job done must self-consciously become teachers. It calls for every segment of the community infrastructure to become part of a culture of deliberate teaching in an educative community.[58] The risk taking in regard to personal disclosure and the loss of privacy that good teaching requires promotes evaluative introspection: What do I have to give and how shall I give it?

The pedagogical method of disciplined conversation leaves no place to hide (which in part explains why so many teachers in schools and universities stay with the safer, more private, didactic mode of teaching). In teaching from one's repertoire of expertise, there is always the potential of reexamining one's own work critically and seeking to do it better. As a lay teacher, one becomes introspective about that teaching and, for example, one's attention to individual clients in delivering health care. The element of the infrastructure of which each individual is a part reaps the benefits. Democracy in education and education in democracy come closer together.

The subtle part of government intervention in all of the above is to raise moral consciousness, not to stifle it through bureaucratic rules. There already exist in most communities voluntary services that fill in many of the gaps in government delivery of human services. For example, at the time of this writing, former President Jimmy Carter is active in the coming together of what he calls "people of faith" representing almost all religious denominations for purposes of assisting the young to be more self-conscious about and attentive to their health. Dramatic increases in longevity are not the product of medical science and practice alone; people are learning to take care of themselves. Indeed, segments of the public virtually led the medical field into greater attention to nutrition and diet in the American family. We must become similarly educationally self-conscious in all aspects of living.

In paying more attention to building social capital through the cultivation of educative communities, we may be less inclined to blame the schools for our malaise and to hold them responsible for the nation's well-being. We can then reasonably expect of them fulfillment of their unique educational mission. Healthy nations have healthy schools. Healthy schools and robust democracies go hand in hand.

Notes

1. Deborah W. Meier, "Get the Story Straight: Myths, Lies, and Public Schools," *The Nation,* September 21, 1992, *255,* 272.
2. Benjamin R. Barber, *An Aristocracy of Everyone: The Politics of Education and the Future of America* (New York: Ballantine, 1992), p. 5.
3. Because the contemporary definition of *civitas* denotes a politically organized community, more than just civility is required for its sustenance and orderly functioning. Also needed is a framework of civil law.
4. Seymour B. Sarason, "And What Is the Public Interest?" *American Psychologist,* 1986, *41,* 899.
5. For further information and elaboration, see Mortimer J. Adler, *We Hold These Truths* (New York: Macmillan, 1987).
6. Thomas K. McCraw, "The Strategic Vision of Alexander Hamilton," *The American Scholar,* Winter 1994, *63,* 31–57.
7. John I. Goodlad, "Common Schools for the Common Weal: Reconciling Self-Interest with the Common Good," in *Access to Knowledge: An Agenda for Our Nation's Schools,* edited by J. I. Goodlad and P. Keating (New York: College Entrance Examination Board, 1990), pp. 1–21.
8. Michael Oakeshott, *Rationalism in Politics and Other Essays* (Indianapolis, Ind.: Liberty Press, 1991), p. 364.
9. Oakeshott, *Rationalism in Politics,* p. 9.
10. Oakeshott, *Rationalism in Politics,* p. 367.
11. See Maxine Greene, *The Dialectic of Freedom* (New York: Teachers College Press, 1988), particularly Chapter Five. This moral community is virtually by definition a caring community; see Nel Noddings, *Caring: A Feminine Approach to Ethics and Moral Education* (Berkeley: University of California Press, 1984).
12. Sarason, "And What Is the Public Interest?" p. 904.
13. For further discussion of self-transcendence, see Robert Ulich, *The Human Career: A Philosophy of Self-Transcendence* (New York: Harper & Row, 1955).
14. Benjamin S. Bloom, *Stability and Change in Human Characteristics* (New York: Wiley, 1964).
15. Erik H. Erikson, *Childhood and Society* (2nd ed.) (New York: Norton, 1963), p. 250.
16. Benjamin R. Barber, "America Skips School," *Harper's Magazine,* November 1993, *286,* 46.
17. National Governors' Association, *Time for Results* (Washington, D.C.: National Governors' Association Publication Office, 1986).
18. Barber, *An Aristocracy of Everyone,* p. 15.
19. Barry L. Bull, "The Limits of Teacher Professionalization," in *The*

Moral Dimensions of Teaching, edited by J. I. Goodlad, R. Soder, and K. A. Sirotnik (San Francisco: Jossey-Bass, 1990), p. 92.

20. Bull, "The Limits of Teacher Professionalization," pp. 91–98.

21. Israel Scheffler, "Basic Mathematical Skills: Some Philosophical and Practical Remarks," *Teachers College Record*, 1976, *78*, 205.

22. Adler, *We Hold These Truths*, p. 20.

23. My colleagues and I have had a difficult time explaining that our use of "moral" in defining teaching, teacher education, and the conduct of schooling pertains to the conditions of sustaining settings in which freedom is experienced and exercised equally by all. We eschew indulging in a litany of behavioral oughts and shoulds—that is, moralizing.

24. Oakeshott, *Rationalism in Politics*, pp. 296–297.

25. This is a modification of the definition put forward by Lawrence A. Cremin, "Further Notes Toward a Theory of Education," *Notes on Education*, vol. 4, 1974, p. 1: "[Education is] the deliberate, systematic, and sustained effort to transmit or evoke knowledge, attitudes, values, skills, and sensibilities."

26. Philip H. Phenix, "Education and the Concept of Man," *Views and Ideas on Mankind*, Bulletin No. 9 (Chicago: Committee on the Study of Mankind, 1961), p. 10.

27. W. Warren Wagar, *The City of Man* (Boston: Houghton Mifflin, 1963; reprint ed., Baltimore, Md.: Penguin, 1967), p. 163.

28. W. Warren Wagar, "Religion, Ideology, and the Idea of Mankind in Contemporary History," in *History of the Idea of Mankind*, edited by W. W. Wagar (Albuquerque: University of New Mexico, 1971), p. 197.

29. Barber, "America Skips School," p. 42.

30. Leo Strauss, *The Political Philosophy of Hobbes: Its Basis and Its Genesis*, translated by E. M. Sinclair (Chicago: University of Chicago Press, 1952).

31. B. F. Skinner, *Walden Two* (New York: Macmillan, 1962).

32. Seymour B. Sarason, *The Creation of Settings and the Future Societies* (San Francisco: Jossey-Bass, 1972).

33. Olaf Stapledon, *Last and First Men* (New York: J. Cape & H. Smith, 1931; reprint ed., New York: Dover Publications, 1968), p. 17.

34. Stapledon, *Last and First Men*, p. 33.

35. Paul M. Kennedy, *Preparing for the Twenty-First Century* (New York: Random House, 1993).

36. Wagar, *The City of Man*, pp. 171–172.

37. John I. Goodlad, "Elementary Education," in *Education and the Idea of Mankind*, edited by Robert Ulich (New York: Harcourt, Brace, and World, 1964), p. 97.

38. For a more extensive analysis, see Paul Theobald and Vicky Newman, "The Implications of Communitarian/Liberal Theory for Public Education," Work in Progress Series No. 4 (Seattle, Wash.: Institute for Educational Inquiry, 1994).

39. James S. Coleman, "Changes in the Family and Implications for the Common School," *University of Chicago Legal Forum*, Volume 1991, pp. 153–170; *Schools, Families, and Children*, The 1985 Ryerson Lecture (Chicago: University of Chicago, 1985); and *Foundations of Social Theory* (Cambridge, Mass.: Belknap Press of Harvard University, 1990).

40. John I. Goodlad, "Beyond Half an Education," *Education Week*, February 19, 1992, pp. 44, 34.

41. "Procedural republic" is the terminology of Michael J. Sandel, "The Procedural Republic and the Unencumbered Self," *Political Theory*, 1984, *12*, 81–96.

42. Oakeshott, *Rationalism in Politics*, pp. 489–490.

43. Gary D Fenstermacher, "The Absence of Democratic and Educational Ideals from Contemporary Educational Reform Initiatives," The Stanley Elam Lecture, Educational Press Association of America, June 10, 1994, pp. 1–2.

44. Don Hopps, "Populism Gone Astray," *Seattle Post-Intelligencer*, July 3, 1994, p. E1.

45. Robert D. Putnam, *Making Democracy Work: Civic Traditions in Modern Italy* (Princeton, N.J.: Princeton University Press, 1993), p. 130.

46. Putnam, *Making Democracy Work*, p. 97.

47. Putnam, *Making Democracy Work*, p. 74.

48. Frank Viviano, "The Fall of Rome," *Mother Jones*, 1993, *18*, 37–40.

49. Wallace D. Loh, "America: A Nation of Nations," *Seattle Post-Intelligencer*, July 3, 1994, p. E3.

50. Laurens van der Post, *A Far-off Place* (San Diego, Calif.: Harcourt Brace, 1974), p. 110.

51. Diana Buell Hiatt, "No Limits to the Possibilities," *Phi Delta Kappan*, 1994, *75*, 788.

52. Larry Cuban, "The Great School Scam," *Education Week*, June 15, 1994, p. 44.

53. Robert M. Hutchins, "The Great Anti-School Campaign," *The Great Ideas Today* (Chicago: Encyclopaedia Britannica, 1972), p. 154.

54. This topic, especially the linking of school, family, and human services generally, deserves more attention than the space limitations of this chapter permit. For a quite comprehensive overview, see Hal A. Lawson, "Toward Healthy Learners, Schools, and Communities: Footprints in a Continuing Journey," Work in Progress Series No. 3 (Seattle, Wash.: Institute for Educational Inquiry, 1993).

55. *The Forgotten Half: Pathways to Success for America's Youth and Young Families* (Washington, D.C.: Youth and America's Future: The William T. Grant Commission on Work, Family and Citizenship, 1988).

56. For further justification and description, see John I. Goodlad, *A Place Called School* (New York: McGraw-Hill, 1984), pp. 323–343.

57. Jacqueline Bugnion, "Overhauling American Education—The Swiss Way," unpublished book manuscript made available to this writer in July 1991.

58. See John I. Goodlad, *Educational Renewal: Better Teachers, Better Schools* (San Francisco: Jossey-Bass, 1994), Chapter Seven.

Chapter Five

Public Schooling and American Democracy

Robert B. Westbrook

The relationship between public schooling and democracy is a conceptually tight one. Schools have become one of the principal institutions by which modern states reproduce themselves, and insofar as those states are democratic, they will make use of schools to prepare children for democratic citizenship. The very notion of democratic "public" education reflects this fact: democratic public schools are ostensibly not only schools supported by public finance but schools that educate every student for the responsibilities and benefits of participating in public life. One reasonable measure of the strength and prospects of a democracy is the degree to which its public schools successfully devote themselves to this task.

By this measure, American democracy is now weak and its prospects are dim. The anemia of public life in the United States—a polity in which even such minimal practices of citizenship as voting do not engage many Americans—is reflected in public schooling that, despite lip service to education for democratic citizenship, has devoted few resources or even much thought to its requirements. We suffer, as Benjamin Barber has said, from a dearth of "civic literacy," which he characterizes as "the competence to participate in democratic communities, the ability to think critically and act with deliberation in a pluralistic world, and the empathy to identify sufficiently with others to live with them despite conflicts of interest and differences in character."[1] In the mid-1970s, a study of Pennsylvania high school seniors who had just completed a high school civics course found that they had little understanding of democracy and its traditions. Most of them believed that "the main characteristic of democracy was that it leaves the citizen alone."[2] But democracy does not leave citizens alone; it brings them together to deliberate on and act in their common interests.

One finds little inclination among educators or the public at large to address this erosion of the understanding and practice of democratic citizenship among young Americans and those who instruct them, or even to see in it a gravely troubling development. As Barber observes, "The logic of democracy begins with public education, proceeds to informed citizenship, and comes to fruition in the securing of rights and liberties. We have been nominally democratic for so long that we presume it is our natural condition rather than the product of persistent effort and tenacious responsibility. We have decoupled rights from civic responsibilities and severed citizenship from education on the false assumption that citizens just happen. We have forgotten that the 'public' in public schools means not just paid for by the public but procreative of the very idea of a public."[3]

Many have decried the shortcomings of American public schools, but few have attributed their difficulties to a weakness of democratic imagination, will, and purpose. Few of the many reports on the dire condition of schooling in the United States which have filled bookshelves recently have anything to say about the education of citizens. When our leaders speak of the failures of public education, they find its purposes and deficiencies quite elsewhere. "We measure every school by one high standard: Are our children learning what they need to know to compete and win in the global economy?," President Bill Clinton declared in his State of the Union message of 1994 (to enthusiastic Congressional applause). This is, indeed, a high standard, but it could conceivably be met without revitalizing democratic education; indeed, the educational purposes of American democracy and those of American capitalism have often conflicted and might be expected to continue to do so. Some have argued that Clinton's standard is more likely to be met by "privatizing" American schools. If our aim is to educate our children for the market, the argument goes, why not use the market to do so if we are more likely to succeed in that fashion? Citizens would hesitate to entrust the education of future citizens to private corporations, but we seldom address the education of our children with their prospective citizenship in mind. We want, above all, for them to have good jobs that will enable them to be full participants in an "American Way of Life" that we have for decades defined as a rich and rewarding private life of material abundance. This is the principal promise to which we have come to hold our schools accountable.[4]

For this reason, the schools cannot and should not be indicted too harshly for failing to educate our children for democratic citizenship. Too often, bashing the public schools has served as an easy substitute for exploring the larger contexts in which their shortcomings can be explained. Why should schools provide an education for public life when American public life, as Walter Lippmann long ago observed, has become a phantom?[5] The practices of the public schools mirror a wider constriction of democratic life in the United States, the near erasure of citizenship as a significant element of the lives of most Americans. Most adult Americans no longer live to any significant degree as citizens, and hence it is not surprising that few feel a compelling need to educate American children for public life. The shortcomings of the school in this respect reflect, as Barber says, a more general "absence of democratic will and a consequent refusal to take our children, our schools, and our future seriously."[6] If one shares Barber's concern, as I do, and believes that freedom as well as democracy is at stake, then it is worth trying to figure out why our public schools do not educate for democratic citizenship and how we might reconstruct them so that they would do so. Here, a little history is helpful.

The Collapse of Common Schooling

The history of American public schooling reflects a more general two-mindedness about democracy that has been a feature of American political culture since the nation's founding. Few among the nation's founders had much good to say for democracy, which in the late eighteenth century remained synonymous for many with mob rule, and insofar as they used the term it was usually as an abusive epithet directed at their political opponents. "The ancient democracies, in which the people themselves deliberated," Alexander Hamilton declared, "never possessed one feature of good government. Their very character was tyranny; their figure deformity: When they assembled, the field of debate presented an ungovernable mob, not only incapable of deliberation, but prepared for every enormity." Democracies, James Madison observed, "have ever been spectacles of turbulence and contention; have ever been found incompatible with personal security or the rights of property; and have in general been as short in their lives as they have been violent in their deaths." Finding themselves faced with an excessively democratic republic bereft of the balancing influences of a monarchy and hereditary aristocracy, the framers of the federal Constitution proclaimed the doctrine of popular sovereignty and then designed a machinery for governing which provided for no institutions or public spaces for popular government beyond a limited franchise. Representative government, they hoped, would limit the dangers of democracy and sustain rule by the best men. Representation, Madison argued, might act as a kind of filter to "refine and enlarge the public views, by passing them through the medium of a chosen body of citizens, whose wisdom may best discern the true interests of their country, and whose patriotism and love of justice, will be least likely to sacrifice it to temporary or partial considerations."[7]

Yet, if the architects of the Constitution were skeptical of the civic virtue of most Americans, they were unwilling to abandon the extra insurance against the threat of democracy which public education for civic virtue might provide. "A well-instructed people alone can be permanently a free people," President Madison told Congress in 1810, seconding the view of his predecessor, George Washington, who had reminded the audience for his "Farewell Address" that "virtue or morality is a necessary spring of popular government" and "in proportion as the structure of a government gives force to public opinion, it is essential that public opinion should be enlightened."[8]

Yet, those American founders with a greater enthusiasm for democracy were not—as their opponents often portrayed them—advocates of rule by an uneducated people. Thomas Jefferson, for example, took issue with the antidemocratic republicanism of the Constitution, and argued that the more democratic a republic was, the more it measured up to republican ideals. A republic, for Jefferson, meant "a government by its citizens in mass, acting directly and personally, according to rules established by the majority; and that every other government is more or less republican, in proportion as it has in its composition more or less of this ingredient of the direct action of the citizens." But Jefferson intended that these citizens would be well educated for their responsibilities, and in 1784 he developed an elaborate plan for "the More General Diffusion of Knowledge" by means of a system of state-supported public schooling. "I know no safe depository of the ultimate powers of the society but the people themselves," Jefferson wrote, "and if we think them not enlightened enough to exercise their control with a wholesome discretion, the remedy is not to take it from them, but to inform their discretion by education."[9]

By the second quarter of the nineteenth century, in the wake of the enfranchisement of most of the white male citizenry and their incorporation into the extra–Constitutional institution of the mass political party, few American political leaders spoke ill of democracy, though many continued to worry over its practices. A general consensus on the necessity of public education for democratic citizenship persisted throughout the nineteenth century, holding within its confines those fearful of the consequences of democracy and those eager to expand its reach. Generally speaking, it was the former who took the initiative in consolidating a system of tax-supported public schools. Such conservative Whigs as Horace Mann and Henry Bernard led a "common school" movement designed to provide the sort of education for these active, enfranchised farmers and artisans which would contain this democratic impulse and forestall any threat it might pose to private property and social order. "It may be an easy thing to make a Republic," Mann remarked, "but it is a very laborious thing to make Republicans; and woe to the republic that rests upon no better foundations than ignorance, selfishness, and passion." For Americans, he argued, "the qualification of voters is as important as the qualification of governors, and even comes first, in the natural order":

> The theory of our government is, not that all men, however unfit, shall be voters,—but that every man, by the power of reason and the sense of duty, shall become fit to be a voter. Education must

bring the practice as nearly as possible to the theory. As the children now are, so will the sovereigns soon be. How can we expect the fabric of the government to stand, if vicious materials are daily wrought into its frame-work? Education must prepare our citizens to become municipal officers, intelligent jurors, honest witnesses, legislators, or competent judges of legislation—in fine, to fill all the manifold relations of life. For this end, it must be universal. The whole land must be watered with the streams of knowledge.[10]

The common school, reformers argued, was the best defense against the common man. As one put it, "the best police for our cities, the lowest insurance of our houses, the firmest security for our banks, the most effective means of preventing pauperism, vice and crime, and the only sure defense of our country, are our common schools; and woe to us, if their means of education be not commensurate with the wants and powers of the people."[11] As Ralph Waldo Emerson observed, such conservatives urged the cause of public education on the grounds that "the people have the power, and if they are not instructed to sympathize with the intelligent, reading, trading, and governing class, inspired with a taste for the same competitions and prizes, they will upset the fair pageant of Judicature, and perhaps lay a hand on the sacred muniments of wealth itself, and new distribute the land."[12]

The working people whom Mann and other reformers feared may not have appreciated the portrait of themselves offered in the literature of common school reform, but they shared with reformers a desire for universal education for citizens (that is, white males). They did not wish to be ruled by ignorance, selfishness, and passion, and they proved eager to educate their children for responsible democratic citizenship. Fierce critics of all forms of monopoly, and often wary of state authority, antebellum spokesmen for American "workingmen" were firm supporters of public education. Rush Welter exaggerates only a little when he characterizes their view of democratic public policy as that of "anarchy with a schoolmaster."[13] Hence, the United States was unique among industrializing nations in that support for public education cut across class lines, a peculiarity that can be attributed to the fact that American workers were enfranchised before bourgeois reformers attempted to deploy the power of the state to educate them. As two historians of social class and schooling in America have said, "the dominant classes feared disorder, articulated their concerns in terms of civic virtue, and pursued educational reform as an instrument of order. The working classes, like working classes elsewhere, strongly desired schooling for their children. But, unlike some other working classes, they were prepared to join in political coalitions favoring public schooling because they had already been mobilized by political parties into the state as voting citizens."[14]

This is not to say that there was not significant political conflict over the shape of common schooling in the nineteenth century, nor to ignore the exclusive character of nineteenth-century American citizenship and common schooling, which was largely schooling for white, northern students. Nor is it to offer a brief for the sort of education for democratic citizenship which the common schools offered their pupils, an education grounded in rote learning from texts such as Noah Webster's spellers and William McGuffey's readers, texts that extolled the virtues of obedience and an unthinking patriotism.[15] Rather, it is to point up the "commonness" of common schooling, the fact that it was schooling for the role that the children it reached would come to share whatever their social class. Whatever the limitations and shortcomings of the civic education these schools provided, as schools putatively dedicated to education for citizenship, they did furnish a setting in which a struggle for a more genuinely democratic civic education might be waged.[16]

This struggle was cut short by the dramatic transformation of American public education in the early twentieth century. Nineteenth-century common schooling had been rooted, like much of American culture, in the hope for a "one-class" society of petty proprietors. Wage labor was perceived as a temporary stage for American workers on their way to independent ownership of productive property; schooling was designed to educate workers who would eventually achieve such a "competence." By the late nineteenth century, it was clear to many that the development of industrial capitalism meant that wage labor would be the permanent condition of most Americans. A new wave of reformers, many of them as fearful of the nation's plain people as their antebellum predecessors, launched a series of "progressive" reforms designed to wrest political power from partisan machines tied to working class voters and vest it in the hands of a new middle class of managerial experts. At the same time, they moved to create a system of public schools which aimed less at common schooling for democratic citizenship than at differentiated schooling devised to accommodate the needs of an economy believed to be divided permanently along class lines. "Increasing specialization in all fields of labor has divided the people into dozens of more or less clearly defined classes," observed reformer Ellwood P. Cubberly. "The employee tends to remain an employee; the wage earner tends to remain a wage earner." Public schools, especially urban ones, had to accommodate this reality, he declared. "Our city schools will soon be forced to give up the exceedingly democratic idea that all are equal, and that our society is devoid of classes, as a few cities have already in large part done, and to begin a specialization of educational effort along many new lines in an attempt better to adapt the school to the needs of these many classes in the city life."[17]

In the first two decades of the twentieth century, reformers in alliance with business interests launched a campaign for "industrial education" that focused on the transformation of the American high school, seeking to change this elite, college-preparatory bastion of the upper-middle class into a socially diverse institution designed to prepare boys and girls for jobs in the higher reaches of blue collar labor and the lower echelons of white collar work. In this, they were quite successful. Between 1890 and 1920, enrollment in high schools grew from two hundred thousand to almost two million students, and the percentage of those fourteen to seventeen years of age in high school grew from 6.7 percent to 32.3 percent. The high school curriculum in 1890 was centered on instruction in classical and modern languages, mathematics, and science, but by the 1920s, students were also studying such things as mechanical drawing, woodworking, ironworking, pattern making, cooking, bookkeeping, stenography, typing, and commercial law. "For a long time all boys were trained to be President," the president of the Muncie, Indiana school board told sociologists Robert and Helen Lynd. "Then for a while we trained them all to be professional men. Now we are training boys to get jobs."[18]

An even more radical effort by the advocates of industrial education to create a dual school system with separate vocational schools controlled by businessmen was, however, a failure. It met with stiff opposition from a coalition of labor unions, teachers, parents, and critics anxious to hang on to the common school tradition. At the 1915 convention of the National Education Association, industrial education supporter J. Stanley Brown accurately (and somewhat ruefully) described this debate as one that pitted parents and various "social, ethical, and religious organizations" who wanted the student "to develop his own life in the way which seemed best to his parent and himself and that his duties as a citizen demand" against "manufacturers, the commercialists, or the industrialists," who were less concerned with schooling the boy to be "the best citizen, the most honest and careful man" than with making "every individual employee subordinate to the production of his particular institution." The defenders of "unitary" schooling managed to defeat the proponents of a separate system for vocational education, but their victory was a Pyrrhic one, for the upshot of this conflict was the creation of the comprehensive high school in which students were "tracked" into separate vocational and liberal arts curricula—in sum, a dual system under one roof.[19]

The leading advocates of industrial education insisted that their reform program was a democratic one since it provided schooling adapted to the particular needs of each student. Because students of different classes faced very different work lives after they left school, reformers argued, they were best served by a differentiated education that took account of this fact. On this rendering, as historian David Nasaw has said, "democracy meant offering every student the opportunity for an education equally adjusted to what school officials assumed would be his or her future vocation." If schools were to be a functional component of a society permanently divided along class lines, these proponents of "social efficiency" argued, they had not only to educate all social classes but to educate them differently.[20]

In a sense, this transformation of the high school did make for a more democratic, or at least a more egalitarian, system of public education. It meant more hours and days of schooling for more children, and greater access to the higher reaches of secondary education for children of the white working class—access that was eventually extended to racial and ethnic minorities as well.[21] However, this was access to schooling that now served above all to reproduce the inegalitarian social order of the larger society, schooling that no longer offered much common schooling for democratic citizenship, the one role that lay in the future of children of all classes.

Civic education did not disappear from American public schools with the triumph of vocationalism, and in the midst of concern about such matters as the "Americanization" of immigrants and the challenge of international communism, calls have gone out for its invigoration. Generally speaking, however, education for democratic citizenship has been increasingly marginalized in public schools, a status perhaps best indicated by its consignment to a narrow range of courses in "social studies."

Arguments that have been advanced for the importance of civic education have defined citizenship in terribly banal and generally nonpolitical terms. In the *Cardinal Principles of Secondary Education* (1918), citizenship is characterized as "a many-sided interest in the welfare of the communities to which one belongs; loyalty to ideals of civic righteousness; practical knowledge of social agencies and institutions; good judgment as to means and methods that will promote one social end without defeating others; and as putting all these into effect, habits of cordial cooperation in social undertakings." This sort of bland mush, with its understanding of citizenship as a set of essentially *social* attitudes and practices, has persisted to this day. Core courses in citizenship have passed from history to civics to various ventures in social science, including courses in "values clarification" in which a host of values are "clarified" but few values in particular are defended as essential to democracy and thereby exemplary.[22]

Even educational reformers who are apparently alert to and concerned about the thinness of American citizenship are unable to muster much of a response. For example, Ernest L. Boyer, reporting on American secondary education for the Carnegie Foundation for the Advancement of Teaching in 1983, noted that "the Jeffersonian vision of grassroots democracy" had come to seem "increasingly utopian," and "civic illiteracy" was spreading. "Unless we find better ways to educate ourselves as citizens," he said, "we run the risk of drifting unwittingly into a new kind of Dark Age—a time when, increasingly, specialists will control knowledge and the decision-making process." But Boyer, like many others, defines this crisis as one of citizens' "ignorance about government and how it functions," and he recommends little more than a few courses in civics. But if students knew more about how American government functioned, they would then only be aware of how fully "the decision-making process" had in fact drifted into the hands of specialists, and the question would remain how they might be educated to stem this drift. Few critics have been so bold as to suggest that democratic civic education is not only a matter of knowing about politics but of acquiring the knowledge, the skills, and the moral dispositions one needs to engage in a full measure of self-government.[23] And few have had the temerity to point out that this larger task would require democrats to put civic education at the heart of public schooling and to figure out how not only courses in civics but the entire public school curriculum might serve this purpose.[24]

On the whole, then, the twentieth century has witnessed the rapid rise to preeminence of schooling for what one report termed "occupational competence" and the relegation of civic education to, at best, an afterthought. Once the principal institution for vocational training, the high school has now become for many students a station on their way to enrollment in a new layer of "differentiated" schooling that emerged with the explosive growth of institutions of mass higher education in the last fifty years. One is far more likely to hear one's child spoken of as "human capital" than as a citizen in waiting. American public schools have become, above all, a vast, variegated system funneling this human capital into its final destination in the hierarchies of the undemocratic world of modern work.[25]

Reconstructing Civic Education

What one makes of this history depends on the democratic theory to which one subscribes. Few Americans openly admit to being antidemocratic; instead, we argue about what democracy should mean. Since the 1920s, American democratic theory has been dominated by thinkers who have advanced views under the banner of democratic "realism" which the founders showed no qualms about openly declaring undemocratic. Such "neo–Hamiltonians," as Barber has termed them, "insist that the public mind must be filtered and refined through the cortex of its betters. Give everyone the franchise, but don't let them do anything much with it. Protect them from the government with a sturdy barrier of rights, but protect government from them with a representative system that guarantees they will not themselves be legislators. In short, let them vote the governors in and out, but don't let them govern themselves. Let them enjoy freedom from government, but don't let them govern themselves freely." Such democrats can regard the collapse of common schooling and the marginalization of civic education with equanimity, for by their lights democratic citizenship is not terribly ill-served by prevailing practice. Since citizenship need not amount to much, there is no need to devote much of our educational resources to training our children for its practice.[26]

The triumph of this neo–Hamiltonian democratic theory has accompanied the steady desiccation of American citizenship since the turn of the century, and has served to legitimate it. Since the 1890s, electoral participation by American citizens has declined dramatically, political parties have decomposed, and public life has become a sideshow for most Americans, if that. Periodically, we are reminded of our citizenship by election campaigns in which candidates are packaged by professional consultants for sale to television audiences whose opinions are packaged by pollsters for sale to candidates. It does not require much education to participate in this sort of spectatorial, consumer politics, and not surprisingly, elections are a market in which many alienated, preoccupied, or uninterested citizens fail to shop.[27] If this be sufficient democracy, then there is little need for a reconstruction of civic education. Neo–Hamiltonians are, to be sure, no less fearful of an ignorant democratic public than their Hamiltonian ancestors, but unlike those ancestors, they do not confront a public widely organized into participatory political institutions. There is little to fear from the uneducated nonvoter, and the "party" of nonvoters is our largest. Hence, neo–Hamiltonians look not to education but to indifference for the protection of social order from the unruly mob; apathy, they argue, has its virtues.

But American two-mindedness about democracy has remained very much in evidence in the twentieth century, and neo–Hamiltonian theory has not gone unopposed. For modern democrats of a more Jeffersonian turn of mind, the neglect of civic education in American public schools is deeply troubling. Among those concerned about democracy and public schooling, perhaps no thinker is more significant than John Dewey. Dewey was not only the most important advocate among modern liberal intellectuals of an expansive participatory democracy, but throughout his career he addressed himself to the pivotal role of the school in fostering such a democracy.[28]

At the heart of Dewey's work as both a philosopher and an activist was a belief that democracy as an ethical ideal calls upon men and women to build communities in which the necessary opportunities and resources are available for every individual to realize fully his or her particular capacities and powers through participation in political, social, and cultural life. This ideal, he said, rested on a "faith in the capacity of human beings for intelligent judgment and action if proper conditions are furnished"—a faith, he argued, "so deeply embedded in the methods which are intrinsic to democracy that when a professed democrat denies the faith he convicts himself of treachery to his profession." Education in a democracy, as Dewey saw it, had to be guided by this ideal and sustained by this faith.[29]

One might reasonably view Dewey's work in the philosophy and practice of education as an effort to reconstruct "common schooling" so that it might remain pertinent to modern industrial democracies. He was a bitter critic of the industrial education movement in the early twentieth century, and he struggled to envision an education for the world's work that would not foster class divisions or preclude schooling for the tasks that democratic citizens had to undertake together. All members of a democratic society, he declared, are entitled to an education that will enable them to make the best of themselves as active and equal participants in the life of their community. "Men will long dispute about material socialism, about socialism considered as a matter of distribution of the material resources of the community," he said, "but there is a socialism regarding which there can be no such dispute—socialism of the intelligence and of the spirit. To extend the range and the fullness of sharing in the intellectual and spiritual resources of the community is the very meaning of the community."[30]

For a child to become an effective member of a democratic community, Dewey argued, he must have "training in science, in art, in history; command of the fundamental methods of inquiry and the fundamental tools of intercourse and communication," as well as "a trained and sound body, skillful eye and hand; habits of industry, perseverance, and, above all, of serviceableness." In a democratic community children have to learn to be leaders as well as followers, possessed of "power of self-direction and power of directing others, powers of administration, ability to assume positions of responsibility" as citizens and workers. Because the world is rapidly changing, children cannot, moreover, be educated for any "fixed station in life," but schools have to provide each child with training that would "give him such possession of himself that he may take charge of himself; may not only adapt himself to the changes which are going on, but have power to shape and direct those changes."[31]

The critical task of Deweyan or neo–Jeffersonian democratic educators, of course, is to figure out what civic education in the public schools for a more expansive citizenship would look like. Dewey himself, alas, had relatively little to say about the particulars of civic education, though most of what he had to say about "democracy and education" is at least indirectly relevant. But since Deweyan democrats are not a particularly noteworthy presence among those few critics who have devoted much attention to civic education in the schools, guidance is hard to come by. The most satisfying extended treatment of this issue I have found is in Richard Battistoni's *Public Schooling and the Education of Democratic Citizens*, though here I can only sketch the bare outline of the proposals he advances.[32]

Beyond providing students with literacy and other basic skills in mathematics, Battistoni argues that the goal of education for democratic citizenship should be that of "developing in students skills and attitudes necessary to direct participation in political affairs, as well as a set of substantive values which underlie our political institutions and procedures." This task, as he sees it, calls for a number of reforms. The civics curriculum must be rethought, and history must be returned to a central place in its offerings—not history as a "parade of institutional and historical facts," not history as the bland pieties of most school textbooks, but history as the story of the conflict-ridden formation of the complex tradition within which all American citizens must exercise their practical judgment.[33] Moreover, civics instruction should openly and unapologetically teach the values that must underlie democratic politics. As Battistoni says: "Fundamental to democratic citizenship are principles such as democratic equality and justice; a belief in every person's ability and responsibility to participate in public affairs; a concern for the dignity of each individual and her or his personal choices, combined with a dedication to cooperating and sharing experiences; a commitment to resolve public disputes through a process of reasoned debate and conflict *transformation*; and an attachment to public affairs and one's fellow citizens."[34]

Unlike most others who have called for a revitalized civics curriculum, Battistoni contends that such a curriculum should include more than courses offered under the rubric of "civics" or "social studies." As he says, "If we want students to be knowledgeable and capable of making decisions about the wide range of issues which constitute contemporary American politics, we should provide them with a broad-based secondary school education which includes the sciences, literature, and the arts as well as history and government. This means that teachers in all high school disciplines must be aware of the connections between their particular lessons and desirable civic skills and attitudes." Teachers of literature have as much to teach future citizens as teachers of history, and for democrats, "compartmentalized learning in secondary schools must come to an end."[35]

As Battistoni cogently argues, not only must civic education educate students for participatory politics but the education itself must be participatory. By this he means not only that learning in the classroom should take the form of joint deliberation but also that students should be encouraged to move beyond the walls of the school and explore the civic life of adults in class assignments and internships. Finally, Battistoni argues that "to provide a more complete civic education for future citizens, we must integrate not only course and activities but also *students* from different backgrounds and interests"—schools must once again be common, and the comprehensive high school must be defended from its critics and "untracked." As Battistoni is well aware, his proposals—particularly this last one—reach deep into the heart of the most bitter conflicts embroiling American society. As he concludes, "Many of the factors mitigating against a renewal of the public high school are part of larger problems in American society as a whole (racial and ethnic conflicts, 'white flight' from urban areas, privatization of interests, economic instabilities, the decline in local and urban communities), and major changes in society may be necessary" before the public schools can provide the sort of education he recommends.[36]

I would imagine that to those given to what Battistoni calls "participatory-republicanism" his proposals will be attractive, or at least of the sort that might initiate a productive argument about civic education. But participatory-republicanism is a minority and adversarial view to which few Americans are committed, or of which not many are even aware. Civic education of the sort Battistoni recommends would be a hard sell, especially to those who have invested so heavily in "differentiated" schooling for "occupational competence." In some respects, to be sure, there need be no conflict between preparing children for a more active citizenship and girding them for competition in "the global marketplace." Education for public life and education for work are not inherently at cross purposes. In the nineteenth century, for example, American democrats believed that petty proprietorship was an essential foundation for democratic citizenship because it cultivated the skills and virtues (above all, the independence) required of good democrats. As Abraham Lincoln told an audience of Wisconsin farmers in 1859, "In these Free States, a large majority are neither *hirers* nor *hired*. Men, with their families—wives, sons and daughters—work for themselves, on their farms, in their houses, and in their shops, taking the whole product to themselves, and asking no favors of capital on the one hand, nor of hirelings or slaves on the other." Such citizens, he declared, "can never be the victim of oppression in any of its forms. Such community will be alike independent of crowned-kings, money-kings, and land-kings."[37]

It is much more difficult—some would say impossible—to make the case for wage labor as a reinforcing influence on democratic citizenship.[38] Yet, insofar as American employers have become disenchanted with a merely docile workforce suited to the unskilled jobs that are becoming in increasingly short supply, and to the extent that they are calling for workers in full command of basic skills and possessed of a disposition for lifelong learning, the purposes of citizenship and capitalism might coincide, at least in part. As Deborah Meier has said recently, if schools take their task to be that of teaching children "to become learners (not learned but a learner)," they will cultivate such habits as "being reliable, someone you can count on, resilient, capable of dealing with frustration, not expecting certainties and absolutes" which are essential to all "decent worthy human vocations. Including the vocation of citizen."[39] But, whether American employers would appreciate employees armed not only with technical skills and these admirable habits but also with the capacity and desire to deliberate on the ends of the enterprise and the economy is another question. Here, one is entitled to greater skepticism about any simple, unproblematic grafting of education for participatory citizenship onto the prevailing aims and purposes of American schools. Dewey, at least, argued that schooling for democracy would only be fully functional when democracy had been extended to the workplace.

Revitalizing Democratic Publics

Even if one could make American public schools more effective vehicles of civic education, it would not be worth doing as long as American public life remains as anemic as it is today. As the neo–Hamiltonians contend, there is no point to educating children for a citizenship that will not be there to practice when they become adults. One could argue, I suppose, that students educated for a more participatory democracy might lead the struggle to create it. In this fashion, the schools would serve as the principal agency of democratic social change; it would be the schools, as George Counts once put it, that would dare to build a new social order.[40] But one might just as easily imagine such students would drift into cynicism when confronted with the thoroughly dysfunctional character of their education; and in any case, one cannot expect adults to commit their tax dollars to schools whose purposes they fail to understand or appreciate. Nor can democrats expect ready assent to their project from those who have turned the schools to their current, often contrary, purposes. The schools simply are not an independent locomotive of social transformation sitting idly on a siding, readily available for democratic engineers who would take the controls.

Thus neo–Jeffersonians must commit themselves not only to a reconstruction of civic education but to a much broader revitalization of American public life—an even taller order. Jefferson himself recognized this task. He called not only for the civic education of all citizens, but for the creation of the public spaces for the exercise of the popular sovereignty which the Constitution had neglected to mandate. He proposed that the country be divided "into wards of such size as that every citizen can attend, when called on, and act in person." Such a ward system, he argued, "by making every citizen an acting member of the government, and in the offices nearest and most interesting to him, will attach him by his strongest feelings to the independence of his country, and its republican constitution." Dewey shared Jefferson's conviction of both the necessity and insufficiency of democratic schooling for the making of a more democratic public life. "It is unrealistic, in my opinion," he wrote in 1937, "to suppose that the schools can be a *main* agency in producing the intellectual and moral changes, the changes in attitudes and disposition of thought and purpose, which are necessary for the creation of a new social order." The defects of schools mirrored and sustained the defects of the larger society and these defects could not be remedied apart from a struggle for democracy throughout that larger society. Schools would take part in democratic social change only "as they ally themselves with this or that movement of existing social forces." Like Jefferson, Dewey believed democracy must rest ultimately on active, face-to-face, local publics. "Democracy must begin at home," he said, "and its home is the neighborly community."[41]

Apart from the civic education it provides to children, the school—that is, the school building—might play a role in this larger project. Recent years have witnessed a revival of interest in "community schools," that is, schools that would serve not only to educate children in a neighborhood but also as wider social centers for adults as well as children, remaining open in the late afternoon and early evening to serve this larger community. For the most part, recent community school initiatives have been conceived as contributing to a more humane, efficient, and democratic means of meeting the social welfare needs of the American poor. Community schools, their advocates have argued, might serve as centers for job training, recreation, health care, adult education, and other social services. In the most imaginative programs, the school curriculum is integrated with provision of these services, as in a school in West Philadelphia in which the studies of middle school students have been folded into their active participation in neighborhood health care services. In their most radical formulations, community school programs foresee what Michael Walzer has termed a "socialization of the welfare state," which would thoroughly decentralize the distribution of social welfare services and solicit the participation of those who receive these services in their management.[42]

This sort of community school project is an important democratic initiative. However, community schools might also well serve efforts to revitalize local, democratic publics, for in many neighborhoods the school is the one remaining public space of any significance. It might conceivably serve as a site for citizens to gather and deliberate, and as such, might serve not only the poor but all American citizens. Anemic citizenship is not only a problem in the inner city. Indeed, few developments have been more damaging to participatory democracy than the mass exodus of American citizens to the suburbs—the preeminent landscape of the overweening claims of private life in this country.

During the early twentieth century, when the rich possibilities of community schools were first broached, some of their proponents grasped the opportunities they might afford deliberative democracy. In Rochester, New York, Edward Ward led a "social centers" movement that for a brief time (1907 to 1911) established local, democratic publics in many of that city's neighborhood schools, and then spread to a number of other cities in the years immediately preceding World War I. Like other neo–Jeffersonian democrats, Ward was distressed that American citizenship had been reduced for most to little more than voting, and that voting had been detached from the joint deliberation with other citizens which would render public opinion informed and reflective. "The people," he said, "is a great vegetable." If the public was to regain its animal spirits, it had to be organized in small, deliberative bodies. As he said, "When the members of the electorate add to their common function of participating in the decision upon public questions, the function of consciously organizing to deliberate upon public questions, then the people become a reasoning, a self-knowing being."[43]

Civic education for children, Ward argued, must be connected with active citizenship for adults. Children who by day went to schools that served adult citizens in the evening could gain a palpable sense of the public life for which they were preparing themselves. "The great central object of the training of youth is the development of good citizenship; the great difficulty is in the visualizing of the business of democracy," Ward observed. Schools that were used for deliberation and voting could give students a "point of contact from which they may go on to the understanding of the civic process as a reality." Young people would be welcomed into the common rooms of their schools to hear their parents deliberate, and here they could make concrete sense of the purposes of their schooling. As Ward put it, "Where the man is, there is the boy's heart, also. When the adults of the community are using the neighborhood building for actual political expression in common council then the idea of citizenship is visualized" and schooling becomes a "civic apprenticeship." If, as Deborah Meier says, the shortcomings of American schooling can be linked to the fact that "what we do in schools bears little resemblance to anything that we can convince kids powerful adults do later on in their lives," then maybe there is something to be learned from this lamentably short-lived social center movement.[44]

There is some evidence that Americans might well take to a more participatory public life. For example, recounting his recent efforts to initiate a "national conversation" about American pluralism, the chairman of the National Endowment for the Humanities (NEH), Sheldon Hackney, reported that he was met with an enthusiastic response from citizens who gathered in local communities throughout the country to discuss such questions as "what holds our diverse society together, what values we need to share if we are to succeed as a democratic society, what it means to be American as we approach the twenty-first century." Not only were these conversations, as Hackney described them, exemplary of the discussions one might expect to find in local, democratic publics, they seemed to whet the appetite for further debate. At the end of the discussions, Hackney says, the question generally asked was, "How can we continue to meet and pursue this subject?" One might well have taken this question as an invitation to help organize more permanent publics, though unfortunately Hackney proposes to move in another direction. The NEH, he said, will make a film on American pluralism for broadcast on television, using "mass communications to broaden the conversational circle." But mass communications do not broaden conversational circles; they preclude them.[45]

Any effort in the present to extend American democracy and shape public schooling for that purpose will encounter enormous obstacles—most of them far more daunting than the myopia of such men of good will as Sheldon Hackney. Whatever lessons we might take from Ward and his Rochester experiment, one must be the lesson of its defeat within a few years at the hands of powerful interests—in this case, machine politicians—threatened by a more democratic politics.[46] In an inegalitarian society, those with much to lose are right to be wary of deliberative gatherings of those with much to gain from its reconstruction. If democracy was in the interest of those who hold the reins of power in the United States, we would have more of it.

It may be, as Michael Walzer has gloomily suggested, that in modern societies citizenship is fated to wither in favor of the more passionate identities of class, ethnicity, religion, and family, which "do not draw people together but rather separate and divide them" and hence "make for the primacy of the private realm."[47] But, to believe this is to guarantee the permanent eclipse of an expansive democratic citizenship. To imagine that American democracy can be reconstructed and revitalized requires, as John Dewey said, an abiding faith in the ability of ordinary men and women to educate themselves and their children for self-government and in their will to use the power at their disposal to wage the long struggle necessary to secure the means of self-government. Democrats of this neo–Jeffersonian sort must expect a torrent of criticism from neo–Hamiltonians who will charge that such a faith is unreasonable and even reckless, and they must be prepared for frustrations, setbacks, and many a long, dark night of the soul.

Notes

1. Benjamin Barber, "America Skips School," *Harper's Magazine*, November 1993, *286*, 44.
2. Pennsylvania study cited in Richard M. Battistoni, *Public Schooling and the Education of Democratic Citizens* (Jackson: University Press of Mississippi, 1985), pp. 4–5.
3. Barber, "America Skips School," p. 44.
4. "Excerpts from President Clinton's State of the Union Message," *New York Times*, January 26, 1994, p. A15. For an astute analysis of Clinton's educational program by a critic concerned about its implica-

tions for democratic citizenship, see B. Todd Sullivan, "Economic Ends and Educational Means at the White House: A Case for Citizenship and Casuistry," *Educational Theory*, 1993, *43*, 161–179. We may perhaps take some comfort in the remark of one leading Clinton advisor on domestic policy, William Galston, that "a wealthy community that determines the worth of all activities by the extent to which they add to its wealth has forgotten what wealth is for. A system of training, education, and culture wholly subservient to the system of production denies the fuller humanity of its participants" (*Liberal Purposes* [Cambridge: Cambridge University Press, 1991], p. 202).

5. Walter Lippmann, *The Phantom Public* (New York: Macmillan, 1925).

6. Barber, "America Skips School," p. 45.

7. Alexander Hamilton, "New York Ratifying Convention First Speech" (1788), in *The Papers of Alexander Hamilton* (New York: Columbia University Press, 1962), vol. 5, p. 39; James Madison, "Federalist X" (1787), in *The Debate on the Constitution*, edited by B. Bailyn (New York: Library of America, 1993), vol. I, pp. 408, 409.

8. James Madison, "Second Annual Message" (1810), and George Washington, "Farewell Address" (1796), in *Messages and Papers of the Presidents*, edited by J. D. Richardson (New York: Bureau of National Literature, 1897), vol. 2, p. 470; vol. 1, p. 212. For a full account of the views of the founders on education see Lorraine Smith Pangle and Thomas L. Pangle, *The Learning of Liberty: The Educational Ideas of the American Founders* (Lawrence: University Press of Kansas, 1993).

9. Thomas Jefferson to John Taylor, May 28, 1816, and Jefferson, "A Bill for the More General Diffusion of Knowledge" (1784), in Jefferson, *Writings*, (New York: Library of America, 1984), pp. 1392, 365, 373; Thomas Jefferson to William C. Jarvis, September 28, 1820, in *The Writings of Thomas Jefferson*, edited by P. L. Ford (New York: Putnam, 1899), vol. 10, p. 161.

10. Horace Mann, "Twelfth Annual Report" (1848), in *The Republic and the School: Horace Mann on the Education of Free Men*, edited by L. Cremin (New York: Teachers College Press, 1957), p. 92; Horace Mann, *Lectures on Education* (Boston: William B. Fowle, 1848), pp. 57–58.

11. Alonzo Potter of Utica, New York, as quoted in Jonathan Messerli, *Horace Mann: A Biography* (New York: Knopf, 1972), p. 373.

12. Ralph Waldo Emerson, "The Conservative" (1841), in Emerson, *Essays and Lectures* (New York: Library of America, 1983), p. 186.

13. Rush Welter, *Popular Education and Democratic Thought in America* (New York: Columbia University Press, 1962), p. 50.

14. Ira Katznelson and Margaret Weir, *Schooling for All: Class, Race, and the Decline of the Democratic Ideal* (New York: Basic, 1985), p. 45.

15. For a good account of common school practice see Jean H. Baker, *Affairs of Party: The Political Culture of Northern Democrats in the Mid-Nineteenth Century* (Ithaca, N.Y.: Cornell University Press, 1983), pp. 71–107. As studies such as Baker's of nineteenth-century American political culture make clear, the schools were not the only nor the most important agencies of civic education. Children learned as much if not more from the rich, expressive rituals and popular culture of the public and partisan life they encountered outside the classroom as they did from the pieties conveyed by their schoolteachers.

16. My assessment of nineteenth-century common schools parallels that which I have offered elsewhere of the partisan politics that helped occasion them. We do ourselves a disservice, I have argued, if we "weave a democratic romance" around the nineteenth-century American political parties as scholars such as Walter Dean Burnham have been prone to do. Nonetheless, this is not to say that "the possibilities of democracy in America have not been adversely affected by the decline of the party" over the course of the twentieth century. "The political party was the one broadly participatory institution in American political life, and for this reason, it was the one institution that held within it the promise of a more expansive democracy. It was the genius of the Populists to see this and to attempt to reconstruct and radicalize the participatory practices of the party system in order to democratize control of the political economy. Their defeat and the subsequent decay of these practices and the partisan culture that fostered them cut most Americans off from the active role in organized public life that might have been theirs." See Robert B. Westbrook, "Politics as Consumption: Managing the Modern American Election," in *The Culture of Consumption*, edited by R. W. Fox and T. J. Jackson Lears (New York: Pantheon, 1983), pp. 151–152.

17. Ellwood P. Cubberly, *Changing Conceptions of Education* (Boston: Houghton Mifflin, 1909), pp. 10, 56–57.

18. Robert L. Church and Michael Sedlak, *Education in the United States: An Interpretive History* (New York: Free Press, 1976), p. 289; Lawrence A. Cremin, *American Education: The Metropolitan Experience 1876–1980* (New York: Harper & Row, 1988), pp. 544–547; Robert and Helen Lynd, *Middletown* (New York: Harcourt, Brace, and World, 1929), p. 194.

19. J. Stanley Brown, quoted in David Nasaw, *Schooled to Order: A Social History of Public Schooling in the United States* (New York: Oxford, 1979), p. 150.

20. Nasaw, *Schooled to Order*, p. 132.

21. See Patricia Albjerg Graham, "What America Has Expected of Its Schools over the Past Century," *American Journal of Education*, 1993, *101*, 83–98.

22. *Cardinal Principles of Secondary Education* (Washington, D.C.: Government Printing Office, 1918), p. 13. On values clarification and democratic values see Battistoni, *Public Schooling*, pp. 92–93.

23. Ernest L. Boyer, *High School: A Report on Secondary Education in America* (New York: Harper & Row, 1983), pp. 105–106. An exception is Battistoni, *Public Schooling*, to which I shall return.

24. To conceive of civic education as a matter of accruing data about politics rather than political "know-how" is characteristic of the modern fetish of "information." Information, no matter how equitably distributed, is less important for democracy than deliberation. As Christopher Lasch remarked, "What democracy requires is public debate, not information. Of course it needs information, too, but the kind of information it needs can be generated only by vigorous popular debate. We do not know what we need to know until we ask the right questions, and we can identify the right questions only by subjecting our own ideas about the world to the test of public controversy. Information, usually seen as the precondition of debate, is better understood as its by-product. When we get into arguments that focus and fully engage our attention, we become avid seekers of relevant information. Otherwise, we take in information passively—if we take it in at all" ("Journalism, Publicity, and the Lost Art of Argument," *Gannett Center Journal*, Spring 1990, p. 1).

25. National Commission on the Reform of Secondary Education, *The Reform of Secondary Education* (New York: McGraw-Hill, 1973), pp. 32–33, 49–61. On the explosion of vocationally oriented higher education, see Daniel O. Levine, *The American College and the Culture of Aspiration: 1915–1940* (Ithaca, N.Y.: Cornell University Press, 1986); and Steven Brint and Jerome Karabel, *The Diverted Dream: Community Colleges and the Promise of Education Opportunity in America 1900–1985* (New York: Oxford University Press, 1989).

26. Benjamin Barber, *An Aristocracy of Everyone: The Politics of Education and the Future of America* (New York: Ballantine, 1992), p. 244. For a brief history of the development of neo–Hamiltonian theory see Robert B. Westbrook, *John Dewey and American Democracy* (Ithaca, N.Y.: Cornell University Press, 1991), pp. 280–286, 543–546.

27. Westbrook, "Politics as Consumption," pp. 152–173.

28. For a much fuller account of Dewey's career as a democratic theorist and activist than I can offer here, see Westbrook, *John Dewey and American Democracy*.

29. John Dewey, "Creative Democracy: The Task Before Us" (1939), in *Later Works of John Dewey* (Carbondale: Southern Illinois University Press, 1988), vol. 14, p. 227.

30. John Dewey, *Lectures on Psychological and Political Ethics: 1898* (New York: Hafner Press, 1976), pp. 444–445. On Dewey's criticisms of industrial education see Westbrook, *John Dewey and American Democracy*, pp. 173–182.

31. John Dewey, "The School as a Social Centre" (1902), in *Middle Works of John Dewey* (Carbondale: Southern Illinois University Press, 1976), vol. 2, p. 93; Dewey, "Ethical Principles Underlying Education" (1897), in *Early Works of John Dewey* (Carbondale: Southern Illinois University Press, 1972), vol. 5, pp. 59–60.

32. Even Battistoni confines himself largely to the high school, and he says nothing about the internal and external structures of authority and power in the school, structures that Dewey contended had to be made more democratic than they were in his time, a criticism that still applies.

33. Battistoni, *Public Schooling*, pp. 187–188. For an even more compelling argument for the centrality of history to civic education see Eamonn Callan, "Beyond Sentimental Civic Education," *American Journal of Education*, 1994, *102*, 190–221.

34. Battistoni, *Public Schooling*, pp. 188–189.

35. Battistoni, *Public Schooling*, pp. 187–190. For a powerful example of the use of literature—in this case, Eudora Welty's story, "Where Is the Voice Coming From?"—to teach civic values see Callan, "Beyond Sentimental Civic Education," pp. 212–214.

36. Battistoni, *Public Schooling*, pp. 190–194.

37. Abraham Lincoln, "Address to the Wisconsin State Agricultural Society" (1859), in Lincoln, *Speeches and Writings: 1859–1865* (New York: Library of America, 1989), pp. 97, 100.

38. For a powerful argument for the incompatibility between wage labor and democratic citizenship see Herbert Croly, *Progressive Democracy* (New York: Macmillan, 1914), pp. 378–405.

39. Deborah Meier, "A Talk to Teachers," *Dissent*, Winter 1994, *41*, 82, 84.

40. George S. Counts, *Dare the School Build a New Social Order?* (New York: John Day, 1932).

41. Thomas Jefferson to Samuel Kercheval, July 12, 1816, in Jefferson, *Writings*, p. 1399; John Dewey, "Education and Social Change" (1937), in *Later Works of John Dewey* (Carbondale: Southern Illinois University Press, 1987), vol. 11, p. 414; Dewey, "Can Education Share in Social Reconstruction?" (1934), in *Later Works of John Dewey* (Carbondale: Southern Illinois University Press, 1986), vol. 9, p. 207; Dewey, "The Public and Its Problems" (1927), in *Later Works of John Dewey* (Carbondale: Southern Illinois University Press, 1984), vol. 2, p. 368. See also Dewey's appreciative account of Jefferson's ward system in "Pre-

senting Thomas Jefferson" (1940), in *Later Works of John Dewey* (Carbondale: Southern Illinois University Press, 1988), vol. 14, pp. 213–218.

42. Michael Walzer, "Socializing the Welfare State," in *Democracy and the Welfare State,* edited by A. Gutmann (Princeton, N.J.: Princeton University Press, 1988), pp. 13–26. On the Philadelphia community schools project see Ira Harkavy and John L. Puckett, "Toward Effective University-Public School Partnerships: An Analysis of a Contemporary Model," *Teachers College Record,* 1991, *92,* 556–581; and Lee Benson and Ira Harkavy, "Progressing Beyond the Welfare State," *Universities and Community Schools,* 1991, *2,* 2–28.

43. Edward J. Ward, *The Social Center* (New York: Appleton, 1913), p. 69. For introducing me to Ward and the social center movement, I am indebted to Kevin Mattson, "Creating a Democratic Public: The Struggle for Urban Participatory Democracy During the Progressive Era, 1890–1920" (Ph.D. dissertation, University of Rochester, 1994), pp. 86–171.

44. Ward, *Social Center,* pp. 17, 128; Meier, "A Talk to Teachers," p. 83.

45. Sheldon Hackney, "Organizing a National Conversation," *Chronicle of Higher Education,* April 20, 1994, p. A56.

46. Community schools—and the deliberative publics that might gather in them—require money to keep them going, and if the activities of citizens are to be the activities of citizens, they must be publicly funded. This places a powerful weapon in the hands of those like the politicians who killed the Rochester movement in its infancy. No American opponent of a more democratic politics is likely to attack it as too democratic, but many lie in wait to contend that it is too expensive.

47. Michael Walzer, "Citizenship," in *Political Innovation and Conceptual Change,* edited by T. Ball, J. Farr, and R. L. Hanson (Cambridge: Cambridge University Press, 1989), p. 218.

Democracy and Access to Education

Linda Darling-Hammond
Jacqueline Ancess

The American democracy has long been a source of admiration and inspiration throughout the world, from Tocqueville in the last century to today's emerging democracies of eastern Europe, Africa, Asia, and Latin America, whose struggles will take us into the next century. So much is democracy an American birthright, so deeply do Americans believe that we embody and define democracy, that we often take its existence and its practice for granted in our own nation. Americans sometimes forget that the achievement of democracy is always a struggle, despite a plethora of twentieth-century images such as the bloodshed in Tiananmen Square, the recent real and symbolic liberation of South Africans from apartheid, the collapse of the Berlin Wall, and the desegregation of America's schools by young African-American students, protected by National Guardsmen from white crowds hurling insults.

As a nation, we sometimes seem unaware that full participation in the rights and benefits of democracy has not been made available to all Americans, and we sometimes seem not to understand that democracy itself is weakened when this is the case. The struggles of African Americans, Native Americans, Latinos, and others who have been disenfranchised are frequently viewed as the plight of isolated groups, and rarely as the struggle of the entire nation to fulfill its values, beliefs, and aspirations. Ironically, efforts to redress inequity in access to opportunity are often perceived as a threat to our democratic government, rather than as a celebration of its core commitment. The prospect of open access to quality education, housing, and employment often triggers the fear of loss by privileged Americans who live the good life that is the American dream. The case has not yet been made persuasively enough that making good on these commitments can enhance and better secure the welfare of all.

America's struggle in confronting issues of inequality is nowhere so apparent as in our tortuous efforts, waged for the better part of a century and not yet concluded, to address the unequal access children have to an education that will enable their full participation and responsible citizenship in our democracy. The fact that U.S. schools are structured such that students routinely receive dramatically unequal learning opportunities based on their race and social status is simply not widely recognized.[1] Nonetheless, evidence of inequality abounds, from wide disparities in school funding across states, within states, and within districts to educational policies and practices that ensure the delivery of unequal learning opportunities. The costs of this inequality are increasingly high, for our society as well as for the individual young people placed at risk by their schools.

In this chapter, we address the nature and costs of educational inequality and its relationship to democracy. We describe schools that defy societally imposed inequalities to support children and their capacity to become democratic members and leaders. We also propose policy changes that are needed to support these kinds of schools and to develop the education our democracy deserves and requires for its own preservation, for the fulfillment of all of its citizens, and for the achievement of its compelling promise that still inspires human beings across the world.

Education for the American Democracy: Recovering Our Roots

Equality and a right to life, liberty, and the pursuit of happiness embody the unique and compelling promise of the American democracy—a promise that intends to make "the good life and the good society"[2] universally accessible, regardless of individual circumstances of birth, religion, race, nationality, or socioeconomic status. So revolutionary was this concept of life and government that Tocqueville called it the American experiment.[3] Public education is central to this vision in two important ways: as a vehicle to the good life for those not born to it by virtue of family wealth and status, and as the foundation for the good society—one in which "the people" can make sound decisions about how government will best serve them and the nation's democratic ideals.

As public education has become the passport to the American dream, it has also become the most powerful icon of equality, mobility, and hope in our society. At the same time, as Thomas Jefferson so keenly understood, it is an essential tool for the preservation of democracy. Popular intelligence coupled with democratic decision making, Jefferson argued, provides the best protection against tyranny. In response to Alexander Hamilton's famous assertion "Thy people, sir, are a beast!" Jefferson was challenged to find a way that "the people" would be enabled to responsibly enact their obligations and privileges in a democratic form of government. Public schools, as the institutions most widely accessible to the people, would be the most effective vehicle for the diffusion of knowledge among them.[4] The mission of public education would be the development of an intelligent populace and a popular intelligence.

Public education for democracy, according to Jefferson, had two central and enduring corollary purposes: (1) to prepare all individuals for citizenship by developing within them the capacity for full and intelligent participation in the processes of deliberation necessary for self-rule; and (2) to identify and develop responsible leadership from the talents and abilities of individuals rather than from family or group privilege, economic wealth, religion, or race.[5] In order for these purposes to be achieved, the state would have to provide all individuals with access to educational opportunities sufficient to prepare them for full and intelligent citizenship. Since intelligent participation is not innate to human nature, argued Jefferson, public education for all was as essential to the preservation of the democratic state as it was to nurturing the capacity of individuals to understand and enact their inalienable rights.[6]

Since not all conceptions of the good society are compatible with one another or with the values underpinning our democracy, citizens must have the knowledge and skills to be able to intelligently debate and decide among competing conceptions, to weigh the individual and the common good, if they are to sustain democratic ideals throughout the complex challenges all societies face.[7] The common good and individual knowledge are inextricably intertwined.

The twin goals of ensuring a popular intelligence as well as an intelligent populace obligate American public schools to ensure a threshold of learning experiences that cultivate in all students the skills, knowledge, and understanding that both predispose them to the values undergirding our pluralistic democracy and arm them with a keen intelligence. It is this democratic threshold that should drive our decision making about funding, standards, assessments, curriculum, classroom practices, and the ways in which adults themselves relate to each other in the educational system.[8]

That this democratic threshold has not always driven decision making about American education should not dissuade us from continuing the struggle to articulate and act on this mandate. As court decisions on education from *Brown v. Board of Education* to *Lau v. Nichols* demonstrate, the struggle to ensure access to the good life and the good society must continually challenge and strengthen our schools. Throughout the twentieth century, this struggle has derived from Jefferson's belief wedding democracy to public education. As we enter the twenty-first century, the promise and the need for enacting a democratic system of education are greater than they have ever been. Our success may well determine the political and economic future of the United States and its form of government.

Schooling in America: A Landscape of Educational Inequality

Much has been made in recent years of the relatively low performance of U.S. students on international assessments, especially in mathematics and science.[9] Still more striking is the finding from the Second International Mathematics Study that in the United States, disparities in student achievement—and in measured opportunities to learn—are many times greater than in other industrialized countries and are comparable only to the level of disparity found in developing nations that do not yet provide universal access to education.[10] In contrast to the vast inequalities in spending and learning opportunities prevalent in the United States, most European and Asian nations we think of as peers or competitors fund schools centrally and equally (often providing higher teacher salaries in disadvantaged or remote communities). They also organize students for a common, nontracked curriculum through high school, and produce a much more narrow spread of achievement on international tests, a spread that is also higher on average than that of U.S. students.

While the United States came sooner than many other countries to the task of educating a wide range of students in public schools, it has not maintained its leadership in the task of equalizing quality across the common school, or in helping schools meet the challenge of creating and sustaining democratic education. As David Tyack reminds us, while schools have delivered opportunities for some, they have dispensed injustice to others.[11] Whether this is an unintended consequence of our commitment to local control, the deliberate use of schools to reproduce an unequal society, the complexity and difficulty of achieving "one best system" in so diverse a society, or some other combination of factors, we are nonetheless concretely confronted with the bruising impact of the layers of inequality dispensed by schools: a growing underclass that is underprepared for the demands of the economy and for full and responsible citizenship, and increasingly denied the promise of democratic life.

The Consequences of Inequality

The increasingly severe social consequences of inadequate and unequal education derive from the convergence of a number of trends that are changing society in profound ways. Briefly, these include:

- A rapidly changing industrial base providing fewer low-skilled manufacturing jobs and more demand for advanced technological skills and problem-solving abilities.[12]
- Major demographic shifts, including a substantial growth in the population over age sixty-five, which will need to be supported

by a shrinking number of young people entering the work force. More of these young workers are—and will increasingly be—the children of immigrants, poor families, and minorities.

• Continuing underperformance of the educational system for these same young people, who by the end of the 1990s will comprise 40 percent of the public school population and more than a third of the entering work force.

• Dropout rates, which continue to hover at 25 percent for all U.S. students, reaching 50 percent for minority youth in central cities, for whom unemployment rates remain almost that high as well.

• Growing rates of crime, incarceration, unemployment, homelessness, drug use, and social dysfunction that victimize both those trapped in an underclass environment and all of those who pay—financially and socially—for its effects on the broader society.

There are many dimensions to these social dilemmas that rest heavily for their resolution on the nature of the education young people receive. First, it is increasingly clear that, as we enter a technologically based information economy, all students—not just a few—must be educated to think critically, work socially, invent, problem solve, and create, not merely to follow directions for completing low-skilled jobs structured by routines. These changes in society mean that the traditional outcomes of our school system—academic success for some and failure for many others—are now more problematic than they have ever been before. While American schools have had high dropout rates and limited success with many graduates in past decades, there were decent jobs on the farm or in the factory to accommodate most of those for whom schooling was not a success.

Now, however, the life chances of students whom schools have failed grow increasingly dim. A male high school dropout in 1986, for example, had only one chance in three of being employed full time; this is half the odds of twenty years earlier. If employed, he earned only $6,700 a year, about half of what a high school dropout earned in 1973.[13] Lack of education is also linked to crime and delinquency. More than half the adult prison population is functionally illiterate, and nearly 40 percent of adjudicated juvenile delinquents have treatable learning disabilities that were not diagnosed in the schools. Meanwhile, prisons fill, along with homeless shelters and welfare rolls, and voter participation declines, a symptom of the growing cynicism about the utility of democratic politics and the prospects for social change.

At the same time, the growth of the U.S. population—and its potential for social renewal—relies substantially on new immigrants and people of color, who have long struggled for voice and opportunity in this country. As we incorporate the largest wave of immigration since the turn of the twentieth century, society's success in embracing and enhancing the talents of all of its new and previously unincluded members will determine much of its future. In addition, repairing the torn social fabric that increasingly appears to pit one group against another is a critical need for securing the continuation of democratic life. This means creating a social dialogue in which individuals can hear one another and converse from a growing common ground, developing an inclusive dialogue that both legitimizes and connects diverse experiences and points of view.

In sum, the United States cannot maintain its standard of living or its democratic foundations unless all students are not only better educated, but also educated for full participation in a democratic dialogue. Self-interest and social interest require that students who have traditionally been allowed to fail be enabled to succeed and become both constructive citizens and productive workers, not just minimally schooled, but highly proficient and inventive, as well as socially committed and responsible.

The Sources of Inequality

The entrenched system used to finance public education in the United States makes systemic inequalities in education inevitable.[14] The reliance on local property taxes ensures that districts with higher property values will have greater resources with which to fund their schools, even when poorer districts tax themselves at proportionally higher rates. In the 1989–90 school year, differences in statewide average per-pupil expenditures ranged from $8,000 in New Jersey to less than $3,000 in Utah.[15] Differences across districts nationwide were much greater, ranging from less than $2,000 per pupil to more than $20,000. Differences in spending among schools also exist within districts, with those serving the most disadvantaged populations receiving the fewest instructional resources.[16] Although states commonly provide aid to offset some of the disparity among districts, the federal government has not sought to equalize spending for poorer states or districts with less ability to pay for education.

The existing system of school finance is particularly harmful to poor urban and rural districts, especially to schools with high concentrations of "minority" students. The racial face of inequality is exacerbated by the continuing segregation of African American, Latino, and Native American students in U.S. schools. In 1986, the percentage of "minority" students in predominantly minority schools remained at 63 percent, virtually unchanged over the preceding fifteen years.[17] Hispanic students have been increasingly segregated over the years, with the proportion located in predominantly minority schools increasing from 55 percent in 1968 to 71 percent by 1986.[18]

African American and Hispanic American students continue to be concentrated in central city public schools, and these students have become the majority "minority" in many of these schools since the mid-eighties (NCES, 1992). These schools are typically funded at levels substantially below those of neighboring suburban districts and of schools in their own districts that serve more-advantaged students. Tracking systems exacerbate these inequalities by segregating many low-income and "minority" students within schools, allocating still fewer educational opportunities to them at the classroom level.

The education of historically disenfranchised Americans—African American students, Native American students, Latino students, and the poor—continues to be characterized by

- Lower levels of tangible school resources
- Reduced access to qualified teachers and high-quality teaching
- Overrepresentation in nonacademic tracks and special education
- Limited access to high status knowledge and challenging curriculum

- High rates of grade retention, suspension, expulsion, and dropping out
- Alienating and dysfunctional school environments[19]

The continuing segregation of neighborhoods and communities intersects with funding formulas and school administration practices that create substantial differences in the educational resources made available to different students. As Silard and Goldstein pointed out in the mid-seventies, these differences—maintained as they are by and within racially distinct neighborhoods and schools—inevitably retard democratic goals for a populace that can work and live together intelligently and harmoniously, peacefully addressing social problems. The connection between inadequate funding and the race and social status of students exacerbates the difficulties of creating either integrated schools or adequately funded ones. The vicious cycle was described early on in the fight for school funding reform: "School inequality between suburbia and central city crucially reinforces racial isolation in housing; and the resulting racial segregation of the schools constantly inhibits progress toward funding a therapeutic answer for the elimination of school inequality. If we are to exorcise the evils of separateness and inequality, we must view them together, for each dimension of the problem renders the other more difficult to solve—racially separate schools inhibit elimination of school inequality, and unequal schools retard eradication of school segregation."[20]

In *Savage Inequalities*, Jonathan Kozol paints a vivid portrait of contemporary disparities in school funding and resources. In 1989, reports Kozol, the Chicago school system spent slightly more than $5,000 per student while neighboring Niles Township High School spent $9,371 per student. In 1990, the New York City school system spent $7,725 per student while neighboring Great Neck spent more than $15,000 per student for a population with many fewer special needs. Kozol contrasts the lack of playgrounds, laboratory equipment, textbooks, and computers in urban schools with the ample resources of spacious suburban schools that support comprehensive sports programs and extensive academic opportunities.[21] He describes inner city classrooms where word processing is taught without word processors[22] and science laboratories that have no lab tables or equipment, in contrast to suburban schools where computers are hooked up to Dow Jones to facilitate the study of stock transactions.[23]

The unequal educational opportunities produced by funding discrepancies affect student achievement. In a large-scale study illustrating how money makes a difference, Ronald Ferguson found that school expenditures are directly and substantially related to student achievement, particularly as they are used to purchase highly qualified teachers and lower class sizes.[24] Eleanor Armour-Thomas and her colleagues confirm these findings: in their study of mathematics and reading achievement in grades three, six, and eight in demographically similar New York City schools, they found that approximately 90 percent of the variance in students' math and reading scores could be attributed to teacher experience and qualifications.[25] Considerable evidence supports the conclusion that differences in achievement between "minority" and white students results primarily from differences in access to high quality teaching and teachers.[26] Jeannie Oakes's nationwide study of the distribution of mathematics and science opportunities across hundreds of schools in 1990 found patterns that are pervasive across communities and across school subjects. On every variable—teacher experience, certification status, preparation in the discipline they are teaching, higher degrees, and teacher and principal perceptions of competence—it is clear that low-income and minority students have less contact with well-qualified teachers. Students in high-minority, low-income schools have only a 50 percent chance of being taught by math or science teachers who are certified, and an even lower chance of being taught by teachers who are fully qualified in the subject areas in which they are assigned to teach. In addition, such students are less likely to have access to college preparatory courses, to "computers and to staff who coordinate their use in instruction, to science laboratories, and to other common science-related facilities and equipment." Oakes concludes that "our evidence lends considerable support to the argument that low-income, minority, and inner-city students have fewer opportunities. . . . They have considerably less access to science and mathematics knowledge at school, fewer material resources, less-engaging learning activities in their classrooms, and less-qualified teachers. . . . The differences we have observed are likely to reflect more general patterns of educational inequality."[27]

Access makes a difference. An unusual natural experiment illustrates how. A randomly selected cohort of African American students and their families were placed in public housing in the Chicago suburbs rather than in the city so that the students could attend largely white and better-funded suburban schools. Compared to their comparable city-placed peers, who were of equivalent income and initial academic attainment, these students were substantially more likely to have the opportunity to take challenging courses, receive additional academic help, graduate on time, attend college, and secure good jobs.[28]

By maintaining unequal access to knowledge and to supportive educational resources, inequitable funding systems put an artificial ceiling on student achievement, locking students in poor schools out of opportunities for high levels of achievement and the life choices that require them. They also deprive our nation of the well-educated populace Jefferson sought as a foundation for democratic decision making and protection of the common welfare. The toll on our democracy is high in both individual and social terms, and will grow larger and more dangerous in the years ahead.

Bureaucracy, Tracking, and Education for Democracy

In addition to equitable access to tangible educational resources, democratic life also requires access to empowering forms of knowledge that enable creative life and thought, and access to a social dialogue that enables democratic communication and participation. Both of these kinds of access are denied to students in most large bureaucratic schooling institutions that segregate students into rigid tracks and consign many to a passive, deadening curriculum. At the same time, such compartmentalized and stratified institutions preclude everyone from an inclusive social discourse that builds the foundations for collective understanding and a sense of shared community.

The bureaucratic structures for schooling that were created at the turn of the twentieth century to batch-process masses of students using factory methods work against democratic goals on many levels. Their size and structures—including the assembly line movement of students through classes, the lack of long-term personal relationships among adults and students, rigid tracks separating groups of students from one another, and the isolation of teachers—preclude most forms of community building and shared discourse. They not only maintain inequalities in access to knowledge, they also heighten divisions among groups, and fail to prepare most young people to become active social participants and leaders. They model and reinforce social stratification rather than inclusiveness, passivity and disengagement rather than active participation, and unthinking acceptance of the knowledge constructed by others rather than critical thought and the development of knowledge.

Access to Empowering Knowledge

In the late nineteenth century, as increasing numbers of individuals from diverse socioeconomic and ethnic groups began to demand secondary school education,[29] the quest for the one best system was shaped by two competing positions vying for dominance. Educators like Charles Eliot and G. Stanley Hall debated whether an intellectually challenging course of academic study for all was preferable to a differentiated course of study that included more practical (and less costly) paths for those students, primarily immigrants and the few children of color provided access to education, who were deemed unlikely to graduate or enroll in college.[30] The *Cardinal Principles of Secondary Education* reinforced the idea of differentiated courses of study by promoting the goal of educating all students to assume their different places in society. Although differentiated curriculum and tracks were presented as a mechanism to democratize schools—to provide equal opportunities for success on the basis of differentiated student interests and abilities—they planted the seeds for unequal educational opportunity, as curriculum in the different tracks granted or deprived access to social mobility.[31]

When rapid industrialization pressured schools to serve an economic agenda, schools increasingly focused on preparing workers for slots in the labor market, providing further justification for a differentiated curriculum. Most students were prepared for low-skilled, rote-oriented factory work,[32] not for full and enlightened citizenship or for powerful forms of inquiry and critical thinking. When the imagination of educators was captured by industrial efficiency, scientific management, and the promise of bureaucracy to increase productivity, their quest for the "one best system" was fulfilled in what is now generally acknowledged as the factory model school.[33] The economic agenda was activated through a vision of students as unequal raw material[34] and schools as a means to place them into a stratified society.

What was lost in this decision was the belief in intellectual development as the proper goal of education for all citizens in a democracy and for whatever future students would pursue.[35] What was rejected, as Sara Lawrence Lightfoot explains, was the positive diversity of the American culture[36] and an appreciation for American pluralism.[37] This decision institutionalized the parameters for unequal educational opportunity, for radically different forms of education for members of different social groups. Such a foundation has paved the way for school organizational policies and practices that have institutionalized inequality through tracking, a pedagogy of disengagement, and norm-referenced tests designed to rationalize differential opportunity.

The role of testing in reinforcing and extending social inequalities in educational opportunities has by now been extensively researched[38] and widely acknowledged. Use of tests for placements and promotions ultimately reduces the amount of learning achieved by students placed in lower tracks or held back in grade.[39] Students placed in the lowest tracks or in remedial programs— disproportionately low-income and minority students—are most apt to experience instruction geared only to multiple-choice tests, working at a low cognitive level on test-oriented tasks that are profoundly disconnected from the skills they need to learn. Rarely are they given the opportunity to talk about what they know, to read real books, to write, or to construct and solve problems in mathematics, science, or other subjects.[40] In short, they have been denied the opportunity to develop the capacities they will need for the future, in large part because commonly used tests are so firmly pointed at educational goals of the past.

The wide use of norm-referenced testing for sorting students has not yet been reduced by the barrage of studies indicating that most such measurements are culturally biased,[41] measure only low-level cognitive skills, ignore creativity and emphasize conformity at the expense of originality,[42] and fail to measure many important dimensions of intelligence and performance.[43] More damaging for instruction are the ways in which the multiple-choice format of standardized achievement tests narrowly defines and measures achievement as the capacity to regurgitate decontextualized, fragmented bits of information.

Because such tests drive curriculum and instruction, and because they do not assess deep understanding or creative problem solving, they diminish the time and opportunity students have for developing the complex skills necessary for participation in democracy—skills such as communication, problem framing and solving, inquiry, analysis, and reasoning.[44] Because these practices are especially predominant in lower-track classes,[45] they contribute to the unequal education of the populations disproportionately represented in those tracks: African American, Latino, and low-income students.[46]

For these reasons and others, students placed in lower tracks are exposed to a limited, rote-oriented curriculum and ultimately achieve less than students of similar aptitude who are placed in more challenging academic programs or untracked classes.[47] Teacher interaction with students in lower-track classes is less motivating and less supportive, as well as less demanding of higher order reasoning and responses.[48] These interactions are also less academically oriented, and more likely to focus on behavioral criticisms, especially for minority students.[49] Presentations are less clear and less focused on higher-order cognitive goals.[50] Learning tasks are less engaging and students are less engaged.[51] Teaching practices are less effective.[52] Teachers prepare less,[53] and they make minimal demands on students, diminishing both the intensity and sense of importance of the educational experiences provided.[54]

Low-track classrooms are often distinctly nondemocratic in their approaches to teaching and learning: they are typically characterized by a noninvolving, autocratic atmosphere, passive activities, and few opportunities to discuss open-ended questions, do cooperative group work, or engage in decision making.[55] Such classes are organized for conformity, compliance, and the development of socialization skills such as punctuality, at the expense of intellectual habits of mind.[56] Retention of facts and lower-level rote skills are emphasized rather than the capacity to analyze. Improvement in skills is an end in itself, not a means to achieving knowledge or broadening one's perspective. For example, students read to improve their score on a standardized test, not to acquire knowledge.[57] In a variety of ways, the curriculum and instruction that characterize low-track classes undermine the development of skills needed for enlightened and responsible citizenship—the ability to deliberate, to think critically, and to develop and express one's voice articulately so as to participate in the shaping of one's society.

In contrast, high-track students receive high-status knowledge, the knowledge and skills required for higher education and necessary for positions of power and leadership.[58] High-track classes are organized for independence, engagement, and critical thinking, the skills necessary for effective participation in democracy. In addition, high-track students are taught by more highly qualified teachers.[59] The assignment of teachers within schools, across schools, and across districts reinforces systemic inequality by creating "ongoing differentials in expenditures and access to educational resources including the knowledge well-prepared teachers rely on in offering high-quality instruction."[60]

The distribution of students to tracks seems based on an economic scarcity model, with places in the upper tracks fixed and rationed, rather than based on the number of students willing and able to profit from the offerings.[61] Since the number of slots in tracks is predetermined by the availability of resources—curriculum costs, qualified teachers, and teachers' time—as well as perceptions of students' future roles in life, access to high-track classes is dependent on factors other than effort and merit.[62] Schools' continuing belief that few students need or will profit from demanding instruction is especially strong with respect to students of color and low-income students. Even after test scores are controlled, race and socioeconomic status play a distinctive role in determining placements to honors courses, vocational and academic tracks, and more- and less-challenging courses within those tracks.[63] As tracking transforms schools into marketplaces where students must compete for a quality education, it teaches both high- and low-track students that society values some individuals more than others. Inequality as a principle and a practice is institutionalized.

The system of curricular differentiation that characterizes the practice of tracking undermines the merit system that Jefferson believed was critical to identifying and securing the best leadership for democracy. Deprived of opportunities to think critically and learn in meaningful ways, students in lower tracks cannot fully develop their potential, which lies dormant and is frequently wasted. Furthermore, because the curriculum and instructional experiences, the knowledge and skills, and the prerequisite courses necessary for admission to the higher tracks are not taught in the lower tracks, there is little mobility between tracks.[64] This practice subverts the American belief that hard work leads to success, that effort, progress, and improvement will be rewarded. The values undergirding belief in the merit system and the marketplace are undermined when one group of individuals is singled out to play by rules that disadvantage them from achieving the system's rewards. This is teaching for despair.[65]

Tracking subverts the purposes of schooling in a democracy by creating two unequal classes of citizens and providing only one class with the skills and knowledge necessary for full participation in society. The values and social structure that tracking establishes, especially in view of the overrepresentation of low-income and "minority" students in lower tracks,[66] set the foundation for an underclass that, excluded from the promise of the good life and good society, is unlikely to have much investment in that society or in its preservation.

This disparity jeopardizes students' experience of democracy and consequently the foundations for democracy. The consequences of systematic labeling, differentiation, and marginalization have produced what John Ogbu terms an "oppositional identity,"[67] a rejection by those long denied education of its appropriateness for them—a definition of their own identity in opposition to the institutions that have rejected them. If society as represented by the institution of public school does not demonstrate the value of all its members, why should the members value themselves, others, or the society? Further, how can all of the members of society engage in the joint construction of community if they are kept separate and disengaged by the structures of schooling?

Access to Democratic Community

Education for democracy requires more than equal access to technical knowledge. It requires access to social knowledge and understanding, forged by participation in a democratic community. In

Democracy and Education, John Dewey noted that "a democracy is more than a form of government; it is primarily a mode of associated living, of conjoint communicated experience."[68] He spoke of the building and extension of associations as one of the ways in which we should evaluate social modes of life, including schools. Given that a society is an association with shared interests, and that all of us belong to a wide variety of societies of different kinds, the worth of these associations can be gauged by asking, first, "How numerous and varied are the interests which are consciously shared?" and, second, "How full and free is the interplay with other forms of association?"[69] How well connected are these associations? How much do they strive to make connections with other groups' perspectives and sets of interests? Dewey noted that, "in order to have a large number of values in common, all the members of the group must have an equitable opportunity to receive and to take from others. There must be a large variety of shared undertakings and experiences. Otherwise, the influences which educate some into masters educate others into slaves. And the experience of each party loses in meaning, when the free interchange of varying modes of life experiences is arrested."[70]

A communication that is, in Dewey's words, "vitally social or vitally shared" is one that allows each person to experience the perspectives of another, and by that connection to develop understanding and appreciation for that person's experience and understanding of the world:

> There is more than a verbal tie between the words common, community, and communication. [People] live in a community in virtue of the things which they have in common; and communication is the way in which they come to possess things in common. . . . Not only is social life identical with communication, but all communication (and hence all genuine social life) is educative. To be a recipient of a communication is to have an enlarged and changed experience. One shares in what another has thought and felt and in so far, meagerly or amply, has his own attitude modified.[71]

Such appreciation of other perspectives provides the foundation for a broader *shared* perspective that in turn allows us to form communities and societies. Paradoxically, it is only by acknowledging the reality and the legitimacy of diverse points of view that we can begin the work of forging a common point of view that takes account of the perspectives of others.

The capacity to achieve associations beyond those of any narrow group is required for the development of democracy, the expansion of knowledge, and the search for truth. Just as inquiry about important problems must cross departmental boundaries, for the same reasons, such inquiry must also cross community and cultural boundaries. The basis of the very earliest universities was that they tried to bring together scholars from all over the known world. They sought to create ways to share diverse perspectives from various geographic areas, cultures, and disciplines as the basis for developing knowledge and finding truth. The same goal of looking for powerful, shared ideas to arise from diverse understandings and experiences of the world undergirds the concept of democratic education that encompasses the many views of its participants—that is, all of the views that will need to be accommodated in the common space that comprises social life.

Here, too, the factory model school, with its "structure of rationalized disempowerment"[72] and "conditions of differential treatment,"[73] creates disengagement, silence, and separation where communication, inquiry, and connections are needed. Students are explicitly divided into status-laden tracks, relationships between teachers and students are depersonalized, and discourse is typically discouraged. Such schools create anonymous conditions for learning rather than communities of shared interest. External controls and rigid rules and procedures must govern where relationships have been so attenuated that they can no longer be the basis of social decisions. In fact, there are no real decisions to be made or communal tasks to be undertaken in the highly controlled environment of the modern school, hence there is little basis for building a democratic social life. "A breakdown in human commitment has resulted from the processes of specialization and centralization that undergird our system of mass education. Transient relationships, a disintegration of common bonds, and a retreat from shared responsibility have developed from organizational mechanisms originally meant to foster efficiency and equity."[74]

In contrast, growing research illustrates the success of smaller schools fostering caring, common learning experiences of relevance to students, sustained and continuous faculty and peer relationships, cooperation, and participation of parents, teachers, and students in making decisions.[75] Communitarian models for schooling provide alternatives to the disengagement, separation, and inequality fostered by bureaucratic methods. Like previous initiatives during the progressive eras of the 1930s and 1960s, reforms fostered by grassroots networks like the Coalition of Essential Schools, the Accelerated Schools Program, the School Development Program, and others are demonstrating that all students can be well educated in settings structured for caring and common high standards.

Policy for Educational Equality and Access to Democracy

The common presumption about educational inequality is that it resides primarily in those students who come to school with inadequate capacities to benefit from what education the school has to offer. In line with the sorting philosophy adopted at the turn of the twentieth century, students must prove themselves "worthy" to receive a rich, challenging, and thoughtful curriculum. If they do not, the fault is thought to be in their own capacities as learners, not in the schools' capacities to teach them. Many policymakers, educators, and members of the public at large do not presume that students are entitled to such a curriculum as a matter of course, and further, that their entitlement is part of the foundation for a strong society.

The fact that U.S. schools are structured such that students routinely receive dramatically unequal learning opportunities based on their race and social status is simply not widely recognized. If academic and social outcomes are to change, however, aggressive action must be taken to change the caliber of learning opportunities students encounter.

At the heart of the educational equality/democracy dilemma is the equity and excellence debate. Can we have them both? And what is the price? Unfortunately, the answer to the first question is usually contingent upon the answer to the second: yes, if the price is not too high—and the assumption generally is that it must be, or we would have achieved it already.

However, the question of cost should also be asked about the high price we pay for inequality. If the per-prisoner price for incarceration, which is more than double the cost of sending a student to the highest-priced school district in the nation, is not too high, what is? If the costs of unemployment, welfare dependency, crime, and social unrest borne of despair and disenfranchisement are not too high, what is? If the cost of a fraying social fabric and dwindling democratic discourse is not too high, then we have lost sight of the goals and underpinnings of this nation. Unequal educational opportunity prevents us from fulfilling the aspirations of our democracy, just as it renders unattainable the rhetoric of the National Education Goals recently articulated by the governors in hopes of keeping the nation in its position of world economic dominance. The challenge before us is to reconcile our economic and political agendas and renew the vows that wed schools to democracy.

These efforts must include equalization of financial resources; access to highly qualified teachers for all students; and fundamental school restructuring, coupling changes in curriculum and testing policies and practices with changes in the dehumanizing structures of bureaucratic school organizations.

Resource Equalization

Progress in equalizing resources to students will require attention to inequalities at all levels—between states, among districts, among schools within districts, and among students differentially placed in classrooms, courses, and tracks that offer substantially disparate opportunities to learn. Equalizing opportunity will require attention to school finance policies, teacher recruitment and preparation policies, and curriculum policies, rather than add-on programs aimed at "remediating" students.

Special programs such as compensatory or bilingual education will never be effective at remedying underachievement while they are layered on a system that so poorly educates minority and low-income children to begin with. The presumption that "the schools are fine, it's the children who need help" is flawed. The schools serving large concentrations of low-income and minority students are generally not fine, and many of their problems originate with district and state policies and practices that place both students and schools at risk.

In the current school reform movement, particularly that part focused on the setting of standards, the missing ingredient has been a serious consideration of students' opportunities to learn. Opportunity-to-learn standards should point the attention of policymakers and educators to those resources and learning experiences required for students to achieve the intellectually and practically challenging learning outcomes necessary for full and effective citizenship. Two kinds of opportunity-to-learn standards should be used to create information and incentives for states, school districts, schools, teachers, and parents to act on in improving and equalizing students' learning opportunities:[76]

1. *Standards for delivery systems* should identify key resources that enable learning and create incentives for the state, school districts, and schools to ensure their equitable availability to all students. These include (1) equitable access to the school funding necessary to provide high-quality education; (2) access to well-prepared teachers, whose knowledge of subject matter, pedagogy, curriculum, and assessment is grounded in deep understanding of how students grow, learn, and develop and how their learning styles and talents may best be addressed and nurtured; and (3) equitable access to the materials and equipment necessary for learning: safe, clean physical facilities; textbooks and instructional materials; and libraries, computers, laboratories, and other resources for inquiry.[77]

2. *Standards for practice* should articulate professionally grounded approaches to the organization and teaching practices of schools. These approaches should be based on knowledge about the teaching and schooling conditions under which children learn well.[78] They should be articulated around important principles of practice, but without prescribing the configuration of school resources or activities, to allow for innovation and for differential approaches to diverse circumstances. These standards of practice are a key component of professional accountability, along with meaningful standards for preparation, licensing, and evaluation of practitioners. Examples of professional standards for schooling and curriculum include those put forth by the National Board for Professional Teaching Standards, the National Association for the Education of Young Children, and the professional subject matter associations, such as the National Council of Teachers of Mathematics.

Standards of practice are better understood by looking at them through an expert lens that can gauge the appropriateness of diverse approaches than by requiring standardized measures and approaches. Like the "critical friends" review proposed by the Coalition of Essential Schools, the school inspection systems in many European countries, and peer review processes in professions like medicine and accounting, a careful examination of teaching and learning by teams of fellow practitioners can evaluate both the quality and appropriateness of unique approaches. A school review that focuses on examining students' learning opportunities can evaluate standards of practice without resorting to inappropriate, standardized measures that might be gathered from afar in a traditional bureaucratic system of regulation.

School Restructuring

Schools need to be restructured as human-scale, learner-centered educational communities that enable adults and children to develop the respectful and responsive relationships that produce more effective teaching and learning. They should embody both the flexibility and the rigor necessary to respond to diversity and to encourage intellectual development. They need to be restructured to allow strong, ongoing relationships among teachers and students and to create occasions for the shared responsibility that enables democratic discourse. Learning experiences need to be restructured so that all children develop the skills that promote inquiry and intellectual habits of mind. Only students who have sophisticated analytic skills, confidence, perseverance, creative problem-solving skills, and the ability to examine issues from multiple perspectives using multiple sources of evidence will be prepared for the personal, economic, and political challenges that currently confront our nation and the world as we enter the twenty-first century.

In addition, providing equity in the distribution of teacher quality requires changing policies and long-standing incentive structures in education so that shortages of trained teachers are overcome and schools serving low-income and minority students are not disadvantaged by lower salaries and poorer working conditions in the bidding war for good teachers. To recruit an adequate supply of teachers, states and localities will need to upgrade

teachers' salaries to levels competitive with those of college graduates in other occupations, and improve professional working conditions.[79] This must occur as part of a general restructuring effort
that places more resources as well as decision-making authority at
the school level and allocates a greater share of education dollars
to classrooms than to the large bureaucracies that oversee them.[80]
Investments in greater teacher knowledge are needed to support
these changes, as better-prepared teachers will be more able to
address diverse learning needs and make responsible decisions
about school practice.

A thinking curriculum also requires a thinking assessment system: one that has the capacity to embrace the complexities of teaching, learning, and schooling, that encourages and provides students,
teachers, and schools with the information and capacity to improve
their individual and collective performance and productivity. While
authentic forms of assessment are being developed, many current
proposals for performance-based assessment view these new kinds
of tests as serving the same screening and tracking purposes as
more traditional tests. The presumption is that the new assessments
will both motivate and sort students more effectively. Others see a
primary goal of assessment reform as transforming the purposes
and uses of testing as well as its form and content. They argue for
shifting from the use of assessment as a sorting device to its use as
a tool for identifying student strengths and needs so that teachers
can adapt instruction more successfully.[81]

In many restructured urban schools engaged in authentic
assessment, students who would normally fail succeed—grad-
uating and going on to college at rates comparable to affluent
suburban schools.[82] Teachers find themselves transforming their
teaching as ongoing assessment reveals how students approach
tasks, what helps them learn most effectively, and what strategies
support their learning. The more teachers understand about what
students know and how they think, the more capacity they have to
reform their pedagogy, and the more opportunities they create for
student success.

Assessment initiatives that embed authentic assessment in the
ongoing processes of teaching and curriculum development share
the view offered by Robert Glaser[83] that schools must move from a
selective mode to an adaptive mode. They must shift from an

approach "characterized by minimal variation in the conditions for learning" in which "a narrow range of instructional options and a limited number of paths to success are available,"[84] to one in which "conceptions of learning and modes of teaching are adjusted to individuals—their backgrounds, talents, interests, and the nature of their past performances and experiences."[85]

Such educational restructuring can enable educators to ensure excellence and equity for all. It can enable schools to embrace what Kornhaber and Gardner refer to as multiple forms of excellence,[86] without fear of lowering standards or watering down curriculum. Rethinking schools to develop thinking schools can expand access to both opportunity and success. Schools alone cannot transform the inequalities of our society. That is a collective responsibility that falls upon all public institutions as well as upon the public will. However, since schools are the first public institution that most individuals encounter in their society, and since they encounter schooling at the most tender, vulnerable moments in their development, schools have a special responsibility as well as a powerful opportunity to teach for democracy—for both intellectual and social development. Schools cannot do this by preaching, but by example. Because individuals will learn what to expect from society's institutions from this first encounter, educators have a special responsibility to be responsive to diversity and capable of supporting multiple forms of excellence. For democracy to survive and flourish, those who have been silenced need to find their voices. Those who have been marginalized need to seek, create, and find a myriad of possible futures for themselves in society. Schools must help widen the narrow straits of the American mainstream, extending diverse tributaries, and negotiating new currents, so that all Americans can have access to the good life and the good society, to the promise of democracy.

Notes

1. Linda Darling-Hammond, "Inequality and Access to Knowledge," in *The Handbook of Research on Multicultural Education*, edited by J. A. Banks (New York: Macmillan, 1995).
2. Amy Gutmann, *Democratic Education* (Princeton, N.J.: Princeton University Press, 1987), p. 14.

3. Alexis de Tocqueville, *Democracy in America* (New York: Random House, 1990).(Originally published 1835.)
4. Gordon C. Lee, "Learning and Liberty: The Jeffersonian Tradition in Education," in *Crusade Against Ignorance: Thomas Jefferson on Education,* edited by G. C. Lee (New York: Columbia University, 1961), p. 17.
5. Lee, "Learning and Liberty," pp. 1–26.
6. Lee, "Learning and Liberty," p. 9.
7. Gutmann, *Democratic Education,* pp. 42–43, 287.
8. Gutmann, *Democratic Education,* pp. 282–291.
9. Curtis C. McKnight and others, *The Underachieving Curriculum: Assessing U.S. School Mathematics from an International Perspective* (Champaign, Ill.: Stipes Publishing, 1987).
10. McKnight and others, *The Underachieving Curriculum.*
11. David Tyack, *The One Best System* (Cambridge, Mass.: Harvard University Press, 1974).
12. Hudson Institute, *Workforce 2000: Work and Workers for the Twenty-First Century* (Indianapolis, Ind.: Hudson Institute, 1987).
13. William T. Grant Foundation, *The Forgotten Half: Non-College Youth in America* (Washington, D.C.: William T. Grant Foundation, 1988).
14. This section draws extensively on two chapters by Linda Darling-Hammond: "Teacher Quality and Equality," in *Access to Knowledge,* edited by J. I. Goodlad and P. Keating (New York: College Entrance Examination Board, 1990), pp. 237–258; and "Inequality and Access to Knowledge," in *The Handbook of Research on Multicultural Education,* edited by J. A. Banks (New York: Macmillan, 1995).
15. Educational Testing Service, *The State of Inequality* (Princeton, N.J.: Educational Testing Service, 1991), p. 4.
16. Darling-Hammond, "Inequality and Access"; William L. Taylor and Dianne M. Piche, *A Report on Shortchanging Children: The Impact of Fiscal Inequity on the Education of Students at Risk,* prepared for the Committee on Education and Labor, U.S. House of Representatives (Washington, D.C.: U.S. Government Printing Office, 1991).
17. Gary F. Orfield, F. Monfort, and M. Aaron, *Status of School Desegregation: 1968–1986* (Alexandria, Va.: National School Boards Association, 1989), cited in Janet W. Schofield, "School Desegregation and Intergroup Relations," in *Review of Research in Education* (17th ed.), edited by G. Grant, (Washington, D.C.: American Educational Research Association, 1991), p. 336.
18. Orfield, Monfort, and Aaron, *Status of School Desegregation.*
19. See Beatriz Arias, "The Context of Education for Hispanic Students: An Overview," *American Journal of Education,* 1986, *95*(1), 26–57; James

A. Banks, "Multicultural Education: Characteristics and Goals," in *Multicultural Education: Issues and Perspectives* (2nd ed.), edited by J. A. Banks and C.A.M. Banks (Boston: Allyn & Bacon, 1993), pp. 3–28; Michelle Fine, *Framing Dropouts* (Albany: State University of New York Press, 1989); Geneva Gay, "Ethnic Minorities and Educational Equality," in *Multicultural Education: Issues and Perspectives* (2nd ed.), edited by J. A. Banks and C.A.M. Banks (Boston: Allyn & Bacon, 1993), pp. 171–194; John I. Goodlad, *A Place Called School: Prospects for the Future* (New York: McGraw-Hill, 1984); John I. Goodlad, "Common Schools for the Common Weal: Reconciling Self-Interest with the Common Good," in *Access to Knowledge*, edited by J. I. Goodlad and P. Keating (New York: College Entrance Examination Board, 1990), pp. 1–21; Jonathan Kozol, *Savage Inequalities* (New York: Crown, 1991); Caroline Hodges Persell, "Social Class and Educational Equality," in *Multicultural Education: Issues and Perspectives* (2nd ed.), edited by J. A. Banks and C.A.M. Banks (Boston: Allyn & Bacon, 1993), pp. 71–89; Michael Sedlak, C. Wheeler, Diana Pullin, and Philip Cusick, *Selling Students Short* (New York: Teachers College Press, 1986); Theodore R. Sizer, *Horace's Compromise* (Boston: Houghton Mifflin, 1984).

20. John Silard and Barry Goldstein, "Toward Abolition of Local Funding in Public Education," *Journal of Law and Education*, 1974, *3*, 324.

21. Kozol, *Savage Inequalities*, p. 157.

22. Kozol, *Savage Inequalities*, p. 198.

23. Kozol, *Savage Inequalities*, p. 28.

24. Ronald F. Ferguson, "Paying for Public Education: New Evidence on How and Why Money Matters," *Harvard Journal on Legislation*, 1991, *28*(2), 465–498. See also William T. Hartman, "District Spending Disparaties: What Do the Dollars Buy?" *Journal of Education Finance*, 1988, *13*(4), 436–459.

25. Eleanor Armour-Thomas and others, *An Outline Study of Elementary and Middle Schools in New York City: Final Report* (New York: New York City Board of Education, 1989).

26. See for example Rebecca Barr and Robert Dreeben, *How Schools Work* (Chicago: University of Chicago Press, 1983); Robert Dreeben and Adam Gamoran, "Race, Instruction, and Learning," *American Sociological Review*, 1986, *51*(5), 660–669; Robert Dreeben and Rebecca Barr, "Class Composition and the Design of Instruction," paper presented at the Annual Meeting of the American Education Research Association, Washington, D.C., 1987; College Board, *Equality and Excellence: The Educational Status of Black Americans* (New York: College Entrance Examination Board, 1985); Jeannie Oakes, *Multiplying*

Inequalities: The Effects of Race, Social Class, and Tracking on Opportunities to Learn Mathematics and Science (Santa Monica, Calif.: The RAND Corporation, 1990); Linda Darling-Hammond and Jon Snyder, "Traditions of Curriculum Inquiry: The Scientific Tradition," in *Handbook of Research on Curriculum,* edited by P. W. Jackson (New York: Macmillan, 1992).

27. Oakes, *Multiplying Inequalities,* p. ix–xi.

28. Julie E. Kaufman and James E. Rosenbaum, "Education and Employment of Low-Income Black Youth in White Suburbs," *Educational Evaluation and Policy Analysis,* 1992, *14*(3), 229–240.

29. Herbert M. Kliebard, "Education at the Turn of the Century: A Crucible for Curriculum Change," *Educational Researcher,* January 1982, pp. 16–24; Jeannie Oakes, *Keeping Track: How Schools Structure Inequality* (New Haven: Yale University Press, 1985).

30. Arthur G. Powell, Eleanor Farrar, and David K. Cohen, *The Shopping Mall High School* (Boston: Houghton Mifflin, 1985).

31. Oakes, *Keeping Track;* Powell, Farrar, and Cohen, *The Shopping Mall High School;* Aage B. Sorensen, "The Organizational Differentiation of Students in Schools as an Opportunity Structure," in *The Social Organization of Schools: New Conceptualizations of the Learning Process,* edited by M. T. Hallinan (New York: Plenum Press, 1987), pp. 103–130.

32. Oakes, *Keeping Track;* Powell, Farrar, and Cohen, *The Shopping Mall High School;* Ray C. Rist, *The Urban School: A Factory for Failure* (Cambridge, Mass.: MIT Press, 1973).

33. Oakes, *Keeping Track.*

34. Kozol, *Savage Inequalities.*

35. Oakes, *Keeping Track.*

36. Sara Lawrence Lightfoot, *Worlds Apart* (New York: Basic Books, 1975).

37. Tyack, *The One Best System.*

38. Stephen Jay Gould, *The Mismeasure of Man* (New York: Norton, 1981); J. R. Mercer, "Alternative Paradigms for Assessment in a Pluralistic Society," in *Multicultural Education: Issues and Perspectives,* edited by J. A. Banks and C.A.M. Banks (Boston: Allyn & Bacon, 1989), pp. 289–303; Oakes, *Keeping Track;* Leon Kamin, *The Science and Politics of IQ* (New York: Wiley, 1974); Bernard C. Watson, "Intellectual Dozens: Talking About Your Mother and Your Father," in *Essays from the Underside* (Philadelphia: Temple University Press, in press); Asa G. Hilliard, "Misunderstanding and Testing Intelligence," in *Access to Knowledge,* edited by J. I. Goodlad and P. Keating (New York: College Entrance Examination Board, 1990), pp. 145–157.

39. Linda Darling-Hammond, "The Implications of Testing Policy for Quality and Equality," *Phi Delta Kappan,* 1991, *73*(3), 220–225.

40. Oakes, *Keeping Track;* Eric Cooper and John Sherk, "Addressing Urban School Reform: Issues and Alliances," *Journal of Negro Education,* 1989, *58*(3), 315–331; Donna G. Davis, "A Pilot Study to Assess Equity in Selected Curricular Offerings Across Three Diverse Schools in a Large Urban School District," paper presented at the Annual Meeting of the American Educational Research Association, San Francisco, 1986; K. Trimble and R. L. Sinclair, "Ability Grouping and Differing Conditions for Learning: An Analysis of Content and Instruction in Ability-Grouped Classes," paper presented at the annual meeting of the American Educational Research Association, San Francisco, 1986.

41. John U. Ogbu, "The Consequences of the American Caste System," in *The School Achievement of Minority Children: New Perspectives,* edited by U. Neisser (Hillsdale, N.J.: Lawrence Erlbaum, 1986), pp. 19–56.

42. Gould, *The Mismeasure of Man.*

43. Howard Gardner, *Frames of Mind: The Theory of Multiple Intelligences* (New York: Basic Books, 1985); Robert J. Sternberg, *The Triarchic Mind: A New Theory of Human Intelligence* (New York: Penguin Books, 1988).

44. Darling-Hammond, "The Implications of Testing Policy."

45. Darling-Hammond, "Inequality and Access"; George F. Madaus, "The Public Policy and the Testing Profession: You've Never Had It So Good?" *Educational Measurement: Issues and Practice,* 1993, *4,* 5–11; Oakes, *Keeping Track.*

46. Darling-Hammond, "The Implications of Testing Policy."

47. Adam Gamoran and Robert Mare, "Secondary School Tracking and Educational Inequality: Compensation, Reinforcement or Neutrality?" *American Journal of Sociology,* 1989, *94,* 1146–1183; Oakes, *Keeping Track;* Adam Gamoran, "The Consequences of Track-Related Instructional Differences for Student Achievement," paper presented at the Annual Meeting of the American Educational Research Association, Boston, 1990; Karl L. Alexander and Edward L. McDill, "Selection and Allocation Within Schools: Some Causes and Consequences of Curriculum Placement," *American Sociological Review,* 1976, *41,* 963–980; Oakes, *Keeping Track;* Adam Gamoran and Mark Berends, "The Effects of Stratification in Secondary Schools: Synthesis of Survey and Ethnographic Research," *Review of Educational Research,* 1987, *57,* 415–436.

48. Thomas L. Good and Jere Brophy, *Looking in Classrooms* (New York: Harper & Row, 1987).

49. Ruth Eckstrom and Ana Maria Villegas, "Ability Grouping in Middle Grade Mathematics: Process and Consequences," *Research in Middle Level Education,* 1991, *15*(1), 1–20; Oakes, *Keeping Track.*

50. Oakes, *Keeping Track.*
51. Donna Eder and Diane Felmlee, "The Development of Attention Norms in Ability Groups," in *The Social Context of Instruction: Group Organization and Group Process,* edited by P. L. Peterson, L. C. Wilkinson, and M. Hallinan (Orlando, Fla.: Academic Press, 1984), pp. 189–208; James Rosenbaum, *Making Inequality: The Hidden Curriculum of High School Tracking* (New York: Wiley, 1976).
52. Ernest Boyer, *High School* (New York: Harper & Row, 1983).
53. Rosenbaum, *Making Inequality.*
54. Powell, Farrar, and Cohen, *The Shopping Mall High School.*
55. Oakes, *Keeping Track.*
56. Goodlad, *A Place Called School;* Oakes, *Keeping Track.*
57. Imani Perry, "A Black Student's Reflections on Public and Private Schools," *Harvard Education Review,* 1988, *58*(3), 332–336.
58. Oakes, *Keeping Track.*
59. Oakes, *Keeping Track;* Davis, "A Pilot Study"; Merilee K. Finley, "Teachers and Tracking in a Comprehensive High School," *Sociology of Education,* 1984, *57,* 233–243; Kaufman and Rosenbaum, "Education and Employment"; Joan E. Talbert, *Teacher Tracking: Exacerbating Inequalities in the High School* (Stanford, Calif.: Center for Research on the Context of Secondary Teaching, Stanford University, 1990); Anne Wheelock, *Crossing the Tracks* (New York: The New Press, 1992).
60. Darling-Hammond, "Inequality and Access."
61. Michael Apple, "Ideology, Reproduction, and Education Reform," *Comparative Education Review,* 1978, *22*(3), 367–387.
62. Maureen T. Hallinan, "Summary and Implications," in *The Social Context of Instruction: Group Organization and Group Process,* edited by P. L. Peterson, L. C. Wilkinson, and M. T. Hallinan (Orlando, Fla.: Academic Press, 1984), pp. 299–340; Sorensen, "The Organizational Differentiation of Students."
63. Adam Gamoran, "Access to Excellence: Assignment to Honors English Classes in the Transition from Middle to High School," *Educational Evaluation and Policy Analysis,* 1992, *14,* 185–204; Jeannie Oakes, Molly Selvin, L. Karoly, and Gretchen Guiton, *Educational Matchmaking: Academic and Vocational Tracking in Comprehensive High Schools* (Santa Monica, Calif.: The RAND Corporation, 1992); Elizabeth L. Useem, "You're Good, But You're Not Good Enough: Tracking Students Out of Advanced Mathematics," *American Educator,* 1990, *14*(3), 24–27, 43–46.
64. Hallinan, "Summary and Implications"; Sorensen, "The Organizational Differentiation of Students."
65. Cornel West, *Race Matters* (Boston: Beacon Press, 1993).
66. College Board, *Equality and Excellence,* pp. 31–33; Gay, "Ethnic Minorities

and Educational Equality"; Goodlad, *A Place Called School;* Hallinan, "Summary and Implications"; Oakes, *Keeping Track.*

67. John U. Ogbu, "Overcoming Racial Barriers to Equal Access," in *Access to Knowledge,* edited by J. I. Goodlad and P. Keating (New York: College Entrance Examination Board, 1990), pp. 59–89; Ogbu, "The Consequences of the American Caste System."

68. John Dewey, *Democracy and Education* (New York: Macmillan, 1916; reprint ed., New York: Free Press, 1966), p. 87.

69. Dewey, *Democracy and Education,* p. 83.

70. Dewey, *Democracy and Education,* p. 84.

71. Dewey, *Democracy and Education,* pp. 4–5.

72. Fine, *Framing Dropouts,* p. 158.

73. Rist, *The Urban School,* p. 18.

74. Valerie Lee, Anthony Bryk, and Mary Lou Smith, "The Organization of Effective Secondary Schools," in *Review of Research in Education,* vol. 19, edited by L. Darling-Hammond (Washington, D.C.: American Educational Research Association, 1993).

75. Lee, Bryk, and Smith, "The Organization of Effective Secondary Schools"; Valerie Lee and Anthony Bryk, "Curriculum Tracking as Mediating the Social Distribution of High School Achievement," *Sociology of Education,* 1988, *61,* 78–94; Michelle Fine, *Chartering Urban School Reform* (New York: NCREST, 1994); Linda Darling-Hammond, Jacqueline Ancess, and Beverly Falk, *Authentic Assessment in Action: Studies of Schools and Students at Work* (New York: Teachers College Press, 1995).

76. This section draws heavily on Linda Darling-Hammond's testimony on Opportunity-to-Learn Standards for the National Governors' Association, Washington, D.C., 1993.

77. Linda Darling-Hammond, *Standards of Practice for Learner-Centered Schools* (New York: NCREST, 1992), p. 3.

78. Darling-Hammond, *Standards of Practice for Learner-Centered Schools.*

79. Linda Darling-Hammond, *Beyond the Commission Reports: The Coming Crisis in Teaching* (Santa Monica, Calif.: The RAND Corporation, 1984).

80. Linda Darling-Hammond, "Teacher Professionalism: Why and How," in *Schools as Collaborative Cultures: Creating the Future Now,* edited by A. Lieberman (New York: Falmer Press, 1990), pp. 25–50.

81. Robert Glaser, "The Future of Testing: A Research Agenda for Cognitive Psychology and Psychometrics," *American Psychologist,* 1981, *36,* 923–936; Robert Glaser, *Testing and Assessment: O Tempora! O Mores!* (Pittsburgh, Pa.: University of Pittsburgh, Learning Research and Development Center, 1990); Linda Darling-Hammond, "Performance-

Based Assessment and Educational Equity," *Harvard Educational Review,* 1994, *66*(1), 5–30.

82. Darling-Hammond, Ancess, and Falk, *Authentic Assessment in Action;* Linda Darling-Hammond and others, *Creating Learner-Centered Accountability* (New York: NCREST, 1993).
83. Glaser, *Testing and Assessment.*
84. Glaser, *Testing and Assessment,* p. 16.
85. Glaser, *Testing and Assessment,* p. 17.
86. Mindy Kornhaber and Howard Gardner, *Varieties of Excellence: Identifying and Assessing Children's Talents* (New York: NCREST, 1993).

Chapter Seven

Curriculum for Democracy

Walter C. Parker

"Let's begin by saying that we are living through a very dangerous time," James Baldwin said in an address to teachers in 1963.[1] It is always a very dangerous time when democratic experiments are the concern, and as if to prove the point, democracies are scarce and their incumbencies brief. All of them, including the United States, are young, and most of them are only nominal democracies: representatives are elected by adults who vote, and whose votes count equally, and individuals have rights. Yet, it is not so much "we the people" who govern in these fledgling democracies as it is power elites who govern. Ordinary citizens' civic competence goes undeveloped or, if nurtured to some extent somewhere along the line, atrophies through disuse. The consequence is the degradation of what Hannah Arendt called the public sphere. Critical discourse is replaced by "rights talk," practical judgment by expertise.[2] Diversity by race, class, gender, language, religion, ethnicity, neighborhood, and so on, is a fact of life in modern democracies. Yet, none of them—not Switzerland, Japan, England, Costa Rica, or the United States—has yet realized *e pluribus unum* (from many, one). They all "tolerate" some degree of pluralism and have achieved perhaps a limited unity, yet to one degree or another they marginalize or repress the former and therefore can only pretend the latter.

These things should matter to educators. Why? Arguing that the first obligation of education is to socialize children, Baldwin reminded his audience that the endeavor becomes meaningful only when educators try to decide what kind of society they are trying to perpetuate. "Thus, for example, the boys and girls who were born during the era of the Third Reich, when educated to the purposes of the Third Reich, became barbarians."[3]

Curriculum developers trying to prepare the next generation of citizens for the purposes of democracy rather than a Third Reich of one sort or another, and specifically for a participatory and multicultural democracy rather than a nominal and homogenizing one, face a daunting array of problems. There are countless ways to interpret and parse these problems, bringing some of them to the fore, bracketing others, and ignoring still others. The particular problem selected for concerted attention by many American educators working in the nineteenth and twentieth centuries was providing young people with equal access to school buildings. Lawrence Cremin called this the popularization of education,[4] and there were numerous lines of opposition. One faction saw it as another incursion of Big Government into the private sphere, this time to tax some parents to pay for the education of others' children. A second saw education as a commodity and, applying the logic of the market, concluded that a wide distribution of schooling would result in lowered curriculum standards and status. Efficiency would be achieved, no doubt, as with Ford automobiles in Detroit, but what is special about an automobile if it looks like all the others and if everyone has it? A third line of opposition was concerned with what it considered to be the negative effects of mixing children of different religions, national origins, ethnicities, races, and classes in common schools.

Busy fighting this battle, just trying to get poor or culturally marginalized children *into* schools, a good number of educators did not concern themselves so much with what went on *inside* schools. Curriculum planning for democracy, then, had to play second fiddle. Yet, play it did. Numerous curriculum committees, commissions, and associations attempted to rouse civic education. The National Education Association's 1916 Commission on the Reorganization of Secondary Education, for example, developed the Community Civics course and the better known course called Problems of Democracy.[5] Also, among the several projects of the Progressive Education Association was the Eight-Year Study.[6] In many ways the largest and most important curriculum research and evaluation study ever undertaken in the United States, this project put community problem solving and the ability to respond intelligently to new situations at the core of the secondary school curriculum. While these initiatives generally failed to consider the curriculum as racialized or gendered terrain, they did attend to its political and economic dimensions, which is to say they did not ignore the fact that the American school curriculum is situated in one of the world's most powerful capitalist, rapidly industrializing nations. They escaped somewhat, therefore, the "social amnesia"[7] that plagues the curriculum field.

Curriculum is, of course, only one realm in the project to educate democrats. There is no need to argue that it is more or less important than other areas, whether family life, media, the political economy, community norms, and realms within the school itself—administration, in-service education of teachers, a school's deliberative practices, and so on. Obviously, these variables are entangled. Assuming, however, that there can be no democracy without democrats, that the schools have an important part to play in the education of democrats, and that the school curriculum is a major feature of school life, educators are justified in attempting to develop a school curriculum for democracy and rousing the public to its support.

My plan in this chapter is as follows: I concentrate throughout on the most basic of all curriculum work, rationale building, without which school work is aimless. The first section introduces the activity of curriculum deliberation and its two key decision points, both utterly dependent on rationale work: content selection and curriculum access/differentiation. The second, more lengthy section represents the search for particular democratic aims toward which an ambitious school curriculum for democracy might be oriented. Three aims are developed, drawing heavily on John Dewey's work, as well as on recent developments in critical citizenship and race theory. This section is followed by a discussion of curriculum principles pertinent to these aims. By connecting curriculum principles in this way to a fresh formulation of democratic aims, the upshot of the chapter is realized: school goals need to mirror broader societal goals; otherwise, school life is conducted not as a laboratory for anything in particular, let alone democratic living, but as an end in itself, and subjects are taught without purpose other than mastery, which is meaningless. Before concluding, I sketch the Problems of Democracy course that was developed for high school seniors near the beginning of this century. While not an instance of the full set of principles given in the prior section, for it did not take diversity seriously enough, nor discussion, it did accomplish much, and should therefore be of tremendous help to planners wishing to do more.

Curriculum Deliberation

Curriculum deliberation is informed discussion with an eye to deciding what should be taught in school. As such, it is a subset of the general, interpretive practice of deliberation, which is the method by which everyday, practical problems are identified and addressed. To situate deliberation still more intimately in common life, we might think of it as a subset of *bricolage*—the improvisational, do-it-yourself, local knowledge with which humans in communities meet situations as they arise. Everyday deliberation breaks down when a community accords technique and expertise greater status than they deserve. This attitude alone can undermine mundane conversation about what is right and what is wrong and how the wrongs might be righted. Precisely this situation has obtained in many industrialized societies, and in their schools. Dewey[8] considered technical rationality an "invasion"; Mary Shelley gave us a more visceral metaphor in *Frankenstein*. Ordinary citizens, whose thinking is not believed to measure up to expert opinion, are marginalized, even stupefied, in matters of public policy formulation. Crime becomes the police department's problem, health the medical community's, and education the school's.

The "crisis" need not be overdrawn, however. I have found across the nation groups of teachers and curriculum supervisors doing precisely what Joseph Schwab described as deliberation:

> Deliberation is complex and arduous. It treats both ends and means and must treat them as mutually determining one another. It must try to identify, with respect to both, what facts may be relevant. It must try to ascertain the relevant facts in the concrete case. It must try to identify the desiderata in the case. It must generate alternative solutions. It must make every effort to trace the branching pathways of consequences which may flow from each alternative and affect

desiderata. It must then weigh alternatives and their costs and consequences against one another, and choose, not the *right* alternative, for there is no such thing, but the *best* one.[9]

Teachers and curriculum supervisors may not deliberate as often as curriculum development requires nor as well as observers external to their circumstances might wish. The former is a problem to which the current "restructuring" movement ought to be concerned, but the latter often is no more than "dueling bricolage." When experts ignore or dismiss teachers' curriculum decision making, they operate quite often, I am afraid, without anything close to a comprehension of what teachers actually do. Theorizing in this interpretive vacuum, they will conceptualize teachers' work using not teachers' but their *own* bricolage, their own know-how, as the standard. As a result, researchers and policymakers inevitably will discover only what teachers cannot do.[10]

Content Selection

To the extent that educators can find time to deliberate, they set about deciding what they want to accomplish and select a sample of content that arguably can get them there. Content selection is wholly bound up with curricular aims or goals, which are societal aims rephrased. "The conception of education as a social process and function," Dewey argued in *Democracy and Education,* "has no definite meaning until we define the kind of society we have in mind."[11] Yet, the vortex around which this goal setting spins, the practical problem that forces deliberation, is deciding what content to teach. Ancillary matters are when, how, to whom, and with what standards. Because content selection is the focal point, curriculum deliberation seems to proceed most productively within a rough ends-means framework: the best reason to select content x rather than content y is that x is judged the better means for the desired end, which is a vision of conjoint living. The process is dialectical, however, as Schwab noted: while the suitability of various content alternatives is being considered, the ends themselves are reinterpreted and revised.

As content is selected, it must somehow be transformed into school subject matter. So difficult is the selection task, let alone this transformation, that some teachers can be seen fleeing the curriculum field in any manner possible—letting the children themselves choose what to study, for example, or "covering" whatever happens to have been included in a particular textbook, or arguing that *what* is studied does not matter as much as *how* it is studied. Professors of education have joined the great escape, too, with any number of stratospheric flights to up-market theory battles that are "merely philosophical" because they are of so little consequence to people working in the curriculum field.[12] School superintendents also have fled, mainly by exchanging their several subject area curriculum coordinators for a "generalist" who "adopts"[13] in science this year, social studies next year, math the next, then reading and language arts, then art and music, then returning to science and repeating the five-year cycle. This practice replaces the whole of curriculum deliberation with one of its parts, materials selection. Moreover, it removes from the local deliberative scene the very professionals whose competencies (such as local knowledge, discussion moderation skills, or programmatic planning) can help frame conversations about curriculum renewal and draw key resources to the task.

Curriculum Differentiation

The pernicious problem of curriculum differentiation or tracking can be addressed by looking to the same rationales that direct content selection. As Michael F. D. Young argued,[14] years after the point had been raised in the Booker T. Washington/W. E. B. DuBois debate,[15] the school curriculum is a mechanism through which knowledge is socially distributed. The consequence of the allocation of knowledge and experience is a roughly corresponding distribution of social roles and status.

Several decades of data show fairly clearly that tracking is an allocation rubric by which old power relations and systems of privilege are maintained. Some students are educated for the board room and the legislature, others for Burger King and the voting booth. In a "wholly racialized society,"[16] cultural minorities are especially disadvantaged by tracking. Middle-class whites, too, are affected by their placement in the secondary schools' aggressively mediocre middle or "general" track. A society aiming as high as democracy will seek at all costs to educate all its students to be democrats, especially if its particular vision of democracy requires that all citizens, not just a few, think and behave democratically. This takes us to the subject of aims.

Social Aims: The Kind of Society We Have in Mind

Toward what *particular* vision of democracy should the curriculum be aimed? Readers may recall the triumphant scene of democratic activists with sledgehammers atop the Berlin Wall only a few years ago, having toppled the German Democratic Republic. Philip Green reminds us, though, of the despair that followed these events "as they watched their democratic . . . revolution ousted from the streets of Berlin and the corridors of its public buildings, to become enmeshed in the monopolistic party politics of the Federal Republic. . . ."[17] It is in this vein that one can appreciate the desire of students in Tiananmen Square in 1989 for something more than democratic politics as usual. Vincent Harding tells of one student in the square who, in an exchange with a Western television interviewer, claimed that what Chinese students and intellectuals wanted from the United States was its "advanced technology." The journalist asked if they were not interested in any other American ideas, such as democracy. The student's response came quickly: "Yes, but only if they are *advanced ideas* about democracy."[18]

This young woman's statement captures the specific moral imperative for curriculum planners wanting to educate democrats: to examine the particular concept of democracy they hold in mind. To quote Dewey, "Since education is a social process, and there are many kinds of societies, a criterion for educational criticism and construction implies a particular social ideal."[19] Do curriculum planners hold a vision of the citizen as occasional voter? As legislator? Is it a vision that subjugates difference? Tolerates it? Fosters it? Curriculum planners and teachers must do what no one else in education has to do: *specify an aim sufficiently to constitute a reasonably distinct target,* one that will justify selecting this content over that, these materials over those, these instructional methods, these experiences, and these modes of interaction.

Nominal democracy is only one kind of democracy. Are there "advanced" ideas to which curriculum planners and teachers concerned with democracy might aspire and which, if taken seriously, might incline them to re-vision a curriculum for democracy? Might they then seek to organize school life in particular ways and choose for concerted attention particular subject matter and instructional methods? I believe there are such ideas, and I will identify and attempt to introduce them in this section. They are drawn, as we shall see, from a burgeoning literature on pluralist democracy, thanks to a surge of critical race and gender scholarship in recent decades. To begin with a conclusion, these "advanced" ideas converge on the conviction that the democratic project can and must be deepened and extended. Together, they address the question, How can people live together justly, in ways that are mutually satisfying, and that leave our differences, both individual and group, intact and our multiple identities recognized?

Participatory Democracy

Critiques of the social formation called "liberal democracy" are plentiful. This form of democracy sets up forms of human coexistence that celebrate individual liberty, popular sovereignty, law, and equality before the law. As well, it separates public from private life, and civil law from religious law. These are the salient contributions of political liberalism to modern democracy, more or less guaranteeing a social space in which, theoretically, a free people can do all that freedom allows. There are shortcomings, however. Individualism's reliance on representative government is so complete that active citizen participation in the civic culture becomes superfluous. Anne Phillips calls this *liberal democratic minimalism*,[20] which holds that voting is a sufficient form of citizen participation. It is sufficient that citizens occasionally exert a preference for policies and representatives. Accordingly, as Tocqueville observed, they step out of their very large private life into a voting booth (well, some of them do), regarding this a magnanimous act of public mindedness, and then relapse into passivity for another four years. Karl Hess gets to the point:

> In politics a person is not a citizen if the person's only function is to vote. Voters choose people who, in turn, act like citizens. They argue. They establish the forms within which people live their lives.

They make politics. The people who merely vote for them merely make politicians. People who argue for their positions in a town meeting are acting like citizens. People who simply drop scraps of paper in a box or pull a lever are not acting like citizens; they are acting like consumers, picking between prepackaged political items. They had nothing to do with the items.[21]

Because ordinary citizens in liberal democracies have rights, their common political language is not limited to talking about those who actually do politics—to "watch talk"—but includes a good measure of "rights talk." Together, spectatorship and free speech make for a pitifully thin moral discourse, and other forms and expressions of democratic engagement are crowded out— deliberation about alternative ways of living together, ways that might be more satisfying and less marked by violence, mental illness, family disruption, poverty, and so on. Jean Bethke Elshtain is blunt: "No substantive sense of civic virtue, no vision of political community that might serve as the groundwork of a life in common, is possible within a political life dominated by a self-interested, predatory, individualism."[22]

The most compelling democratic alternative to liberal democracy is a vision of public life that takes popular sovereignty more seriously. It relies on the key notions of participation, civic virtue, and common good. Called participatory or *strong* democracy, it defines democratic politics not as the negotiations of elected party and interest-group elites but as "a self-governing community of citizens who are united less by homogeneous interests than by civic education and who are made capable of common purpose and mutual action by virtue of their civic attitudes and participatory institutions rather than their altruism or good nature."[23] Representatives in a strong democracy would not become obsolete, nor would they be, as now, virtually the only people in a society practicing democracy.

Creative Democracy

Tied to the participatory ideal is a view of democracy as a process and path. Dewey called this *creative democracy*, by which he meant that democracy is a way of individual living with others, a way of being. It has no end other than the "way" itself. It follows that there is no period or place, either in the past or today, that can serve as a model of democracy.[24] This is not an easy view to hold, particularly in Great Britain and the United States, for democracy was what these nations thought they were fighting two world wars to "save."[25] Still, viewed as a creative, constructive process, democracy is not already accomplished, needing only protection, but a path that citizens in a pluralist society try to walk together. It is this trek—this commitment—that unites them, not a culture, language, or religion. The ratification of the Constitution and the several democratic struggles that followed hardly closed the book on democracy in the United States; they hardly dispensed with its possibilities. Democracy is not now "done," like so much baked bread. The "miracle of Philadelphia" was an important step on the path, and the Civil Rights Movement another, but the work continues.

The path notion in no way mitigates the importance of tradition and initiation, but it holds a dynamic view of the traditions involved. Richard Rorty exemplifies this point with his hope that children will be taught to consider themselves "heirs to a tradition" that sponsors a continual deepening of democracy and a rethinking of its tenets. He calls this a tradition "of increasing liberty and rising hope." Children should think of themselves "as proud and loyal citizens of a country that, slowly and painfully, threw off a foreign yoke, freed its slaves, enfranchised its women, restrained its robber barons and licensed its trade unions, liberalized its religious practices and broadened its religious and moral tolerance, and built colleges in which 50 percent of its population could enroll—a country that numbered Ralph Waldo Emerson, Eugene V. Debs, Susan B. Anthony, and James Baldwin among its citizens."[26]

This is a tradition that asks democrats to "live out the true meaning of their creed," as Martin Luther King, Jr., said, doing what is needed to close the gap between the real and the ideal. It is a perennial gap, because the real and the ideal both are continually reformulated, but in its most rudimentary form the creed defines the path. It guarantees certain individual rights and does not allow even the majority to abrogate them. Everyone is to be regarded as equal to everyone else and in possession of the fullest measure of human dignity. Law making and enforcement are not to be the province of the rich, elders, priests, or experts, but the shared tasks of everyone (popular sovereignty). Procedures for institutional change are to be respected so that change can be accomplished without leaving the path altogether.

Multicultural Democracy

The first two ideas emphasize, first, wider and deeper forms of popular sovereignty and, second, democracy as a way of life rather than an attainment. The third idea, which we could call multicultural democracy, concentrates on what is perhaps the most crucial intersection in this problem space, the juncture of democracy and diversity. It brings to the first "advanced" idea the question, Who is and is not participating and on whose terms? And to the second, How wide is the path?

Fueling this third idea is the new pluralism that has swept through democratic theorizing, replacing the longstanding assumption that traditional democratic institutions had effectively solved the problems posed by diversity. Much of the new work stems from the postmodern and post-structural literatures—literatures that not only allow but *foster* difference, literatures that resist the theistic urge to gather all into one. I am referring especially to recent analyses of race relations and racial formation,[27] and to feminist critiques of the patriarchy, which has suffused liberalism and Marxism alike, conveniently rendering private life as "women's work."[28]

This third idea challenges the ability of liberal democracy to hold pluralism as a central tenet while at the same time denying or punishing or, at best, "tolerating" diversity. According to the principles of liberal democracy, unity arises from diversity (*e pluribus unum*). At the same time, in what Nancy Fraser aptly calls "actually existing democracies,"[29] numerous groups live on the outskirts of the political community and are not by any stretch of the imagination included in the *unum*. One wonders at the size, history, and constitution of the blind spot. While people of color, women, the poor, gays, and lesbians are marginalized, liberal democracy celebrates pluralism as a present, continuing, and necessary feature of a democratic state.

How is the contradiction managed? In the first place, according to the myth's supporters *e pluribus unum* is not so much a process or path as an accomplishment, the key benchmarks of which include the Federalists' brilliant constitutional accommodation of political factions and numerous eighteenth- and nineteenth-century accommodations of diversity of religion and national origin.[30] Any serious attention to diversity today, the argument goes, now that the deal is done, the bread baked, and the envelope pushed as far as it can go, will therefore result in what Arthur Schlesinger calls "the disuniting of America."[31] Of course, this is a fantastic misconception. Contradicting the second idea, creative democracy, it construes the situation in such a way that the status quo becomes a jewel not to be disturbed. James Banks is direct: "The claim that multicultural education will divide the nation assumes that the nation is already united. . . . Multicultural education is designed to help unify a deeply divided nation rather than to divide a highly cohesive one."[32]

Second, liberal democracy's individualism is highly abstract and impersonal. It is necessarily "difference-blind."[33] Its citizen is a character of *in*different sex, race, social class, religion, national origin, and in some polities, sexual orientation. This is liberal democracy's neutrality premise. However, in societies where group identities are politicized and matter greatly in the conduct of public affairs, indifference will serve especially the interests of whichever groups presently enjoy positions of power. That is, formulations that pretend neutrality reproduce the status quo, and the failure to acknowledge this fact only intensifies its effect. Members of dominant groups are predictably the last to see the very categories in which their superior status allows them to prosper.[34]

To summarize, liberal democracy's basic tenets of individual liberty, human dignity, equality, and popular sovereignty need to be preserved, but extended and deepened. Accordingly, a new sense of citizenship needs to be forged, one that embraces individual difference, group difference, and political community all at once. In order to do this, democrats will not be able merely to replace liberalism's excessive individual self-interest with a new politics of *group* self-interest. That would be no gain. Pluralism itself needs to be reformulated in order to avoid the essentializing tendencies of much liberal and radical thinking about diversity that considers men to be such and such because they are men, and Japanese to be so and so because they are Japanese. In the same way, women are this way, blacks are that way, Hispanics are . . . , lesbians are . . . , the working class is . . . , and so on down a stereo-type-littered civic back alley from which no one, and no group, escapes.

Identities, both individual and group, are socially constructed abstractions located only temporarily at the intersections of numer-ous categories—historical, psychological, cultural, and sociologi-cal. The perilous challenge is to recognize individual and group identities without etching them in primordial stone,[35] and to unite them horizontally in a democratic moral discourse that is capable of embracing more than mere "rights talk." Here is Dewey's vision of a larger public that embraces the little publics.[36] The larger one is not, let us be clear, a broad-based *cultural* comradeship. In mod-ern, culturally diverse states, this is not only unrealistic but unde-sirable. When pursued by dominant groups, the wish for cultural bonding becomes a repressive, assimilationist, even totalizing ambi-tion. Dewey's vision of the larger public is instead an approach to democratic life that strives to construct a moral grid that binds cit-izens together in a broad *political* comradeship—one that not only tolerates diversity but actively appreciates it as a democratic virtue.[37] The democratic project, then, requires a critique of the forms of liberalism that make genuine pluralism impossible and of the forms of pluralism that make political community impossible. This will not be easy work; in fact, it may prove too difficult to succeed.

Curriculum Aims

Educators will argue over these social ideals and whether they should double as aims for the curriculum. Some will prefer to think that the school curriculum has only one aim, "achievement," which they will argue is walled off from the sociopolitical realm. Others will admit that the school is not insulated, that it stands on moral ground. They will prefer the aims of liberal democracy, how-ever, because these aims do make a good beginning and they are at least somewhat secured in convention. Others will prefer the aims of liberal democracy because they are convinced, with the founders, that wider participation will breed mob rule, which in turn will invite a police state—a Third Reich of one sort or another. The latter is among the more thoughtful oppositions to the "advanced" aims sketched above, but it puts educators in the position of having to choose between perpetuating the exclusive minimalism of liberal democracy and the release of mob passion, unchecked, to demagogues.

Civic education is a way out of this impasse. Without it, a strong democracy would indeed undo itself. Even Barber harbors no romantic notions of what "we the people" would do if, uneducated for it, we were to participate in more than the ritual voting act:

> Give the uneducated the right to participate in making collective decisions, and what results is not democracy but, at best, mob rule: the government of private prejudice once known as the tyranny of opinion. For Jefferson, the difference between the democratic temperance he admired in agrarian America and the rule of the rabble he condemned when viewing the social unrest of Europe's teeming cities was quite simply education. Madison had hoped to "filter" out popular passion through the device of representation. Jefferson saw in education a filter that could be installed within each individual, giving to each the capacity to rule prudently. Education creates a ruling aristocracy constrained by temperance and wisdom; when that education is public and universal, it is an aristocracy to which all can belong.[38]

Let us to turn, then, to an examination of civic education curricula relevant to this "installation." This is a leap, to be sure. It is one that many avoid, some by ignorance and some by resistance. Illustrating the first, Council for Basic Education researcher James Banner claims that we cannot move ahead productively with civic education because of the "striking absence" of "what everyone would recognize to be straightforward curriculum thinking. . . . None of those who urge upon us the reassertion of civic themes in education offers any guidance as to how these themes would be reinstated in the course of instruction."[39] Illustrating the latter, philosopher Bernard Murchland, in a statement that alone could earn the ivory tower its reputation among practitioners, avers that "it is premature to be worrying about the curriculum." So many details still need to be worked out, he argues. Is civic education a kind of intelligence? A set of behaviors? A disposition?[40]

Certainly, much theorizing still is needed, but people actually working in the curriculum field cannot and do not wait to get the plans "just right" before acting. I present in this section a set of curriculum principles that should help curriculum planners move ahead on the practical matter of content selection. To begin with conclusions, the field of study most relevant to educating democrats is the one known for centuries as the *practical.* Its subject matter is public problems, its method is deliberation, and its aim is right action. The Greeks called it *phronesis* or the practical reasoning necessary to do the right thing in real (versus hypothetical) settings.[41] A curriculum for *phronesis* is required because the aims discussed earlier specify citizens whose main task is not the rule-bound reproduction of what has come before (recall, there are no models) but a principled, creative *praxis*—identifying and negotiating obstacles as they arise, building and applying ideas, easing out of the various ruts of weak democracy, and working toward strong democratic ideals that are revised and clarified in the course of working toward them.

The centerpieces of such a curriculum are study and practice. Democracy is what is studied; democracy is what is practiced. The claim favors a genre of curriculum planning that we might call "teaching the aim." If participatory, creative, multicultural democracy is the chosen social aim, then let it serve also as the core K-12 curriculum aim, the one to which students and teachers direct their efforts. Following are seven principles that I would suggest for determining such a curriculum (Table 7.1 provides a summary).

Teach the aim. Preceding and pervading the other facets of the curriculum is a direct relationship of curricula to the aims of strong

Table 7.1. Curriculum for Democracy.

Weak Democracy	Strong Democracy	Curriculum Principles for a Strong Democracy
Minimalist	Participatory	Teach the Aim
Protectionist	Creative	Knowledge-in-Use
Marginalist	Multicultural	Face-to-Face Discussions
		Reflective Citizen Action
		Diverse Perspectives
		Democratic Values
		Multiple Associations

democracy. Teachers and curriculum supervisors should be able to articulate the relationship of curricula to aims, and not a very great leap of faith should be required. Teaching the aim should counter long-standing habits in curriculum guides of posting goals for which little curriculum or instruction can be found.

Knowledge-in-use. Pro-democratic curricula need to sponsor a dialectical view of knowledge development and application (for example, Theodore Sizer's "knowledge-in-use"[42]) so that participation is not postponed to dutifully, and wrongly, follow knowledge acquisition. This is what Dewey criticized in *Democracy and Education* as "object teaching," which required that purposeful action (such as participatory democracy) wait until positive understandings (of a discipline's findings and methods, for example) had been formed. Much substantive knowledge should be developed, and this alone will require planned, sustained intellectual labor by students; but its development cannot be insulated from the practice of democracy. To the contrary, the development of a fund of democratic knowledge will depend on its situated use and revision in real and simulated civic activity. Two such activities are primary: discussion of public problems and citizen action.

Face-to-face discussion. Curricula need to emphasize civic discourse, particularly face-to-face discussion. Discussion of the public's problems, the causes of which they are effects, and alternative courses of action need to become centerpieces of the curriculum— taught, modeled, studied, practiced, and assessed. This elevates democratic deliberation to the high point of the school curriculum. Discussion itself should be studied, and discussion competence developed. Who associates in discussion? Is difference repressed, tolerated, or respected? How do particular discussion forums advantage some groups and disadvantage others? How is participants' cultural self-knowledge addressed? How is knowledge of American constitutional democracy brought to bear? How can consensus be reached and obstacles overcome? What about persons who disagree with a consensus? Discussion, then, is prominent in the curriculum, not only as instructional method but as subject matter and as a form of democratic action.

Reflective citizen action. Curricula need to sponsor citizen action/ advocacy along with critical reflection on such action. Discussion itself is a species of democratic action, perhaps its highest form, for in discussion alternative ways of living are imagined, encountered, created, and argued; differences are brought face-to-face and common ground is explored; power relations based on normally unspoken fixtures of social life (such as race, class, or gender) can be negotiated; shared understandings of problems can be forged; and agreeable policies may be devised. Yet, a more assertive form of democratic action also must be developed, for democrats are expected to advocate reasoned positions and actually to exert influence on the course of public affairs.

Diverse perspectives. An intimate familiarity with difference can be developed in the K-12 school years if multiple perspectives, including conflicting perspectives, are incorporated into learning. This means exposing students to multiple cases of the topic at hand (not only the U.S. Constitution but others, not only ethnic diversity in the U.S. but elsewhere around the world, not only racial segregation in South Africa but elsewhere). It also means the rigorous study of culture, broadly defined.[43] Oppressed cultural groups often develop cultures of resistance and struggle, just as dominant cultural groups typically develop cultures of privilege. As a facet of the democratic curriculum, then, "diverse perspectives" admits critical analytic concepts, such as power, conflict, and racism, without which multicultural education lacks rigor.

Democratic values. Curricula need to sponsor reasoning with and about democratic values. This guideline has two meanings. First, students are taught to grapple with democratic values during discussion so that they will listen as well as talk, appreciate that not all their demands can be satisfied, restrain themselves from policies that punish difference and needlessly constrain liberty, and attend to such things as inclusion and exclusion. In short, students need to learn to recognize and oppose repression and discrimination.[44] Second, reasoning with democratic values means that students directly study public controversies, contemporary and historical, in which democratic values, such as liberty and civic virtue, difference and community, are at loggerheads.

Multiple associations. Both the formal curriculum (such as the study and practice of democracy) and the informal curriculum (for example, school governance and climate) should bring a diverse student body into numerous small and large associations in which the democratic way of life is imagined and practiced, and the tensions of democratic life dealt with firsthand. This principle overlaps each of the others, particularly "diverse perspectives." Its unique contribution, however, goes to the heart of creative democracy, which is the "mode of associated living, of conjoint communicated experience"[45] discussed earlier. What is distinct about this mode is that the interplay among various groups (ethnic groups, peer groups, and age cohorts, for example) is wide-ranging, frequent, and unrestricted, and that this interplay creates a broader public space—a bigger public—that incorporates these differences without homogenizing them.[46]

Interactions

I want to demonstrate briefly the interaction of these principles, showing them to be an interdependent set. The meaning of any one principle is protean and thoroughly dispersed across the other principles. For purposes of this demonstration, I will focus on the third principle, "face-to-face discussion" of public conflict, defining and supporting it with reference to the others, particularly "multiple associations" and "diverse perspectives."

Discussion of public conflict is an exemplar of the first principle, "teaching the aim," because discussion can be understood to be the constituting activity of public life. Discussion creates publics. When two or more people are gathered—whether in a tavern, in a church basement, at a Rotary luncheon, or on a street corner—and are talking or exchanging in some way ("acting and speaking together"[47]) and their topic is a *common* problem requiring decision, they constitute a public. A public, then, in the most straightforward sense, is a group of people discussing common problems with an eye to decision.

Once formed, publics change the lives of the people they include, as well the lives of those they exclude. Contrary to the very North American aphorism "talk is cheap," talk in fact matters. In the Soviet Union, *glasnost* allowed talk, and the rest is history; likewise, conversations in church basements produced the Civil Rights Movement. For these reasons, democratic governments do not grant free speech; they protect it. (There is a huge difference.) In talk, shared understandings are created, different perspectives are heard, social policies are done and undone, alternative possibilities are envisioned, and plans are made. A curriculum that features sustained, rigorous study and practice of discussion educates children in the daily labor of strong democracy.

But is discussion education a feasible aspect of the curriculum? It is, and it can be implemented without providing costly excursions away from the school site, because the school itself is a most promising site for discussion education. It is difficult to imagine a better one. The association of diverse groups there is quite vigorous: students, teachers, boys, girls, rich, poor, Black, White, Jew, Buddhist, Filipino, Hispanic, European, administrators, counselors, parents, nurses, police, guests, the press. Power and status suffuse all of these groups.

Public schools are places where the bigger public congregates and where the array of little publics gathers and engages in common activity. At least this is the possibility public schools afford. The problems that arise in them (academic, interpersonal, within groups, and between groups), around which discussion is made necessary and around which it becomes a supreme associative practice, are precisely the sorts of problems through which a diverse body of young people gradually can be initiated into democratic *praxis*, which is to say, into "an impassioned and significant dialogue"[48] and increasingly critical levels of civic competence; that is, into wondering and worrying together—deliberating—about how we ought to live together.

Discussion, then, is not merely an "instructional method." That view has undermined schools and impoverished them as civic places. Rather, discussion is a shared life-world wherein civility might be nurtured and alternative futures made.

For these reasons, discussion *competence* becomes important and, in turn, discussion education becomes central to democratic education. It is not enough to have a "community of learners" if blather counts as discussion. Discussion needs to be constrained by norms of civility: listening as well as talking, taking turns, criticizing ideas rather than persons, supporting claims with reasoning, and so on. Furthermore, it needs to be constrained by traditional canons of inquiry such as double-checking the facts, suspending judgment, interrogating positions one has taken early in the inquiry, subjecting claims to peer scrutiny, and in general allowing positions to develop *through* discussion rather than only defending positions held before.[49] In this way, discussion is more a forum for forging public understandings than it is a platform to which participants bring and defend opinions. It is more (and better) than debate or negotiation. Competent discussion is a way out of the tyranny of prior belief and stubborn opinion, not a way in.

Discussion competence involves something more, without which discussion may be disciplined but not democratic: reasoning with democratic values and, dialectically, reconsidering them. A shared commitment to justice, equality, and human dignity fashions the talk about *both the issues at hand and the talk itself.* Competent discussants are able and inclined to notice what is missing, to scan the social horizon to ascertain which values, interests, and experiences are absent from the table or present but ignored. They pay attention as well to what is dismissed through the habits of condescension built into dominant discourses (what Lisa Delpit calls "silenced dialogues"[50]). Because better meanings are those formed dialogically, systemic exclusions of meanings and persons disables discussion and, therefore, the products of discussion.

The Problems Approach

The Problems of Democracy (POD) course should be worth considering at this point for three reasons. First, it affords readers an opportunity to reflect upon and situate the curriculum principles just articulated. Second, it demonstrates that "straightforward curriculum thinking" on civic education, contrary to Banner's claim,[51] indeed has been taken up by curriculum developers not only recently but throughout the century. Third, the problems approach to democratic education, of which POD is one example, is an estimable one. Like most curriculum programs that have been developed in the United States, it did not take seriously enough the question of diversity generally and the pervasiveness of bigotry in particular. However, it did treat democracy as a creative endeavor, not an attainment, and it did push the concept of citizenship education further than it had been pushed before or than it has been since.

POD was designed by a 1916 commission of the National Education Association that was called to attempt a sensible articulation of college and high school curricula. Its work soon broadened to a reformulation of the entire secondary curriculum. A subcommittee assigned to "social studies" worked out a comprehensive curriculum for grades seven through twelve ending in a "culminating course . . . with the purpose of giving more definite, comprehensive, and deeper knowledge of some of the vital problems of social life, and thus of securing a more intelligent and active citizenship."[52] This became POD. It would rely heavily on what students had learned in a course of study called Community Civics (CC) in grades seven through nine and the history (European and American) learned in grades seven through twelve. Careful to mollify the social sciences competing for dominance over the secondary school curriculum, the planners clarified that POD would not "discard one social science in favor of another, nor attempt to crowd the several social sciences into [POD] in abridged forms." Rather, it would have students "study actual problems, or issues, or conditions, as they occur in life, and in their several aspects, political, economic, and sociological."[53] In this way, students might "acquire the habit of forming social judgments" (practical reasoning), which would necessitate "drafting into service the materials of all the social sciences as occasion demands for a thorough understanding of the situations in question."[54]

A brief examination of the CC course is necessary if we are to understand what the authors were wanting to accomplish with POD. CC was at heart a problems course. Its problems were those that modern life had spawned, and their examination was made through a set of dimensions of community life called "elements of community welfare." The term "community" in CC meant a "community of interests," not a place. The course hoped "to lead the pupil (a) to see the importance and significance of the elements of community welfare in their relations to himself and to the communities of which he is a member; (b) to know the social agencies, governmental and voluntary, that exist to secure these elements of community welfare; (c) to recognize his civic obligations, present and future, and to respond to them by appropriate action."[55]

The elements of community welfare were to include health, protection of life and property, recreation, education, civic beauty, wealth, communication, transportation, migration, charities, correction, government agencies, and voluntary agencies. Advice also was given on how to provide instruction on an element. Teachers were first to devise an approach that would "lead pupils to realize its importance to themselves, to their neighborhood, and to the community." Second, they were to plan a "concrete" and "detailed investigation" to consist largely of firsthand observation and study of local conditions pertaining to the particular element. Teachers were advised not to attempt intensive instruction on all the elements listed, for surely this would "result in superficiality, kill interest, and defeat the purpose of the course."[56]

Ninth-grade CC sought to lead students to "new points of view and new relations." It tried to push students to identify with the broader communities of interest that industrialization had made inevitable. Thus, "national" and "world community" were brought to the fore. The course's objective, just a little more than fifty years after the end of the Civil War and in the midst of another wave of immigrants, was to encourage the subordination of "conflicting group interest" to "the common general interest." The referent for the latter was mainly the nation, as opposed to state and local polities, and from there outward to "internationalism." Again, studies were to be concrete, only now the objects were national and world problems.

Returning to POD, the problems recommended for the POD course required for their proper deliberation knowledge formulated by historians and social scientists, but above and beyond this, by the students' own judgment. Disciplinary knowledge cannot speak for itself, after all, or leap up and apply itself prudently to policy alternatives. Furthermore, problems had to meet the committee's twin criteria for selection: immediate interest to the class and vital importance to society. They also were allied closely with the "elements of community welfare" at the heart of CC. A handful of illustrative problems were given: fluctuation in the cost of living, the impulsive action of crowds, power and effects of tradition, the church as a socializing agent, and immigration.

Problems were to have been studied "in some of their aspects and relations" in history and CC courses, but they "may now be considered more comprehensively, more intensively, and more exhaustively."[57] In particular, they would be studied "from different angles," or disciplinary vantage points. Economic, sociological, and political viewpoints, especially, would now be brought to bear. For example:

I. Economic relations of immigration
   A. Labor supply and other industrial problems
   B. Standards of living, not only of the immigrants, but also of native Americans affected by immigration
II. Sociological relations of immigration
   A. Movements and distribution of population; congestion in cities
   B. Social contributions of immigrants; art, science, ethics
III. Political and governmental relations of immigration
   A. Political ideals of immigrants; comparison of their inherited political conceptions with those of the United States
   B. Naturalization; its methods, abuses

Conclusion

Lest planners be overwhelmed at the prospect of educating democrats, it may be helpful to represent the problem as a straightforward curriculum project: clarify the aims and teach to them. That is, arrange educational experiences and settings so that students study and practice democracy. The particular subject matter to be studied and practiced is, as always, problematic. Reasonable people will disagree on its selection. Still, linking curriculum deliberation to particular democratic ideals is crucial, for it clarifies and specifies the moral ground, thereby providing principled guidance on two critically important decision points faced by all local planners: which understandings and intellectual frameworks will be selected for study (content selection), and which students, if any, will be helped to achieve them (curriculum access/differentiation)?

In this chapter, I formulated and clarified three democratic ideals, and suggested seven curriculum principles aimed at achieving these ideals. The principles were construed as an interdependent set, and their relatedness was briefly demonstrated. They converge on the field called the *practical*, in which problems are the subject matter, practical reasoning is the method, and doing the right thing is the aim. Deliberation, then, is the basic labor of strong democracy—the labor necessary to create, deepen, and extend democracy in an ongoing manner. Because it must be learned and practiced, deliberation should be joined with problems as the core subject matter in a curriculum for democracy.

The Problems of Democracy course was only mentioned, but I wanted to do at least this because POD is a promising example of curriculum work *already being done* that expresses quite well a number of the principles identified here. Other work in the problems genre also deserves attention: "The School for Individual and Community Development" project of the 1930s and 1940s,[58] for example, or Maurice Hunt and Lawrence Metcalf's program for exploring social taboos in the 1950s,[59] Donald Oliver and James Shaver's "jurisprudential" approach in the 1960s,[60] and more recently, Fred Newmann's *Education for Citizen Action* and Lawrence Kohlberg's "just community" work.[61]

I write at a time when "curriculum standards" for precollegiate education are being produced for most of the academic disciplines that are well secured in the schools. Though a few of the standards projects are relevant to the education of democrats— the civics and history projects, for example[62]—this disciplinary activity should give democratic educators pause. Recall that little work on curriculum for democracy has ever emanated from the academic disciplines. This is not to deny what academic scholars have accomplished, only to point out their historically limited direct usefulness on the matters to which this chapter has attended. When they have turned their attention to the K-12 curriculum, scholars in the disciplines generally have worked to hone and convey their disciplines' topical and methodological structures[63]—*their* standards. This has been helpful, but it has been undermined by the presumptive claim that this material—academics' own bricolage— would make an appropriate aim for precollegiate schooling.

Disciplinary knowledge has much general relevance to democratic aims; its questions, findings, and canons of inquiry are, as W.E.B. DuBois and Michael Oakeshott argued so well, essential to a liberating, cosmopolitan education. Yet, disciplinary knowledge has no final or singular relevance where *praxis* is concerned. Recall that the architects of the Holocaust enjoyed probably the best disciplinary education the West had to offer.

Disciplinary concepts and generalizations taken from the inventories of knowledge amassed in each field and then delivered as objects of inquiry to students through their teachers are abstracted from the practical world. In many ways, they are not problems at all. After all, they are derived from sets of data that scientists choose to gather, define, and organize; they are not "acting situations"[64] in which humans sense that something is wrong or inadequate and are trying to figure out what action to take. In other words, the problems stockpiled by the social sciences often are not, as Dewey put it, "set by actual social situations which are themselves conflicting and confused,"[65] which are the situations requiring deliberation.

I conclude on this knotty problem of the academic disciplines' relationship to building a curriculum for democracy by way of urging readers to appreciate the principles "teach the aim" and "knowledge-in-use." The task before those who would write curriculum standards, let alone those who would try something more difficult still—to educate democrats—is not merely one of content selection but of figuring out how to intersect the teaching and learning of that content with deliberating on and acting for the common good. It is at this intersection that we find an appreciation for *praxis* and *phronesis*—that is, for the lived, shared world. Educators have in the problems-approach literature what are probably the best curriculum statements to date that attempt to do just this. Much work is still needed, of course. On the democratic path, there always is. However, planners committed to educating democrats rather than "barbarians" need not start from scratch.

Notes

1. James Baldwin, "A Talk to Teachers," reprinted in *Multicultural Literacy*, edited by R. Simonson and S. Walker (Saint Paul, Minn.: Graywolf Press, 1988), p. 3.
2. Hannah Arendt, *The Human Condition* (Chicago: University of Chicago Press, 1958); Mary Ann Glendon, *Rights Talk* (New York: Free Press, 1991); Ronald Beiner, *Practical Judgment* (Chicago: University of Chicago Press, 1983).
3. Baldwin, "A Talk to Teachers," p. 4.
4. Lawrence A. Cremin, *Popular Education and Its Discontents* (New York: Harper & Row, 1990).
5. Commission on the Reorganization of Secondary Education of the National Education Association, Committee on Social Studies, *The Social Studies in Secondary Education*, Bureau of Education Bulletin No. 28 (Washington, D.C.: U.S. Government Printing Office, 1916).
6. Wilford M. Aikin, *The Story of the Eight-Year Study* (New York: Harper & Row, 1942).

7. Russell Jacoby, *Social Amnesia* (Boston: Beacon, 1975).

8. John Dewey, *The Public and Its Problems* (Chicago: Swallow, 1927).

9. Joseph J. Schwab, *The Practical: A Language for Curriculum* (Washington, D.C.: National Education Association, 1970), p. 36.

10. Walter C. Parker and Janet E. McDaniel, "Bricolage: Teachers Do It Daily," in *Teacher Personal Theorizing*, edited by E. W. Ross, J. W. Cornett, and G. McCutcheon (Albany: State University of New York Press, 1992), pp. 97–114.

11. John Dewey, *Democracy and Education* (Carbondale: Southern Illinois University Press, 1985), p. 103.

12. Schwab, *The Practical*.

13. *Adoption* is school jargon for deciding which textbooks to purchase.

14. Michael M.F.D. Young (ed.), *Knowledge and Control* (London: Collier-Macmillan, 1971), p. 27. See also Walter C. Parker, "The Urban Curriculum and the Allocating Function of Schools," *Educational Forum*, 1985, *49*(4), 445–450.

15. See W.E.B. DuBois, *The Souls of Black Folk* (New York: New American Library, 1985).

16. Toni Morrison, *Playing in the Dark: Whiteness and the Literary Imagination* (Cambridge, Mass.: Harvard University Press, 1992).

17. Philip Green (ed.), *Democracy* (Atlantic Highlands, N.J.: Humanities Press, 1993), p. 18.

18. Vincent Harding, *Hope and History: Why We Must Share the Story of the Movement* (Maryknoll, N.Y.: Orbis, 1990), p. 33.

19. Dewey, *Democracy and Education*, p. 105.

20. Anne Phillips, *Democracy and Difference* (University Park: Pennsylvania State University Press, 1993).

21. Karl Hess, *Community Technology* (New York: Harper & Row, 1979), p. 10.

22. Jean Bethke Elshtain, "Feminist Discourse and Its Discontents: Language, Power, and Meaning," *Signs*, 1982, *3*(7), 617.

23. Benjamin R. Barber, *Strong Democracy* (Berkeley: University of California Press, 1984), p. 117.

24. Phillips, *Democracy and Difference*, p. 2.

25. Green, *Democracy*, p. 4.

26. Richard Rorty, "The Opening of American Minds," *Harper's Magazine*, July 1989, *286*, 22.

27. Among this rapidly growing literature are Bell Hooks, *Talking Back* (Boston: South End Press, 1989); Michael Omi and Howard Winant, *Racial Formation in the United States* (New York: Routledge, 1986); Edward Said, *Orientalism* (New York: Pantheon, 1978); Cornel West, *Race Matters* (Boston: Beacon, 1993).

28. Mary Dietz, "Feminism and Theories of Citizenship," in *Dimensions of Radical Democracy*, edited by C. Mouffe (London: Verso, 1992), pp. 63–85; Nancy Fraser, "Rethinking the Public Sphere: A Contribution to the Critique of Actually Existing Democracy," in *Habermas and the Public Sphere*, edited by C. Calhoun (Cambridge, Mass.: MIT Press, 1993), pp. 109–142.

29. Fraser, "Rethinking the Public Sphere," p. 109.

30. Lawrence H. Fuchs, *The American Kaleidoscope: Race, Ethnicity, and the Civic Culture* (Middletown, Conn.: Wesleyan University Press, 1990).

31. Arthur Schlesinger, *The Disuniting of America* (New York: Norton, 1991). See the review of this book by Gloria Ladson-Billings, "Through the Looking Glass: Politics and the Social Studies Curriculum," *Theory and Research in Social Education*, 1993, *21*(1), 84–92.

32. James A. Banks, "Multicultural Education: Development, Dimensions, and Challenges," *Phi Delta Kappan*, 1993, *75*(1), 23.

33. This is Charles Taylor's term in Amy Gutmann (ed.), *Multiculturalism and the "Politics of Recognition": An Essay by Charles Taylor* (Princeton, N.J.: Princeton University Press, 1993).

34. John U. Ogbu, *Minority Education and Caste: The American System in Cross-Cultural Perspective* (New York: Academic Press, 1978).

35. Phillips notes that the point has always been rather easily grasped where social class is concerned, for modern people do not generally believe that one's social class is fixed or natural. This is why people can at least imagine the elimination of class distinctions. Ethnicity, race, and gender, however, are not eliminatable, and the tendency, perhaps for this reason, has been to reify them.

36. Dewey, *The Public and Its Problems*.

37. This is Amy Gutmann's thesis, *Democratic Education* (Princeton, N.J.: Princeton University Press, 1987).

38. Benjamin R. Barber, "America Skips School," *Harper's Magazine*, November 1993, *286*, 44.

39. James M. Banner Jr., "Thinking about Civic Education," in *Civic Learning for Teachers: Capstone for Educational Reform*, edited by A. H. Jones (Ann Arbor, Mich.: Prakken, 1985), p. 26.

40. Bernard Murchland, "Civic Education: Parsing the Problem," in *Civic Learning for Teachers: Capstone for Educational Reform*, edited by A. H. Jones (Ann Arbor, Mich.: Prakken, 1985), p. 34.

41. A careful discussion of practical competence can be found in William B. Stanley and James A. Whitson, "Citizenship as Practical Competence: A Response to the New Reform in Social Education," *International Journal of Social Education*, 1992, *7*(2), 57–66. See also J. T. Dillon (ed.), *Deliberation in Education and Society* (Norwood, N.J.: Ablex, 1994).

42. Theodore R. Sizer, *Horace's School* (Boston: Houghton Mifflin, 1992).

43. Marion Brady develops the entire school curriculum around the single concept of culture, in *What's Worth Teaching?* (Albany: State University of New York Press, 1989).

44. Gutmann, *Democratic Education*.

45. Dewey, *Democracy and Education*, p. 93.

46. I elaborate on this principle in "Schools as Laboratories of Democracy," *Educating the Democratic Mind*, edited by W. C. Parker (Albany: State University of New York Press, 1996).

47. Arendt, *The Human Condition*.

48. Maxine Greene, *The Dialectic of Freedom* (New York: Teachers College Press, 1988), p. 2.

49. This is David Mathews's point in *Politics for People* (Urbana: University of Illinois Press, 1994).

50. Lisa D. Delpit, "The Silenced Dialogue: Power and Pedagogy in Educating Other People's Children," *Harvard Educational Review*, 1988, *58*(3), 280–298.

51. Banner, "Thinking about Civic Education," p. 26.

52. Commission on the Reorganization of Secondary Education, *The Social Studies in Secondary Education*, p. 52.

53. Commission on the Reorganization of Secondary Education, *The Social Studies in Secondary Education*, p. 53.

54. Commission on the Reorganization of Secondary Education, *The Social Studies in Secondary Education*, p. 56.

55. Commission on the Reorganization of Secondary Education, *The Social Studies in Secondary Education*, p. 23.

56. Commission on the Reorganization of Secondary Education, *The Social Studies in Secondary Education*, p. 24.

57. Commission on the Reorganization of Secondary Education, *The Social Studies in Secondary Education*, p. 54.

58. Paul R. Hanna, "The School: Looking Forward," in *Democracy and the Curriculum*, edited by H. Rugg (New York: Appleton-Century, 1939), pp. 381–405.

59. Maurice P. Hunt and Lawrence E. Metcalf, *Teaching High School Social Studies: Problems in Reflective Thinking and Social Understanding* (2nd ed.) (New York: Harper & Row, 1968).

60. Donald W. Oliver and James P. Shaver, *Teaching Public Issues in the High School* (Logan: Utah State University Press, 1974).

61. Fred M. Newmann, *Education for Citizen Action* (Berkeley, Calif.: McCutchan, 1975); F. Clark Power, Ann Higgins, and Lawrence Kohlberg, *Lawrence Kohlberg's Approach to Moral Education* (New York: Columbia University Press, 1989).

210 DEMOCRACY, EDUCATION, AND THE SCHOOLS

. See my "The Standards Are Coming," *Educational Leadership,* 1994, *51*(5), 84–85.

. See Jack L. Nelson's critique of the periodic "zeal of otherwise disinterested historians and social scientists" in his "Charting a Course Backwards," *Social Education,* 1990, *54*(7), 434–437.

. Hans-George Gadamer, "The Problem of Historical Consciousness," in *Interpretive Social Science: A Reader,* edited by P. Rabinow and W. M. Sullivan (Berkeley: University of California Press, 1979).

. John Dewey, *Logic: The Theory of Inquiry* (New York: Holt, 1939), p. 498.

Oratory, Democracy, and the Classroom

John Angus Campbell

For democracy in the classroom to be a reality, it must rest on robust, sustained practice. As a practice, democracy is not a matter of affirmation only—whether on the part of educators or of students. Democracy is most secure when the art required for its foundation has become second nature, when its truths seem self-evident because they are grounded in the daily experience of a whole community and do not rest on the opinions of select individuals, however articulate or correct. At first glance, the inequality in power and knowledge between instructor and students makes "democracy in the classroom" sound like an oxymoron; but inequalities in knowledge and power are a fact in any real democracy and the classroom is but one arena where democratic practice must struggle to find expression under local constraints.

Establishing democracy in the classroom is particularly urgent in our time because of the challenge posed to democratic order by the information age. What possible meaning can there be in training students to exercise choice and to examine and criticize alternatives when the choices in today's world are increasingly technical and require experts to explain them? The inequalities between teacher and student in the classroom, far from making the classroom unrealistic, faithfully mirror the conditions of postmodern life and the challenges to democratic practice that it poses. Previous chapters have discussed various general and many particular conditions necessary for democracy in the classroom.

In this chapter, I argue that while the contemporary challenges facing democratic educators are distinct in form, they are not new in principle. To meet these challenges, I recommend a particular model of democratic practice based on the ancient art of rhetoric—the civic language of democratic order and the embodiment of democratic epistemology.

The Art of Rhetoric and
the Ground of Democratic Practice

The tension between the commonsense knowledge of the many and the expert knowledge of the few is a cognitive fault line running through western education.[1] The periodic shiftings along this venerable fissure continue to reverberate in the academy and in the larger culture.[2] The recent defeat of the super collider, for example, has been termed "the revenge of the 'C' students." Yet, one might wonder in what subject the grade was given and to which students the remark referred. Were the "C" students the legislators who failed to grasp the national interest in physics, or were they the physicists who failed to adapt their argument to a popular forum?

The clash between the orators and the philosophers, between the ideals of education rooted in common sense (*phronesis*) and the thought of the many and the educational and cultural ideals rooted in precise knowledge and the expertise of the few, is epitomized by the terms "rhetoric" and "episteme" (science, or broadly, "expertise").[3] Not only do these terms designate different approaches to knowledge, but they are themselves the fruit of a dispute over the proper aims and ideals of education and its relation to culture.[4]

The democratic roots of rhetoric can be traced, for heuristic purposes, to the very first syllable of the term.[5] "Rhe" is a Greek root that means "to say" or to engage in "logos" or discourse. It carries the connotation of fullness.[6] "Rhe" implies an inclusive and popular speech in which the substance of what is said is inseparable from the form. If, for instance, one has said, "It was big," one has communicated an intelligible attribute of something; but if one has said, "It was BIIIG!" one has said much more.[7]

The fullness or amplitude of speaking suggested by "rhe" is given specificity by the second syllable. "Tor" is the *nomen agentis* or agent of the word.[8] "Tor" occurs in such words as the various forms of the word "history": '*istoria,* '*istorikos,* '*istorein,* '*istor.* By the same token that a *histor* adjudicates differences in accounts of events from various sources, so a *rhetor* speaks forth or orates possible lines of argument.[9] The "speaking forth" one would expect of an "orator" in ancient Greek, as in modern English, suggests a broad flexibility that can be spacious or concise as circumstances require, always assuming an audience of the many and always requiring the exercise of judgment on the part of the speaker.

The earliest use of the term *rhetoria* (as a noun) is in Isocrates' essay *Against the Sophists* and occurs in his defense of an educational program centered in oratory:

> Those who desire to follow the true precepts of this discipline may, if they will, be helped more speedily towards honesty of character than towards facility in oratory [*pros rhetoreian*]. And let no one suppose that I claim that just living can be taught; for in a word, I hold that there does not exist an art [*techne*] of the kind which can implant sobriety and justice in depraved natures. Nevertheless, I do think the study of political discourse can help more than any other to stimulate and form such qualities of character.[10]

Isocrates may have had high ethical standards in his school of oratory, but his modesty, a modesty founded in realism, about the capacity of his art—or any art—to make a *techne* of virtue or practical wisdom, left his program vulnerable to attack. The specific greatness of Isocrates' conception of oratory, as revealed in this passage, is the training it provides in how to deliberate on political questions and how to act and speak.[11] Indeed, as Harry Hubbell points out, "It is this insistence on the value of a general education [provided by his oratorical program] which makes Isocrates the successor of the sophists of the fifth century."[12]

With the addition of the suffix "*ic*" to "*rhe*" and "*tor,*" philology takes a nasty turn. Edward Schiappa has pointed out that the word *rhetorik* (our term "rhetoric"), the technical term for the study of speeches and speech making, was almost certainly the invention of the archenemy of oratory and its program of education in practical reason: Plato.[13] Schiappa notes, "Plato was a prolific coiner of words ending with -*ike*, denoting 'art of'." Such terms were central to Plato's project of inventing a proper philosophic vocabulary and are particularly evident in his "analysis of the relationship between *techne* and *episteme*—art or skill and knowledge." "Ike" terms occur by the dozens in *Gorgias, Euthydemus*, and *Sophist*, and Schiappa observes that Plato was particularly keen on coining "ike" terms for the verbal arts: "Words like eristic (*eristike*), dialectic (*dialectike*), and antilogic (*antilogike*) all originated in Plato's writings."[14] The effect of the suffix "ic" is to make the adjective into a noun. When, with Plato, the implied noun is a "*techne*" such as analytics, dialectics, poetic, or politics, we get as many "arts" as there are descriptive terms.[15]

The advantage for Plato in being able to define Isocrates' art is unmistakable. Schiappa makes the point exactly: "If Plato could identify the 'product' of his rival Isocrates' training as something unnecessary or undesirable, so much the better for the reputation of Plato's school. Gorgias, it should be remembered, was the teacher of Isocrates, hence a dialogue on public discourse titled *Gorgias* that included thinly veiled references to Isocrates would easily have been recognized in the fourth century as an attack on the training afforded by Isocrates."[16]

Rather than destroying Isocrates' "art," Plato provided the perfect term to thematize it and then granted this art such meager legitimacy as to perpetually marginalize its practitioners.[17] Though orators and the teachers of oratory have usually found ready employment over the centuries (as advisors to princes, or as teachers of composition as well as of speech) and materially have probably fared better than philosophers, the Isocratic ideal of practical reason has never enjoyed the prestige of theoretic reason.[18] Even Aristotle, who as philosophers go may be regarded as the best friend rhetoric ever had, exacts a high price for philosophically domesticating the practical reason of the orators. Though his definition of rhetoric—"the faculty of discovering the possible means of persuasion in reference to any subject whatever"[19]—is in its way magnificent, finding subject matter (what the later tradition called "invention") is only part of the practical reason of the public speaker.[20] The difference between the Aristotelian contemplative classification of kinds of proof and the performance- and speech-based Isocratic view of practical reason is well captured in John Poulakos' sophistic definition of rhetoric: "the art which seeks to capture in opportune moments that which is appropriate and attempts to suggest that which is possible."[21] An orator must do more than think logically. An orator must make practical judgments on the spot—including when to modify or abandon a prepared speech or when to remain silent.[22]

The derivation of the term "rhetoric" and the pedagogic spite that motivated its differentiation from "episteme," or exact knowledge, is of more than antiquarian interest.[23] Through varying pathways, including its positivistic incubation in the German universities of the nineteenth century, the Platonic/Aristotelian ideal of "episteme," coupled with the increasingly technological character of society, has made contemporary education, particularly contemporary higher education, an increasingly specialized affair.[24] In the absence of any common language, method, or informing ideal, exposure to "disciplinary" learning has effects upon undergraduates that are, alternatively and depending on one's frame of mind, sad and amusing.

In all too many of the classes a student in a modern university attends (especially in a large modern state university), there is an implicit assumption—sometimes made explicit—that the broader world of experience is to be seen through the terminology and methodology of that subject. In the absence of an opportunity to develop true expertise in the relevant discipline, students who pay (or whose parents pay) large sums of money to gain an education develop a peculiarly "schooled" form of "common sense." When asked a question by an instructor, they do not trust their own native notions of what seems probable or likely—but use the special language of the discipline or method to give the answer they think the instructor wants. After only a quarter or a semester or two of this "higher education," and whatever its actual contribution to a student's learning, students become cagey. The defining mark of the cagey student is that she does not really use her own resources when addressing a question, but tries to repeat the "right answer" from the book or from something that the professor said earlier.

Any competent educator is familiar with caginess and, out of self-defense, has become cagey herself. Though the particular approach will vary with the discipline, the generic tactic of the cagey educator is to tempt the student into thinking, usually through a practical and certainly concrete example, and then to demonstrate (when it works) that the student really does understand. When instructors do this, they are starting down (or rather up) the path that leads back to the ideals of oratorical education exemplified by Isocrates. Isocrates, in contrast to Plato (as readers of this book are no doubt aware), grounded education in *phronesis,* or "common sense," as opposed to *episteme,* or roughly "science." My argument in this chapter is not that we should select one over the other, but that we need to reintegrate the two branches of our common educational tradition. To do this we need to rediscover in the midst of our current practice and theory the fork where what once were parallel grooves in the path to knowledge diverged into separate roads traveling across the fields of hostile neighbors.[25]

Though he does not link his program to Isocrates and the tradition of oratorical education, Charles Anderson has recently offered a radical assessment of the ills of the contemporary university and a remarkably cogent plan for their remedy. Anderson's *Prescribing the Life of the Mind: An Essay on the Purpose of the University, the Aims of Liberal Education, the Competence of Citizens, and the Cultivation of Practical Reason* paints a picture of the excessive and divisive attention to theory on the part of academic enterprises and prescribes close attention to practice as an antidote.[26] Following his own advice, Anderson moves beyond critique to offer five positive and concrete steps for educators to follow in nurturing their students' intelligence by drawing their attention to practice:

1. *Mastery:* leading from what is received, teaching positively and without apology the "right way" to do things
2. *Critical reason:* critique of one's own practice and that of others, of the received enterprise, and of the limits of one's own vision
3. *The arts of judgment:* experiencing the relativizing moment, the confrontation with inconvenient facts and/or incommensurable views within the enterprise
4. *Creativity:* realizing how little creativity is a matter of inspiration and how much a matter of judgment—a defiance equally of the rules (sheer mastery) and of those who oppose the enterprise in principle (sheer criticism)

5. *Transcendence:* the opening of new horizons for reflection and practice by genuinely moving beyond what experience has shown to be unworkable.[27]

In Anderson's account, it is attention to method, to theory, and to the "hard and fast rules" (or in the humanities, to a nihilistic joy in not finding them) that is vitiating the telos of reason in the contemporary academy. This chapter aims to advance Anderson's project by underscoring a precondition for its success—democracy in the classroom—and by providing a practical example of democracy in action. As Anderson's proposal reflects his own discipline of political science, I will explore a complementary paradigm from an entry-level course in my own field—the site where the dispute between the orators and the philosophers (the advocates of *phronesis* and *episteme*) began—a class in public speaking.

Democratic Community: The Condition of Practical Reason

Despite his many transgressions against the knowledge claims of the orators, Plato never more clearly recognized the organic connection between speech and thought than in his critique of writing in the interview between Pharaoh and the god Theuth in his dialogue *Phaedrus.* In this myth, when Theuth praised writing while extolling his many gifts to humanity, Pharaoh warned that writing would not make anyone more intelligent but would make readers seem to know things they did not understand.[28] Pharaoh's prophecy has been fulfilled in the caginess of students in the modern university. The defect, however, is not in reading or writing themselves, but in reading as a solitary self. When reading is in the service of an interpreting community and is not done in social or intellectual isolation, then reading becomes intelligent, for it becomes an active and articulate mediation between common sense and expertise. A community of peers—a pedagogic *polis,* if you will—supplies the necessary condition for making reading social and intelligent, and thus an engine capable of driving Anderson's five-part telos of the mind. Within community, practical intelligence has an object and an occasion; without community, theoretic intelligence is stillborn.

Mastery: The Telos of Community

Anderson's aim to teach the "right way" to do something may sound authoritarian, but reflection shows it is radically democratic in that it clearly and explicitly distinguishes practices that will work from those that will not, thus making an appeal not to the authority of the professor but to the authority of the discourse community of which the professor—and by increasing degrees, the students—are members. Helping students to understand why "x" rules are standards for the relevant community and how the community forms the rules into a hierarchy is vital to democratic education, for it is through this process that the teacher prepares the student for full citizenship, as it were, in the domain of discourse under examination. While of course there is a difference in "power" in the relation of the professor to the students, this difference is trivial and irrelevant. The issue is not the "power" of the professor and the "powerlessness" of the student but the empowerment of both student and professor through their mutual demonstration of discursive competence. Teaching the "right way" is not authoritarian, for experience—in any domain—is spontaneously hierarchical.[29] Reflection on experience empowers students because it enables them to grasp the hierarchy of rules in its lair—in the living act of increasing mastery of a discipline—and to avoid the autistic path of *episteme*, which predictably degenerates into the students' passively taking down the *dicta* of the professor. The classroom is never more democratic than when students and instructor stand on equal footing, though on different rungs of the ladder of mastery, before the common rules of the craft. If one aims to follow the radically democratic path of traditional oratory and integrate theory with practice, one must transform one's classroom into a civic forum in which it is possible to consider the regularities of common experience and invite one's students to turn its lessons into rules.

The task of the public speaking teacher—and of all practical Isocratic educators in whatever field—is the reclamation of intelligence. To reclaim intelligence, one must transform caginess back into real common sense and from there tempt common sense to betray itself by committing acts of intelligence. Once common sense has revealed the intelligence of the student, one must confront the student publicly with the incriminating facts and get her to take responsibility for the consequences.

Two elements are useful here: a sense of the concrete and a sense of play.

Early in my own course, usually on the second day (after I have sketched the assignments and set forth the emphasis on persuasive speeches on controversial subjects), I have the students sit in a circle. Each student is to say something about what has brought them to the class, what topics they would be interested in hearing about, and what topics they themselves are considering speaking about. The aim of the exercise is not to break the ice (though it does) but to begin to establish a specific reference for later discussions of rhetorical strategy and audience adaptation. Subsequent and "prescriptive" discussions of the right way are to have reference to the site of application. This exercise establishes a prior and shared experience of reality as the ground against which questions about message design and persuasive strategy are to be seen. "What would work?" or "How would that apply?" are questions that always have some concrete audience—this class or some other group in some setting with which the student is familiar—as their focus.

Play is a necessary ingredient in a public speaking class, and I should hope in other courses as well, in that it is an antidote to the single greatest killer of intelligence in universities—baseless, unreasoning seriousness. Without a sense of the ridiculous, true seriousness is impossible, for perspective is impossible. It is partly for this reason that occasional brief rounds of impromptu speeches are a staple of most speech classes. Each student brings a topic that asks for an attitude toward a current event or controversy or that requires a moral choice. The topics are placed in a hat and each student picks one and delivers a minute or two-minute address, sits down, and the next student does the same. (I pick one and give an impromptu speech myself.) At the end of the speeches we reflect on our individual and collective experience.

Three things are particularly remarkable in this exercise. First, the speeches move most students beyond fear and self-consciousness and cause them to glimpse their possible future mastery in prepared speeches. Second, everyone has an observation. Third, in the course of reflection many pointers or "rules of thumb" about public speaking emerge.

The common discovery of rules is of particular interest, because since the rules emerge from experience, they show that the source of the rules of the speaker's art is the practice of public speaking. Further, since the teacher facilitates the discovery of these rules, the ground for her authority is not in the institution or in her degree but in her own mastery. There is an additional important point here. It is notorious that rhetoric in general and public speaking in particular are relativistic enterprises. (Indeed, I have a law I call *Campbell's first law:* there is no formula for success in public speaking that will not serve equally well, in some other circumstance, as a recipe for disaster.) And yet, within any particular situation there are only a very limited number of possibilities for message design. It is a paradox of public speaking—real to a logician, merely apparent to a rhetorician—that an instructor in public speaking at one and the same time is teaching respect for rules and a readiness to set them aside. This is why classical oratory, and its successor, the modern class in public speaking, is the wellspring of the liberal arts. Public speaking is the supreme and original site at which one learns the delicate art of judgment—of recognizing and negotiating the necessary tension between opposite and inescapable demands of living. The ability to engage the student in critical reflection about common rhetorical situations based on a small number of rules and abstract models distinguishes the teacher from the apprentice—and the serious teacher from the hack.

When students become dependent on rules, they want more. In oratory the situations are so diverse and particular, the rules would soon outstrip the art and even then would never succeed in explaining it. To teach public speaking well one must teach it as a way of thinking. Quintilian demonstrated keen sensitivity to oratory as thought in the artful way he gave instruction in that part of the art which most lends itself to schematic formulation—the topics. As Mike Leff notes, Quintilian "disclaims any intention to devise a fully rigorous and exhaustive topical system."[30] Quintilian's reason, Leff observes, could not be clearer: "In practical situations the arguer does not have time to run through a long list of topics until he discovers the one that fits the particular situation." Most tellingly of all, "Mere rules do not produce eloquence, and to possess nothing more than knowledge of a system of topics is to possess a dumb science (*mutam scientiam*)."[31] Quintilian's whole point is not to get the student to memorize a system (which the student would certainly do if given one), but to train his mind—which is something quite different.[32] While of course a teacher must provide elementary guidelines, it is even more important that one teach students the capacity to generate rules as rules are needed or to recognize them when they are emergent in rhetorical situations. Rules accepted on faith produce wooden speeches—and worse, a wooden and gimmicky understanding of the art. The fun happens when mind happens, when students use rules as initial guidelines to the right way and then, through the arduous discipline of judging the particulars of their own cases, transcend them. If in the elementary exercises students recognize their own innate abilities, they lay a foundation for understanding the later assignments—and larger situations beyond the classroom—as equally rhetorical problems to be addressed. In grasping the nature of what Edwin Black calls "rhetorical questions,"[33] students cross the line, almost without knowing it, between oratorical practice and rhetorical theory.

Once democratic practice has brought out intelligence, intelligence in turn requires varied yet exacting standards of rigor. If one has led one's class to advert to the standards immanent in practice, one is in a position to teach the "right way"—even within the changes and chances of emergent situations—with authority and without apology. The rules and the "right way" now emerge with the authority of the instructor's mastery as confirmed by the student's own lived experience and maturing capacity for judgment.

Democratic Community: The Condition of Critical Reason

Critical reason in the speech class typically emerges in three forms. First, of course, there is the critical reasoning present in the arguments of the student speeches; second, there is the critical response to the subject spoken about by the class *qua* audience; and third, there is the critique of presentational form: strategy, message design, adequacy of evidence, audience adaptation, and delivery.

For critique to be worthwhile, a real speech needs to have been given in the first place. A real speech is not "an essay on its hind legs"—a well-organized and adequately researched presentation on some subject. A real speech is an expression of concern in which the student's common sense has been informed by appropriate evidence, fact, and opinion—and *vice versa*. A real speech is equally a presentation in which appropriate evidence, fact, and opinion have been ordered by the student's common sense. A speech class can only perform its Isocratic function of training minds to act effectively in the world of opinion and practical affairs if it becomes a real forum—a forum in which real speeches are heard and examined critically.

The greatest challenge the speech teacher faces in encouraging students to give real speeches is negotiating the celebrated western "subject/object" split. While the most recent sponsor of this split, the philosophy of academic positivism, has been roundly rebutted, the split itself is kept in place by the strong, ingrained pedagogic practices that require students to be alienated from their sense of reality in order to pass courses in particular "disciplines." Under these circumstances, the "benefits" of "higher education" are frequently indistinguishable from injuries.

For example: The first round of persuasive speeches is in progress. Over a course of days, the speeches have displayed the usual range of seemingly benign imperfections. Here is a speech with no point; here is another with twelve! Here is a speech crammed with technical evidence incomprehensible to the audience. Here is a light speech backed with little thought and no research. Here is an adequate speech, if one could listen to it, but that is all but impossible because of the speaker's odd dexterity in jingling change, chewing gum, and talking all at once. Here is a speech that is being read. Here is a speech so obviously memorized that the speaker looks out at the class as though his body had been snatched by space aliens.

Then there emerges a paradigm speech—a speech that captures the essential something missing that is difficult to detect amongst the various strengths and weaknesses of the others. Here is a speech that so literally fulfills the technical letter of the assignment for organization, research, outline, proof, and adequacy of presentation while so totally, and with such consistent fidelity to principle, violating its spirit that even a professor of rhetoric must pause in reverence before the absolute.

An instructor's best gift at this moment is her silence. She should allow the class discussion of the substance of the message to proceed as normal, signal the transition to critique of presentational form, and wait for someone to ask the one question on which the fate of the entire course—indeed of a liberal education—hinges. Someone almost always will. A hand will be raised and someone will ask, "And why did you speak on this subject?" Out of dozens of such moments during many classes over many years, one moment in particular stands out. A young woman had just given a perfect "look-at-the-neatly-labeled-dead-butterflies-under-the-glass-case" speech on the subject of drug abuse in high schools. Another student had just posed the fateful question. With a clear and unmistakable authority—indeed, as though it were the voice of another person—the student responded: "Because my best friend died of an overdose during our junior year." The effect of this remark on the class was, of course, electric, but its main effect was on the speaker. The student then proceeded to pour out details about the impact of this experience on her and its urgency for others with brothers or sisters still in high school. The logic of this second speech was sharp, the evidence at once personal yet public. What before had been at best adequate content and "correct" delivery was now transformed into brilliance as the student spoke with feeling, emphasis, tone, movement, and commanding presence. Brief as it was, this second and real speech was nothing short of a rhetorical ressurection. Seeing a lifeless body rise to an occasion never ceases to impress a class, though to a speech teacher (and contrary to much in the art that holds only for the most part) it is the apodictically certain result of right reason—the recovery of *phronesis*. The answer to the follow-up question (and there always is one), "Why didn't you include that in the speech?" was equally revealing—and though I hear this answer often, it is always shocking. With complete candor and naivete she said, "Because I did not think it was relevant." If any one statement is a damning indictment of what a university "education" does to a young person's mind and illustrates the intellectual integrity and urgency of the Isocratic alternative, this is it.

With the advent of even a single real speech such as this brief second speech, insight and critique now have a presence in the classroom and will begin their transformative work. Experience has spoken with the authority of a Columbus. A public continent of meaning has been discovered that is (oddly) inaccessible to "disciplined" reason. Yet, anyone who has an arguable thesis will discover this continent if she will head west, stay on course, resist the temptation to turn back, trust the trade winds, and ride that inner gulf stream peculiar to each yet common to all.

The class is now in a position to understand what before they could only have heard (and probably did) but could not comprehend. Kierkegaard aptly phrased the decisive moment in the recovery of truly critical reason that should be the epistemic motto for every contemporary Isocratic educator: authentic subjectivity is objectivity.[34] In *Postscript*, Kierkegaard's Johannes Climacus says, "It is commonly assumed that no art or skill is required in order to be subjective."[35] The problem, he goes on, is in the failure to distinguish between being a subject "in the proper sense" and "a bit of a subject" or a subject "so called." The "so called" subject—our "cagey student"—can receive sense impressions and mouth approved platitudes, and even give speeches that seem to fulfill the letter of the assignments. The shift to authentic subjectivity requires more than serving time; it requires catching on. Authentic public speaking (certainly in our highly technical age) may require nascent expertise—at the very least, careful research, a feel for the subject, and appropriate conceptual rigor. It almost never involves the stereotypically romantic (and I suspect sometimes well rehearsed) throwing aside of one's "prepared" speech to give a few words directly from one's heart! The peculiar rigor of authentic subjectivity, however, is grounded in a principled and uncompromising repudiation of the false rigor of mere academic (that is, epistemically induced) *rigor mortis* and in its place offers a ringing affirmation—"ringing" because truth is striking when incarnate—of the personal meaning and social urgency of what is being said.

In Anderson's terms, with the advent of the objectivity that is authentic subjectivity, the received enterprise has been relativized. The limits of a previous vision of the nature of public speaking have now been transcended and a new horizon of practice—demanding yet achievable—emerges into view. With the advent of authentic speaking, and as circumstances and cases require, the instructor can move back and forth between considering the adequacy of reasoning or presentational form, or technical rhetorical mastery, and discussion of "substance"—the unity of form and content that is what the speech is about.

Democratic Community and the Arts of Judgment: Experiencing the Relativizing Moment

In one sense, "experiencing the relativizing moment" is the norm in a speech class—since everything discussed is debatable. One might suppose that prolonged exposure to a steady succession of relativizing moments would produce a profound and indeed cynical relativism in students. As Darwin has taught us, given sufficient variation, world enough, and time, anything imaginable could happen, and probably has. In this spirit, any speech teacher can tell us that Plato's *Gorgias* is not entirely a fiction. There really are Poluses who major in speech. Worse, there are Callicleses who not only majored in speech but went on to careers of distinguished venality. But what of it?

A colleague of mine in philosophy told of an ethics course he taught, and recounted his shock when years later he read in the paper that one of the students in that class had become a criminal. If the examples of virtuous orators recommended by Isocrates to his students are not always sufficient to make a student of oratory virtuous, the knowledge taught by philosophy is no better. Socrates is no more to blame for the occasional ethically failed philosophy student than is Gorgias—or by implication Isocrates—for Callicles.

When we move beyond what rarely happens to what usually happens, we discover that there are ethical norms intrinsic to the art of speech that usually or for the most part foster the development of a deliberating community capable of self-restraint. Indeed, though he was careful in asserting it, Isocrates was correct that oratory—even political oratory—is capable of offering models for the formation of moral character. From the standpoint of the ethical culture of oratory, what is unreal in Plato is his embarrassment in the presence of history, his fear that the inevitable singularities and indeterminacies of ordinary life—especially as revealed in the public life of the mind—will lead to the abandonment of personal and civic virtue. It is the indeterminacies of common life that create the possibility of personal and civic virtue—for it is here that judgment must be trained and exercised.

To appreciate the redemptive quality of the relativizing moment as it emerges in the speech class and how it enables rather than defeats practical reason and civic virtue, it is important to recontextualize Plato's destructive critique of Isocrates' educational program.

Central to the way in which Plato's Socrates misformulated rhetorical relativism and thereby discredited the teachers of oratory is what Steve Fuller has called the Socratic Conflation—the confusion of sophistic relativism with antirealism.[36] Protagoras' maxim, "man is the measure of all things," of which Callicles presents a caricature, need not "mean the solipsistic individual, who is a standard unto himself. . . . *Anthropos* in its original Sophistic use referred to the 'average man' in a community, in terms of whose standards one could tell whether one was in the right or the wrong. . . . Socrates obscured for future generations the possibility that relativism might be aligned with realism—that there might be spatiotemporally indexed 'facts of the matter.'"[37] There is an enormous difference between Callicles' cynicism and the deference to local standards implied in Protagoras' counsel to, when in Athens, do as the Athenians do. This issue of the existence of particular facts—moral as well as epistemological—that are binding, real, yet not universal, is central to properly framing the relativizing moment as it emerges in the speech class. It is equally central to understanding how oratorical education negotiates in the name of virtue and reason the confrontation with inconvenient facts or incommensurable views within the enterprise of practical reason.

The speech class is essentially a deliberating community. Much of its discussion concerns what Eugene Garver has called "essentially contested concepts."[38] That there is no single right answer to these concepts, at least none to which the community can permanently agree, does not mean that discussion is pointless—let alone an invitation to nihilism. What emerges in a deliberating community through common concern about issues is a common concern to resolve them at least temporarily, with minimum friction and with mutual respect. In the course of deliberation, speakers and audiences switch roles, and alliances between persons and issues are made and renegotiated. In a deliberating community, persuasive speeches and arguments do not address merely fixed attitudes. Some of the most important attitudes emerge in the course of discussion. The ability to deliberate—to continue moving talk in productive ways and attitudes in new directions—is both a civic skill and, in an open society, a moral virtue.[39] In this sense Isocrates was more right than he dared to admit—to teach public speaking is, in fact, to teach civic virtue. Indeed, it is to teach the architectonic virtue on which the vitality of all other virtues depends.

The experience of shared concern produced by the process of deliberation radically recontextualizes the confrontation with inconvenient facts or incommensurate views of the enterprise spoken of by Anderson, for it places them within a context of what Ralph Dahrendorf has called "warm" as opposed to "cold" liberalism.[40] Liberalism is "cold" when it places individual liberty above all else and inevitably weakens the collective—and coercive—values of tradition and its "warm" positive community. The coolness of liberal institutions is congenital, for their very ground is purely negative. Liberalism affirms one's right to be different, but it has no informing vision of how to be (other than, of course, being "oneself," which may be the problem, and being tolerant—the need for which would hardly arise if everyone were "liberal.") Who I am is at once a gift, a choice, a destiny, and a highly ambiguous work of art, and "tolerance" is a mixer, not something taken "neat." It is because I am someone—a Jew, a Buddhist, a Mohammaden, a secularist, or a Christian—that I must be tolerant, and thus "tolerance" is a necessary solvent and necessarily a weak cement.

"Warm" institutions, by contrast, create community, but at the cost of imposing limits on individual self-expression for the sake of collective identity, memory, hope, tradition, and the common good. The deliberating community of the speech class is not a medium between these extremes, but negotiates the tension between the opposite pulls of "cold" negative freedom and "warm" intimate community. In providing a place where individuals have a name and a reputation and will be listened to with respect, the speech class provides—at least for the time of the class—a sense of public identity and rootedness within a common deliberative enterprise. In its relative communal warmth—relative to other university courses—the speech class momentarily checks the empty and negative liberal freedom merely to be different by requiring individuals to explain themselves in ways others can understand. By placing the vagaries of individual choice and difference under the norms of communal judgment—backed only by the persuasive power of opinion—the public speaking class facilitates the possibility of a liberal education by reinventing civility.

By placing the shock of the relative into the "warm" but critical context of a deliberating community, the speech class makes possible the local and temporary resolution of issues that otherwise would defy decision in an absolute sense. There is nothing value neutral or spectatorish about this process, and its partisan, or multipartisan, spirit is among its greatest gifts to rigorous mental discipline. Speech education defies the ethos of education that gives pride of place to mere anemic expertise, for it seeks through deliberation to remedy the silence that is the inevitable product of *episteme's* pedagogy of estrangement and intimidation. Where the "common sense" of a class has indeed been reclaimed, and the class has developed a public opinion of its own, "reason" becomes particular, nuanced, and often very precisely adapted to its circumstances. What a speech teacher witnesses in the classroom, particularly in the final round of presentations (indeed, this is one of the chief joys and privileges of the profession) is a community, aware of itself as a community, making up its mind. Increasingly one finds speeches that manifest better general research in the library sense, but also better use of the particular resources unique to the speakers' local public. Above all, one sees young men and women—who have no intention of being "eloquent"—realize aspects of their potential as reflective, engaged, articulate, and *effective* human beings.

The relativizing moment in the speech class, and how it invites and hones the arts of judgment, is found not only in the "essentially contested" nature of the subjects discussed and in the need to make observations in a manner that is timely and appropriate, but in the very "rules" of the art of speaking. To find Anderson's "incommensurable views of the enterprise" in rhetoric and oratory, one need look no further than the enterprise itself. The rules of public speaking are a series of situated maxims.

Kierkegaard's story of the man who escaped from a mental institution and resolved that to evade detection he would repeat one thing that was certainly true is a good case in point. It did not require too many repetitions of "the world is certainly round" for people to recognize he was not quite right in the head.[41] In the spirit of this example, the rules of rhetoric work fine so long as you have what cannot be subject to a rule—the judgment that lets you know how to apply them. Francis Bacon put this point aptly: "The better sort of rules have been not unfitly compared to glasses of steel unpolished, where you may see the images of things, but first they must be filed: so the rules will help, if they be laboured and polished by practice."[42]

In its demand for judgment trained through practice, rhetoric is not entirely singular. It is notorious that genius in any subject is above the rules—and the few true masters of any art, indeed even of most rigorous sciences, feign the rules to cover their art. In this they win the uncritical admiration of the many in their disciplines who are deceived by their apparent rigor. By the same token, they win the discerning applause of the few who are deceived with their eyes open. The *cognoscenti* in any field see the feigning and celebrate it as the secret of the art that the uninitiated think was produced only by knowledge of the rule. Thus it follows that one does not always begin a speech with a joke; one does not always begin a speech with a startling statement. The best way to begin a speech is with an act of judgment about the best way to begin this speech before this audience on this occasion.

The situated character of oratorical art does not mean that "rhetoric" is a "point no point" the content of which vanishes the closer one approaches. Rather it means that the point only emerges through participation in the life of a community and that "teaching" this civil and civilizing art epistemologically as well as pedagogically is inherently temporal, social, democratic, and moral. It is temporal because it emphasizes the imperative of action over thought; it is social because it is done only in the context of a specific culture or tradition; it is democratic because it shapes material, premises, maxims, and facts that are common. It is at once moral and political because it reclaims the individual as a constitutive voice in sustaining community. It is teachable, despite its modesty of fixed rules, because human beings learn in some of the most exacting senses through a complex process of imitation that does not rely on exact propositions. This brings us to the creative core of the enterprise of oratorical/rhetorical education.

Creativity As Applied Judgment

In the public speaking class, true creativity is rarely manifest by loosening the constraints that give the assignments their integrity. Real speeches in the various forums in which they appear in society—and many of these are connected with work—are, like the assignments in class, highly stylized. That is, the constraints or decorum of the situation require that a presentation be of a certain type, be given in a certain manner, and be of a certain length. True creativity in public speaking occurs within the constraints of such conventions. While people joke—often with considerable justification—about the difference between "the real world" and "the university," in the speech class this distinction is—or ought to be—minimal. The speech class is primarily a forum, and in being a forum it prepares students to participate effectively in other forums—whether within the university or beyond it.

Students who deliberately set out to do something "creative" almost always end up wanting the constraints that facilitate creativity removed. True creativity is only possible where constraints provide boundary conditions. I learned the creative necessity of constraints—of insisting on respect for the integrity of the class as a forum—early in my career from students whose creative genius at evasion outstripped by far my uncertain grasp of the rationale of my craft. One example will suffice.

In one course, there was a young man who distinguished himself as particularly articulate. He always participated well in class discussions and frequently talked to me after class. Without ever having seen him give a prepared speech, I assumed he really must be a very good speaker. When he came to me before the first presentation, which called for an informative speech, and wanted to modify the assignment, I was fully prepared to grant his request. He wanted to give a speech on the aerodynamics of kites, and wanted my permission, since he was the first speaker, to arrive early and display various kites from the ceiling. That sounded fine. However, he then wanted to wear a costume and give the speech as "Kite Man." I thought, "Oh hell, why not?" and told him to go ahead. The speech was just fine—entertaining as well as informative. He even heightened the dramatic effect by hiding behind the door and just at the point when his classmates thought he was not going to show he burst out at them in this elaborate kite outfit. As I recall, he even wore a tail.

The speech was well received. I gave him an "A." I came away with the nagging feeling that I had been had, but could not quite say why. Before the second speech—our first persuasive presentation—he came to me again, wanting the class to be a particular kind of audience and himself to be a particular kind of speaker. Though I cannot now remember the details, the situation he described was interesting and I thought there would be some value in letting him go ahead. Again, the speech was very good, but this time my uneasy feeling burst through to me with its name. This fellow was using the course as a place to perfect his skills as an actor. When he came to me before the third speech with a similar creative modification of the assignment, I said no. The results were, at last, truly instructive. His speech was adequate, but scarcely more than a "C." This young man had an enormously difficult time addressing the class as himself and in treating the class as an actual audience with whom he shared common interests! While he had done an adequate amount of research on his subject, when it came to thinking oratorically—drawing on his own resources and making use of the resources of the attitudes of his classmates to develop his subject—he was at a loss. As long as he was dealing with imaginary situations he was fine; but when it came to giving a real speech, as himself, before a real audience—this fellow needed a course in public speaking. With two assignments yet to go, at last I recovered my senses and proceeded to give him one.

In my current course, I use a combination of lecture and practical exercises to underscore the possibilities of creativity when directed toward making appropriate judgments within the constraints of real situations. In introducing the persuasive speaking assignment, I offer a visual diagram to illustrate the meaning of Aristotle's definition of rhetoric. Having explained that the intellectual aim of a persuasive speech is not persuasion absolutely but the discovery of the means of persuasion particular to the case, I draw a large yin/yang symbol on the board. I point out that the yin and the yang are united by a shared tension. I make the connection with Aristotle's definition of rhetoric by pointing out the two islands of identity floating in a sea of difference. "These two points—the white within the black and the black within the white are what you are looking for. Find the point of agreement, however small, between you and your opponent and you are thinking rhetorically."

I then quickly poll the class for current topics that divide them. Once these are discovered, I set "pro" and "con" teams of two students each conferring with their partners to build their respective cases. As I set them off to do their work, I give the assignment a special twist that distinguishes it from debate. "Each team is to argue its own side of the case, but from the standpoint of the values and ideals of the team on the other side. The idea is not to show the other side up, but to win them over." What eventuates from this exercise is not so much a debate—though there are moments that are certainly that—but intense public deliberation. One way of viewing the aim of the assignment is to see it as creating the conditions for persuasion by initiating a debate within the mind of the opposition. I never fail to be struck with the way this exercise underscores the peculiar objectivity of oratorical reason. Though the responses may vary to such questions as "Should women soldiers be allowed in combat?" or "Should we support 'three strikes and you're out' for violent crimes?" there are clearly "right" and "wrong" ways of framing each side of these issues. When a team examining the first question (particularly but not necessarily a team of men) or a situationally insensitive individual of either sex offers a paternalistic argument—the individual inevitably is booed, particularly by the women in the class. When anyone on any issue says something that rings false or, conversely, makes a point that is telling—there is always immediate audience response. This exercise illustrates with remarkable precision that rhetorical questions can be as intellectually demanding as questions in mathematics or chemistry and—in their different settings—can have comparably exacting answers.

"Creative genius" is sometimes displayed in this assignment, but it always emerges as a refinement of practice within the tight constraints of convention. Creativity emerges as a well-placed appeal or well-conducted line of questioning. Those who internalize the point of the exercise and take it as a guide to thinking through the rhetorical problems posed by the topics they have selected for their formal speeches often provide memorable examples of creativity as applied judgment. One case was particularly remarkable.

Two summers ago in a night class, I had a student from north-ern Idaho whose attitudes toward gun control and various other subjects from crime to sex education were several degrees to the right of what his liberal Seattle audience was prepared for. Mike's speeches could be counted on to elicit animated discussion, for they were always controversial. Though Mike was well informed and his presentations were well researched, his speeches were not well organized; they were always brimming with information, pre-dictably exceeded the time limit, and were not helped by his knack for always leading from the aspect of the case most likely to infu-riate his audience. A week after the yin/yang exercise, Mike was the kick-off speaker for the fourth and final round. With few notes, he faced the class and asked, "How many of you have ever heard of Simon Weisenthal?" After a moment's hesitation several hands went up. He then asked, "What does he do?" One of the students asked, "Isn't he the fellow who hunts Nazis?" "That's right," Mike responded. "Why do you suppose he does it? Do you think he is trying to rehabilitate them?" He paused, looking straight at the class, and said, "He does it for vengeance." Mike then dispensed with the usual deterrence argument and gave a pro capital pun-ishment speech based on the social value of vengeance.

The speech left the class stunned. The ensuing discussion was both hot and cold at the same time. There was heat from the inher-ent interest of the subject and the bold clarity with which Mike had cast his "outrageous" position. The coolness came from a kind of chastenedness that Mike's audience felt in having clearly lost con-trol of the moral ground of the debate. While it is doubtful that any-one was persuaded, it is equally doubtful that anyone could have been no matter what was said. As Aristotle put it, the aim of rhetoric is not, any more than with medicine, health, but to bring the patient as near to health as the situation allows. Here Mike had achieved something almost better than persuasion. He had con-vinced his audience that his position was not grounded in values foreign to their own, but was a legitimate offshoot of the common stock. He effectively repositioned the debate as a disagreement within the values of his audience and not merely (as in his other speeches) as a difference between the audience and a right-wing alien. In his question and answer period, while demonstrating his usual competent command of the relevant sources of information, Mike demonstrated as well an ability to defend himself by inviting his questioners to follow him in consistently thinking through their common values. An additional effect of the speech was that afterwards speaker after speaker got the point and became creative in the same way. With varying degrees of artistry and success, speaker after speaker repositioned his or her knowledge in relation to his or her intelligence. I can never remember a final round that was so consistently a sustained public forum and so little a "class."

Local Knowledge, Imitation, and Transcendence: The Necessary Tension

Even if a speech class reclaims reason, as I have argued it can and does, there is an obvious objection from within the very enterprise I have sketched. By attending so closely to the particular, is it not the case that the class simply teaches its members to speak to themselves? This, unfortunately, is exactly what happens in some instances. I have had students return a quarter or so after a course and say how much they enjoyed the course, but then add that when they tried some of the things that worked in the class, they did not have the same affect in the new situation. While each of us can learn to improve our teaching, it is also the case that, as in this instance, a certain number of our students will only get half the point.

Rhetorical reason has a particular aspect and a universal aspect. The particular aspect looms large, for rhetoric is concerned primarily with specific situations. "How can one move from here to there on this issue in this community in this particular situation?" The answers one generates to questions of this sort are particular in essence and only universal by accident. One discovers the universal within the particular when one reflects on what one is doing when one is solving one's local problem. Kenneth Burke's interpretation of American sociologist and economist Thorstein Veblen's "trained incapacity"[43] well frames the "benefit" obtained by the student of a speech class who—in learning to speak to the audience in front of him—learns only to speak to that particular audience. (This effect also shows that the reclamation of "common sense" is not always to be equated *simpliciter* with the awakening of intelligence.)

Rhetorical reason transcends the particular through reasoning by example and by a much misunderstood process known as "imi-tation." In reasoning by example, rhetoric follows law, or perhaps vice versa. The key is to learn to read experience by figuring out what is to count as similarity and what is to count as difference between one's earlier learning and the case at hand. As Edward Levi notes of law, first one sees similarity, then one determines "the rule of law inherent in the first case . . . ; then the rule of law is made applicable to the second case."[44] The tricky part, though, is that "the classification changes as the classification is made." The universal element in public speaking emerges through an identi-cal process of continually rethinking similarity and difference.

The problem with rhetorical imitation is that it is difficult to say exactly what is to be "imitated," that is, to specify what "simi-larity" means. To do something "similar" may require one to do something literally very different than what was done in a prior sit-uation. To be sure, rhetoric abounds in precepts and rules, but as we have indicated in our classroom examples, these rules are in the nature of training wheels on a bicycle, useful for starting out, but permanently necessary only for those who cannot distinguish the mature art from a way station on the road to mastery. When one understands the living essence of oratory and rhetorical rea-son as timely action, examples of successful practice loom large and the rules recede. Once the rules have provided a secure train-ing ground for the student to exercise her powers of judgment, it is judgment alone that remains. As Mike Leff has aptly observed, "A command of paradigm cases allows the orator to move from concrete usage in the past to concrete problems in a case at hand without recourse to disembodied precepts."[45]

Machiavelli addresses a similar point in *The Prince* when he urges the prince to imitate examples of earlier princes,[46] but the question "in what way" is left open. It is here that what in rhetoric may seem an exposition of rules or advice is a sketch of the condi-tions to be considered in reaching a judgment. Garver insightfully notes that success is not the supreme or governing aim of a Machi-avellian prince. There is one hard and fast rule the prince must fol-low, and this rule captures the complexity of imitation and rhetorical argument by example. The invariable rule is: never hire mercenaries.[47] Worse than occasional defeat is losing the power of independent action; and worse for the student of oratory than an occasional lapse in information is being separated from her living understanding of the subject at hand by dependence on written notes disinterred from the library and quoted (complete with references to source, date, and page number) because this is a university and reading what one does not understand to people who do not expect to understand is what "doing research" means. (After twenty-something years of running what amounts to an epistemological emergency room, I sometimes believe the university is the last place in society where true mindlessness would be detected.)

Perhaps the universalizing element in rhetoric can be summarized as the ability to size up what is required of a situation and always to act out of one's own resources to address it. John Henry Newman captured this implicit universalizing and transcendent moment in rhetorical reason when he said, "You must be above your knowledge, not under it, or it will oppress you."[48] While knowledge of many kinds may be required to meet this moment of decision, knowledge alone is never sufficient.

Competence, Community, and Differentiated Consciousness: The Culture of Deliberation and the Aims of Education

As daily experience in the university suggests, and as Anderson has argued, the excessive attention to "disciplines" and disciplinary learning and to theory within disciplines has fragmented the university and alienated educators from any sense of common mission and (aside from recognizing the need for technical training to become employable) has alienated students and the public from "higher education." The program of practical reason that I have sketched here through examples from the public speaking classroom is aimed not at giving a decisive victory to practical over theoretical learning, but at reorienting practical and theoretical reason in the interest of saving intelligence from its own excesses. What I have sought to illustrate through examples of training in public speaking is not the cognitional superiority of public speaking as a mode of intellectual discipline, but what it means concretely to mediate between the worlds of common sense and theory in an academic subject. I have tried to present the public speaking class both as a forum for practical reason and as a forum in which practical reason and specialized learning join in dialogue. This dialogue occurs partially through the research of the student in preparing the speech, partially through the communal response to the message, and partially through the capacities of speakers and audiences together to achieve higher viewpoints from the moving platform of deliberation.

It is often remarked that the tragedy of knowledge is that while human beings quest after truth, they have an inability to grasp it (or as Dr. Johnson somewhere observes, "The desire to know is the weakest of human passions"). Even if by "truth" one means the most important or timely insight, achieving truth is problematic. The famous western "subject/object" split has, however, introduced a gratuitous element into the "tragedy" of knowledge by denying epistemic status to one mode of intelligence: commonsense knowing. Indeed, absent this split and, while always problematic and subject to revision, knowledge becomes a far more realistic, practical, and indeed "comic" enterprise.

Alfred North Whitehead's "fallacy of misplaced concreteness" aptly captures how the Isocratic program of education would socially rehabilitate theory without compromising its integrity as theory.[49] The fallacy of misplaced concreteness occurs when abstract intelligence fails to advert to the difference between theoretic and commonsense knowing and treats the everyday world as though it were a concrete instance of a general rule. The first recorded victim of this fallacy was the Greek philosopher Thales, who, oriented to the theoretically interesting order of the stars, fell into a well through failure to advert to the theoretically uninteresting ground beneath his feet. The milkmaid who rescued the great theorist may be understood synecdochically as "common sense." As Bernard Lonergan has poignantly observed of this example, Thales might have avoided the well because he was not blind, and the milkmaid might have taken an interest in the stars because she was human.[50]

Theoretical and commonsense knowing, as this example well illustrates, have built-in limitations which, left unchecked, guarantee blindness. This blindness is not genetic, for its cause is arrogance. The arrogance in theoretical knowing is that in privileging abstract clarity, it sacrifices as "uninteresting" what it cannot understand in its own mode. The arrogance in commonsense knowing is that in demanding a concrete sensual image for what properly can be grasped only by imageless insight, it mirrors the fallacy of misplaced concreteness. Carl Sagan's observation in one of his "Cosmos" programs that he was about to show his viewers "ultimate reality from the side" is a particularly hilarious illustration of confusing the imageless insight of the theoretical physicist with a sensual thing you could take a picture of and show someone! The readiness of his audience to believe him illustrates the commonsense expectation that any important truth—including ultimate truth—could be made clear at a glance. (Sagan's implicit claim that physics is ultimate truth is another matter and a further illustration of the original fallacy.)

The arrogance of knowledge, the principled refusal of intelligence in either of its modes to give way to the legitimate demands of the other mode, may be remedied (or at least given therapy) by education, providing that by education we mean increasing mastery through deliberation, which at its most general is a civic virtue and at its most particular is a professional skill. The educational program I have sketched here, though leading from common sense, aims to bring about a perpetual deliberation between common sense and theory and between the competing claims of the mind for knowledge and of life for action. The advent of articulate dialogue between common sense and theory as an event in the education of an individual constitutes a "differentiation of consciousness"—an epochal before and after of meaning in the life of that person.[51] The differentiation of consciousness is never complete. What "differentiates" in consciousness through deliberation are common sense and theory. What abides following this differentiation is reflective awareness of the unity of the mind amidst the diversity of its acts and the infinitely problematic relation of thought to life.

Acquisition of knowledge marks a person as informed. No amount of information makes anyone educated. The mark of an educated person is the ability to make distinctions within and about what she knows—and thereby show that her knowledge is intelligent and practical. Fostering skill in negotiating the common sense/theory boundary and the knowledge/action boundary can be an aspect of education in any discipline. Indeed, we might call this project "deliberating across the curriculum." Were fostering skill in students to negotiate these tensions accepted as central to the aim of the university, the university could in fact be a "community of learning," for it would have a unifying "vision across all disciplines."

Notes

1. Bruce A. Kimball, *Orators and Philosophers: A History of the Idea of Liberal Education* (New York: Teachers College Press, Columbia University, 1986), pp. 17–42; Brian Vickers, *In Defence of Rhetoric* (Oxford: Clarendon Press, 1988), pp. 148–213; Nancy S. Struever, *The Language of History in the Renaissance: Rhetoric and Historical Consciousness in Florentine Humanism* (Princeton, N.J.: Princeton University Press, 1970), pp. 5–39; Walter R. Fisher, *Human Communication as Narration: Toward a Philosophy of Reason, Value, and Action* (Columbia: University of South Carolina Press, 1987), pp. 57–84; Jerrold E. Seigel, *Rhetoric and Philosophy in Renaissance Humanism: The Union of Eloquence and Wisdom, Petrarch to Valla* (Princeton, N.J.: Princeton University Press, 1968), pp. xi–xvii, 3–30; Samuel Ijsseling, *Rhetoric and Philosophy in Conflict: An Historical Survey* (The Hague, The Netherlands: Martinus Nijhoff, 1976), esp. Chapters One and Two; Mario Untersteiner, *The Sophists*, translated by K. Freeman (Oxford: Oxford University Press, 1953), esp. the Introduction and Chapter One. For the additionally complicating and illuminating role of orality and literacy in this dispute, see Tony M. Lentz, *Orality and Literacy in Hellenic Greece* (Carbondale and Edwardsville: Southern Illinois University Press, 1989); Jacqueline De Romilly, *The Great Sophists in Periclean Athens,* translated by J. Lloyd (Oxford: Clarendon Press, 1992), esp. Chapter One.

2. The contemporary urgency of the dispute between "theoretical" and "practical" knowledge and between deliberation and demonstration is evident in many fields. For medicine and ethics, see Albert R. Jonsen and Stephen Toulmin, *The Abuse of Casuistry* (Berkeley: University of California Press, 1988); see also the perceptive study by James Michael Tallmon, *Casuistry and the Quest for Rhetorical Reason: Conceptualizing a Method of Shared Moral Inquiry,* unpublished doctoral dissertation, University of Washington, 1993. For science, see Marcello Pera, "The Role and Value of Rhetoric in Science," in *Persuading Science: The Art of Scientific Rhetoric,* edited by M. Pera and W. R. Shea (Canton, Mass.: Science History Publications, 1991), pp. 29–54; Charles Bazerman, *Shaping Written Knowledge* (Madison: University of

Wisconsin Press, 1988); Alan G. Gross, *The Rhetoric of Science* (Cambridge, Mass.: Harvard University Press, 1990); Lawrence J. Prelli, *A Rhetoric of Science: Inventing Scientific Discourses* (Columbia: University of South Carolina Press, 1989); Steve Fuller, *Philosophy, Rhetoric, and the End of Knowledge* (Madison: University of Wisconsin Press, 1994). For the human sciences, see Herbert W. Simons (ed.), *The Rhetorical Turn: Invention and Persuasion in the Conduct of Inquiry* (Chicago: University of Chicago Press, 1990); John S. Nelson, Allan Megill, and Donald N. McCloskey, *The Rhetoric of the Human Sciences: Language and Argument in Scholarship and Public Affairs* (Madison: University of Wisconsin Press, 1987); George L. Dillon, *Contending Rhetorics: Writing in Academic Disciplines* (Bloomington: Indiana University Press, 1991); John Bender and David E. Wellbery (eds.), *The Ends of Rhetoric: History, Theory, Practice* (Stanford, Calif.: Stanford University Press, 1990). An outstanding historical account of the implications of theoretical vs. practical wisdom for contemporary civilization is Stephen Toulmin, *Cosmopolis: The Hidden Agenda of Modernity* (New York: Macmillan, 1990); two nuanced and searching studies of practical reason are Eugene Garver, *Machiavelli and the History of Prudence* (Madison: University of Wisconsin Press, 1987), and "The Arts of the Practical: Variations on a Theme of Prometheus," *Curriculum Inquiry*, 1984, *14*, 165–182. For practical reason and education, see Ian Westbury and Neil Wilkof (eds.), *Science, Curriculum and Liberal Education* (Chicago: University of Chicago Press, 1978). A groundbreaking statement of the major contemporary issues in the rhetorical and philosophic traditions is Thomas B. Farrell, *Norms of Rhetorical Culture* (New Haven, Conn.: Yale University Press, 1994).

3. Perfect knowledge in Latin is *scientia,* and in Greek, *episteme.* See Jonsen and Toulmin, *The Abuse of Casuistry,* pp. 58–65; Kimball, *Orators and Philosophers,* pp. 26–29; for the long shadow cast by this tradition, see Neal Gilbert, *Renaissance Concepts of Method* (New York: Columbia University Press, 1960).

4. Kimball, *Orators and Philosophers,* pp. 13–29.

5. De Romilly, *The Great Sophists in Periclean Athens,* pp. 1–24; Thomas M. Conley, *Rhetoric in the European Tradition* (New York: Longman, 1990), pp. 4–5; George Kennedy, *The Art of Persuasion in Greece* (Princeton, N.J.: Princeton University Press, 1963), pp. 27–29; Susan C. Jarratt, *Rereading the Sophists: Classical Rhetoric Refigured* (Carbondale and Edwardsville: Southern Illinois University Press, 1991), pp. 98–107; Vickers, *In Defence of Rhetoric,* pp. 151–155; see also Kenneth Cmiel, *Democratic Eloquence: The Fight over Popular Speech in Nineteenth-Century America* (Berkeley: University of California Press, 1991), esp. pp. 23–54.

6. Renato Barilli, *Rhetoric,* translated by G. Menozzi (Minneapolis: University of Minnesota Press, 1989), p. vii; see also Edward Schiappa, *Protagoras and Logos: Philosophy and Rhetoric* (Columbia: University of South Carolina Press, 1991), p. 44.

7. See Geoffrey N. Leech and Michael H. Short, *Style in Fiction: A Linguistic Introduction to English Fictional Prose* (London and New York: Longman, 1987), p. 17. As Leech and Short point out, "The elaboration of form inevitably brings an elaboration of meaning."

8. Schiappa, *Protagoras and Logos,* p. 44.

9. Gerald Press, *The Development of the Idea of History in Antiquity,* McGill-Queen's Studies in the History of Ideas, Number 2 (Kingston and Montreal: McGill-Queen's University Press, 1982), pp. 24ff.

10. George Norlin (trans. and ed.), *Isocrates in Three Volumes,* Vol. II, Loeb Classical Library (Cambridge, Mass., and London: Harvard University Press/William Heinemann, 1980, 1982, 1986), p. 177.

11. Harry Hubbell, *The Influence of Isocrates on Cicero, Dionysius and Aristides* (New Haven, Conn., and London: Yale University Press, 1913), p. xi.

12. Hubbell, *The Influence of Isocrates,* p. xi.

13. Schiappa, *Protagoras and Logos,* and "Did Plato Coin RHETORIKE?" *American Journal of Philology,* 1990, *111,* 457–470.

14. Schiappa, *Protagoras and Logos,* p. 44.

15. Schiappa, *Protagoras and Logos,* p. 44.

16. Schiappa, *Protagoras and Logos,* p. 45.

17. Nor, it hardly needs remarking, is the attack on Isocrates limited to the *Gorgias.* See R. L. Howland, "The Attack on Isocrates in *The Phaedrus,*" *Classical Quarterly,* 1937, *31,* 551–559. Indeed, as Howland points out (p. 551), the attack on Isocrates is also particularly prominent in *The Protagoras.*

18. On the diversity of employment opportunities for rhetoricians, see Patricia Bizzell and Bruch Herzberg, *The Rhetorical Tradition: Readings from Classical Times to the Present* (Boston: Bedford Books of St. Martin's Press, 1990); Seigel, *Rhetoric and Philosophy in Renaissance Humanism,* pp. xi, xvii, 3, 30.

19. John Henry Freese (trans.), *Aristotle: The "Art" of Rhetoric* (Cambridge, Mass.: Harvard University Press, 1932), p. 1355b. See also George A. Kennedy, *Aristotle on Rhetoric: A Theory of Civic Discourse,* Newly Translated with Introduction, Notes, and Appendixes (New York: Oxford University Press, 1991). As Kennedy puts it (p. 36), "Let rhetoric be [defined as] an ability, in each [particular] case, to see the available means of persuasion." In a note, Kennedy comments: "The actuality produced by the potentiality of rhetoric is not the written or oral text of a speech, or even persuasion, but the art of 'seeing' how persuasion may be effected."

20. For an excellent discussion of the role of the topics in Aristotle's view of invention, see William M. A. Grimaldi, *Rhetoric: A Commentary* (New York: Fordham University Press, 1980), pp. 1–2; see also his examination of topoi in *Studies in the Philosophy of Aristotle's Rhetoric* (Wiesbaden, Germany: Franz Steiner, 1972), pp. 115–135. See also Carolyn Miller, "Aristotle's 'Special Topics' in Rhetorical Practice and Pedagogy," *Rhetoric Society Quarterly*, 1987, *17*, 61–70. For a penetrating account of invention in the larger rhetorical tradition, particularly as it pertains to performance, see Michael C. Leff, "The Topics of Argumentative Invention in Latin Rhetorical Theory from Cicero to Boethius," *Rhetorica*, 1983, *1*, 23–44.

21. John Poulakos, "Toward A Sophistic Definition of Rhetoric," *Philosophy and Rhetoric*, 1983, *16*, 36; and his "Rhetoric, The Sophists, and The Possible," *Communication Monographs*, 1984, *51*, 215–226.

22. On rhetoric and the tradition of prudential reason, see Victoria Kahn, *Rhetoric, Prudence, and Skepticism in the Renaissance* (Ithaca, N.Y.: Cornell University Press, 1985); Eugene Garver, *Machiavelli and the History of Prudence* (Madison: University of Wisconsin Press, 1987).

23. See, for example Jarratt, *Rereading the Sophists*, pp. 107–117; and Dillon, *Contending Rhetorics*, pp. 19–40; and Eugene Garver, *Aristotle's Rhetoric: An Art of Character* (Chicago: University of Chicago Press, 1994).

24. Kimball, *Orators and Philosophers;* Jarratt, *Rereading the Sophists*, p. 161.

25. For an account of Isocrates' teaching methods, see Werner Jaeger, "Isocrates' Teaching Methods," *American Journal of Philology*, 1959, *80*, 25–36.

26. Charles Anderson, *Prescribing the Life of the Mind: An Essay on the Purpose of the University, the Aims of Liberal Education, the Competence of Citizens, and the Cultivation of Practical Reason* (Madison: University of Wisconsin Press, 1993).

27. Anderson sketches these goals, which I have paraphrased, in Chapter Six, "The Cultivation of Practical Reason," pp. 96–120.

28. Reginald Hackforth (trans.), *Plato's Phaedrus* (New York: Bobbs-Merrill, 1952), pp. 157, 275a.

29. Bernard J. F. Lonergan, *Insight: A Study of Human Understanding* (New York: Harper & Row, 1978), pp. 4, 33, 116, 174, 220–277, 286, 365, 375.

30. Michael C. Leff, "The Topics of Argumentative Invention in Latin Rhetorical Theory from Cicero to Boethius, *Rhetorica*, Spring 1983, p. 33.

31. Leff, "The Topics of Argumentative Invention," p. 34.

32. Quintilian, *The Institutio Oratoria of Quintilian*, translated by H. E. Butler, 4 vols. (Cambridge, Mass.: Harvard University Press, 1963).

33. Edwin Black, *Rhetorical Questions: Studies in Public Discourse* (Chicago: University of Chicago Press, 1991).

34. Søren Kierkegaard, *Concluding Unscientific Postscript to the Philosophic Fragments: A Mimic-Pathetic-Dialectic Composition: An Existential Contribution,* edited and translated by R. Thomte with the collaboration of A. B. Anderson (Princeton, N.J.: Princeton University Press, 1980), pp. 116–117.

35. Kierkegaard, *Concluding Unscientific Postscript,* p. 116.

36. Fuller, *Philosophy, Rhetoric, and the End of Knowledge,* p. 320.

37. Fuller, *Philosophy, Rhetoric, and the End of Knowledge,* p. 320.

38. Eugene Garver, "Rhetoric and Essentially Contested Concepts," *Philosophy and Rhetoric,* 1978, *1,* 156–172.

39. Eugene Garver, "How To Develop Ideas: The Contribution Philosophy Can Make to Improving Writing," *Teaching Philosophy,* 1983, *6,* 97–102.

40. Cited in Maciej Zieba, "The Liberalism We Need," *First Things,* 1994, *40,* 24–25.

41. Kierkegaard, *Concluding Unscientific Postscript,* p. 174.

42. Francis Bacon, *The Advancement of Learning,* Book II, XVIII, p. 13.

43. Kenneth Burke, *Permanence and Change* (Los Altos, Calif.: Hermes Publications, 1954), pp. 48–49.

44. Edward H. Levi, *An Introduction to Legal Reasoning* (Chicago: University of Chicago Press, 1949), pp. 2–3.

45. Levi, *An Introduction to Legal Reasoning,* p. 312.

46. Garver, *Machiavelli,* Chapters Three and Four.

47. Garver, *Machiavelli,* p. 37.

48. John Henry Newman, *The Idea of A University* (Garden City, N.Y.: Doubleday, 1959), p. 161.

49. Alfred North Whitehead, *Science and the Modern World* (New York: Mentor Books, 1964), p. 52.

50. Lonergan, *Insight,* p. 182.

51. The term "differentiation of consciousness" is an expression used by both Eric Voegelin and Bernard Lonergan. For Voegelin, see John A. Campbell, "A Rhetorical Interpretation of History," *Rhetorica,* 1984, *2,* 227–266; for Lonergan, see John A. Campbell, "Insight and Understanding: The Common Sense Rhetoric of Bernard Lonergan," in *Communication and Lonergan: Common Ground for Forging the New Age,* edited by T. J. Farrell and P. A. Soukup (Kansas City, Mo.: Sheed and Ward, 1993), pp. 3–22.

Chapter Nine

Teaching the Teachers of the People

Roger Soder

In autocratic regimes, the central question for political philosophers is, What is the proper education of the prince? In democratic regimes, however, the question—for everyone, not just political philosophers—becomes, What is the proper education of the people? For in a democratic regime, the people rule. The people are self-governing. They rule either directly or through those they choose to represent them. If they are to rule wisely, or as Plato suggests in the *Laws*, "to rule or be ruled with justice,"[1] then the people must understand and act upon their rights and responsibilities as citizens living and working in a democratic regime. It is possible that such understanding and acting (a working knowledge, if you will) can be obtained through casual, nonpurposeful ways. Watching the behaviors of football players and referees might suggest notions of abiding by rules and of fair play. Watching even just a bit of television news shows will suggest notions of the behavior of a president, of representatives, of judges, and the like. Much of childrearing devolves on notions of sharing, waiting one's turn, honesty, and trust. But the matter of preparation for self-governance is, for most people, too important to be left to chance or to casual observation.

For this reason, the contributors to this book (as well as many others) have argued that we must turn to the schools for formal instruction of the young in notions of citizenship in a democratic regime, for reasonable responses to the question, "What is the proper education of the rulers?" Although the question itself can be stated with clarity, the reasonable responses are a bit more problematic. Consider, for example, a young and as ever careful Abraham Lincoln speaking to the people of Sangamo County during his campaign for the legislature in 1832. He saw the need for at least a "moderate education" that would lead to the appreciation of the "value of our free institutions." But beyond that, Lincoln was not inclined to go: "Upon the subject of education, not presuming to dictate any plan or system respecting it, I can only say that I view it as the most important subject which we as a people can be engaged in."[2]

Education itself is a complex matter. Many have known the frustration expressed by John Adams: "Education is a subject so vast, and the systems of writers are so various and so contradictory, that human life is too short to examine it, and a man must die before he can learn to bring up his children. The philosophers, divines, politicians and pedagogues who have published their theories and practices in this department are without number."[3]

Democracy is contested ground. The interrelationships between education and democracy, as discussed elsewhere in this volume, are complex and contested. But beyond these difficult matters lies equally rocky terrain. Beyond developing reasonable responses to the role of schools in the proper education of the people, we must address a further question: What must teachers of the people know in order to provide the proper education of the people? To put it another way, what does it mean to be an educated person, who happens to be a teacher, in a democratic regime?

Teachers as Political Agents

The argument for teachers as political agents has been put forth perhaps most succinctly in *The People Shall Judge*, a collection of readings compiled by the College of the University of Chicago. As expressed in the preface to the collection, the argument is as follows:

> This book expresses the faith of one American college in the usefulness of liberal education to American democracy. If the United States is to be a democracy, its citizens must be free. If citizens are

to be free, they must be their own judges. If they are to judge well, they must be wise. Citizens may be born free; they are not born wise. Therefore, the business of liberal education in a democracy is to make free men wise. Democracy declares that "the people shall judge." Liberal education must help the people to judge well.[4]

Thus, we deny that teaching is teaching is teaching, no matter where you are, no matter what the political circumstances. It has been suggested that teaching is context free, free of moral consideration, free of political consideration—that the only thing that matters is teaching one's subject (or teaching to the test). To claim, however, that one is, say, a math teacher, doing nothing but teaching algebra, and that one can become a math teacher simply by learning the subject of mathematics, is to claim a great deal. Teaching in a democracy is not at all the same thing as teaching in a dictatorship. One expects different outcomes, different behaviors. In a dictatorship, one expects only certain people to participate in the affairs of the regime, and one expects the subjects of the regime to follow the party line without question. In a democracy, we have to make sure that everybody has access, that everybody has the tools to participate. It is not much of a democracy when only a few of some sort of Mandarin class know how to use the regime and profit from it, while the many (for whatever reason of class or gender or ethnicity) are denied access. If people do not have access, if they do not have the tools to participate, then democracy and self-governance have little meaning. Moreover, in a democracy, all people—not just a Mandarin class, but *all* people—have to be able to think critically; they must be able to engage in free and open inquiry. In a democracy, we have to reject the kind of thinking depicted in Tennyson's "Charge of the Light Brigade"—theirs not to reason why, theirs but to do and die. We have to reject the contemptuous (and frighteningly widespread) views of the Grand Inquisitor in *The Brothers Karamazov*, that the people must be ruled, *want* to be ruled, by miracle, mystery, and authority. In place of this kind of thinking, we must side with John Dewey, who talked about democracy in terms of the free play of facts and ideas, secured by effective guarantees of free inquiry, free assembly, and free communication.

If teachers are in large part political agents, if teaching is at heart a moral and political endeavor and only secondarily a matter of technique or subject matter or teaching to the test, then there are significant implications for how teachers need to be prepared. Teacher preparation programs limited to the acquisition of an undergraduate major followed by an add-on program of various methods classes combined with a student teaching experience are clearly inadequate and wrong. Teacher preparation programs must be grounded in something more than pedagogy or tricks of the trade. But to focus exclusively on the need to change teacher preparation programs is to ignore the plain fact that virtually all intending teachers spend some 75 percent of their higher education time taking courses in the departments of the arts and sciences, either as part of their general education or in conjunction with their teacher preparation program. Ultimately, it is to the arts and sciences, then, that we must turn in considering the grounding of teaching as a moral and political endeavor.

The grounding must begin with an assessment of what the intending teacher needs in order to be an effective political agent. Where is that teacher to learn about the responsibilities of living and working in a democracy? Where is that teacher to develop the understanding of the institutions and procedures and habits of mind that Ralph Lerner considers necessary for making a political regime actual?[5]

The faculty in teacher education and the faculty in the arts and sciences must address a most difficult question: "If teaching is at heart a political matter, if teachers are political agents, if the main purpose of schooling is to teach students their moral and intellectual responsibilities for living and working in a democracy, then what should be the liberal education of the intending teacher provided by the arts and sciences such that intending teachers can fulfill effectively and ethically their moral and political responsibilities as teachers?"

There are many conceptual, practical, and procedural difficulties in addressing this question. Many of the difficulties have a common source: to address this question means to say what one thinks is important. We cannot dodge the matter of importance by saying we will include everything in the undergraduate program that everybody thinks is important. Students are enrolled for a limited time. Not all favorite texts, courses, experiences, and ideas can be attended to, so decisions have to be made. Is it important that intending teachers have some basic working understanding of the Constitution of the United States? Of the founding of the republic? Should they have some familiarity with notions of rights? Of liberty? Of freedom? Of the duties of a citizen in a democracy? Of the relationship, if any, between free, common, public schooling and the American democracy? Should they know something of the arguments in *The Federalist* papers? In the anti-*Federalist* papers? What kind of grounding should intending teachers have in matters of ethics? Of moral dimensions?

Who is to decide what is important? One approach would have those in schools and colleges of education approach their colleagues in the arts and sciences, saying, Here is our sense of what the intending teacher should know about the moral and political dimensions of teaching in a democracy prior to entering our teacher education program. What courses do you currently offer (and what courses might you offer or alter) that address what we think the teacher should know? Another approach would have faculty in education and the arts and sciences decide collectively what the prior knowledge should be.

There are problems with both approaches. For education colleagues to decide in advance what is needed might be welcomed by some in the arts and sciences (at long last, they are dealing with fundamental issues over there), but might be seen by others as an affront (Why should we without question gear our courses to the dictates of the education people?). Collective action might be seen as good (Isn't it wonderful for us to be engaging with them?), but for some, collective action is an oxymoron, and it will be hard enough to get the education people to agree on what is important, and next to impossible when you add in political science, philosophy, French literature, art, music, and all the rest. These are some of the difficulties that must be faced in addressing the question of what the intending teacher should know in order to assume and carry out with virtue his or her obligations as moral and political agent. The difficulties are formidable. To address the question may seem a task beyond our powers. As Leo Strauss reminds us, however, "We cannot define our tasks by our powers, for our powers become known to us through performing our tasks."[6]

I will now attempt to perform the task of outlining what it is the intending teacher should have as working knowledge about the political dimensions of teaching in a democracy. In performing this task, I turn first to a consideration of what others have said teachers should know of these matters. This consideration is followed by an outline in some detail (or at least beyond what I will suggest are the usual generalities) of the basic working knowledge of the political dimensions of teaching that every public school teacher might be expected to have. The focus in this chapter, then, is primarily on the political rather than on the moral dimensions of teaching.

I appropriate this task with more than a little caution. My wariness stems in part from the recognition that matters of political philosophy and schooling are complex and contested. In much larger part, however, my wariness stems from the silence, the overwhelming silence that one senses from the many who have moved into this terrain only to return mute. Much has been said about the importance of schools in a democracy and about what children should learn in schools, but many of those very same people, who speak with great certainty about the schooling process, lapse into uncharacteristic silence as to the education of educators in these matters.

Perspectives on Democracy, Schools, and Teachers

Along with matters of commerce, trade, and law, the relationship of democracy and schools was given due attention during the formation of the American republic. Although actual support for the schools rarely matched the rhetoric proclaiming the necessity of schools for the republic, it is difficult to disagree with Richard Hofstadter's conclusion that a "signal fact" of our national experience is "our persistent, intense, and sometimes touching faith in the efficacy of public education."[7] We note, for example, the long preamble in Thomas Jefferson's "A Bill for the More General Diffusion of Knowledge," in which he argues that the most effectual means of preventing the perversion of a republic into tyranny is "to illuminate, as far as practicable, the minds of the people at large." To this end, he prescribes in great detail the administration of schools, school building construction, curriculum, and the like. The subjects to be studied are specified: "Reading, writing, and common arithmetic, and the books which shall be used therein for instructing the children to read shall be such as will at the same time make them acquainted with Grecian, Roman, English, and American History." Little is said, however, of what teachers should know, other than: "An overseer shall be appointed annually by the Aldermen at their first meeting eminent for his learning, integrity, and fidelity to the commonwealth, whose business and duty it shall be, from time to time, to appoint a teacher to each school, who shall give assurance of fidelity to the commonwealth."[8]

In his first annual address to Congress, George Washington asked for aid for education in one form or another. He argued that education contributed "to the security of a Free Constitution" in various ways:

> By convincing those who are intrusted with the public administra-
> tion, that every valuable end of Government is best answered by the
> enlightened confidence of the people; and by teaching the people
> themselves to know and to value their own rights; to discern and
> provide against invasions of them; to distinguish between oppres-
> sion and the necessary exercise of lawful authority, between bur-
> thens proceeding from a disregard to their convenience and those
> resulting from the inevitable exigencies of Society; to discriminate
> the spirit of Liberty from that of licentiousness, cherishing the first,
> avoiding the last, and uniting a speedy, but temperate vigilance
> against encroachments, with an inviolable respect to the Laws.[9]

In "A Plan for the Establishment of Public Schools" (1786), Benjamin Rush acknowledges the need to ensure certain characteristics of teachers: "Let our teachers be distinguished for their abilities and knowledge. Let them be grave in their manners, gentle in their tempers, exemplary in their morals, and of sound prin-
ciples in religion and government."[10] Four years later, Noah Webster argued that "with respect to morals and civil society . . . the effects of education are so certain and extensive that it behooves every parent and guardian to be particularly attentive to the characters of the men whose province it is to form the minds of youth. From a strange inversion of the order of nature, the cause of which it is not necessary to unfold, the most important business in civil society is in many parts of America committed to the most worthless characters."[11] He speaks of the "want of good teachers in

the academies and common schools. By good teachers I mean men of unblemished reputation and possessed of abilities competent to their stations. That a man should be master of what he undertakes to teach is a point that will not be disputed, and yet it is certain that abilities are often dispensed with, either through inattention or fear of expense."[12]

Robert Coram makes an interesting connection between form of government and education in "Political Inquiries" (1791):

> In several states we find laws passed establishing provisions for colleges and universities where people of property may educate their sons, but no provision made for instructing the poorer rank of people even in reading and writing. Yet in these same states every citizen who is worth a few shillings annually is entitled to vote for legislators. This appears to me a most glaring solecism in government. The constitutions are *republican* and the laws of education are *monarchical*. The *former* extend civil rights to every honest industrious man, the *latter* deprive a large proportion of the citizens of a most valuable privilege.[13]

Coram, however, had little to say as to how teachers might best be prepared to prepare citizens for a republic.

In his "Discourse on Education" (1796), Samuel Doggett recognized that the current corps of teachers was less than adequate, but he was optimistic about the future: "It is most painful and gloomy to the patriot and philanthropist to observe that the instruction of our youth has, through mistake or deficiency of patronage, too generally fallen into inadequate hands. But we are animated, happy in the consideration that the good sense of the people is now rapidly correcting this mistake. Raptures of enthusiasm fill our hearts in anticipating the golden era when Socrateses shall again be schoolmasters."[14] Again, we find little here regarding the proper preparation for these Socrateses.

In the twentieth century, the relationship between democracy, education, and the schools and teacher preparation has received due consideration. Again, without cataloging the whole, some of the salient observations can be reviewed, beginning with those traditionally considered in the centrist camp, followed by those on the political left and right.

Views from the Center

Surely a central figure, one who wrote and spoke at some length about the relationship of education and democracy, is Robert Maynard Hutchins. Although Hutchins was aware of the complexities of the democracy/education relationship, he apparently found the matter of what teachers need to know in order to teach students civic responsibilities could be dismissed with ease: "The prospective teacher's general education would be identical with that of the lawyer, doctor, and clergyman. With a good education in the liberal arts, which are grammar, rhetoric, logic, and mathematics, he has learned the basic rules of pedagogy. The liberal arts are, after all, the arts of reducing the intellect from mere potentiality to act. And this is what teaching is."[15]

Elsewhere, Hutchins expands on the notion: "Most of the argument about teacher-training is beside the point. The argument revolves around the question of whether a prospective teacher should take a lot of courses in the school of education or take a lot of courses in the subject-matter departments. The answer is that the teacher should understand his subject and should understand education; but, first of all, he should himself be educated. He should have a good general education."[16] As to what this general education should be, Hutchins says:

> Clearly, the object of general education is the training of the mind. Clearly, too, the mind should be trained for intelligent action. Or, to put it another way, the object of general education is to produce intelligent citizens. . . . A program of general education which is based on ideas, which leads the student to understand the nature and schemes of history, to grasp the principles of science, to comprehend the fine arts and literature, and to which philosophy contributes intelligibility at every stage, is the kind of program that we must now construct. It may seem, at first glance, remote from real life, from the facts, and from the social order. On the contrary, if we can construct it, we shall find that it may give us at last a land fit to be free.[17]

Undeniably, these are fit sentiments, but they are also sentiments that give little direction for the preparation of teachers.

Others, too, in what we might call the centrist position assert the need for education in a democracy, but provide little in the way of guidance for what teachers should know. Four examples follow.

A 1951 yearbook of the National Council for the Social Studies, suitably entitled *Education for Democratic Citizenship*, tells us that "it is clear that education for democratic citizenship is not solely the responsibility of social studies teachers; it should encompass the entire school program and permeate all aspects of school life."[18] Nothing, however, in any of the fifteen nicely written chapters addresses what teachers need to know and be able to do.

A 1967 research bulletin of the National Council for the Social Studies notes that "a recent study of the political beliefs of public school teachers indicates that many of them are either hostile to or uncertain about many democratic principles."[19] Moreover, we are told:

> Perhaps the most acute educational problem reflected by political socialization research is the proclivity of our schools to approach the task of political socialization in a one-sided manner, especially in schools serving mainly lower or working-class children. . . . Overemphasis on conformity appears to be associated with authoritarian school atmospheres where docile children are prized above active, deeply probing thinkers; where strict adherence to authoritative pronouncements is preferred over student inquiry into pressing, sociopolitical concerns; where strict obedience to rules is stressed to the exclusion of inquiry into the need for rules.[20]

The most the authors can say about teacher education is the need to develop better political socialization strategies. "These new strategies should involve reconstructing teaching methods and course content in order to help overcome tendencies in our schools that encourage closed-minded attachments to political beliefs and that breed intolerance and unreasonable resistance to potentially beneficial socio-political changes."[21]

More recently, the American Federation of Teachers weighed in with its *Education for Democracy: A Statement of Principles*, in which it argues that education is important for a democracy, and that available evidence suggests a decline in understanding of democracy and history, a lack of understanding of the "responsibility for preserving and extending their political inheritance."[22] Further, the authors argue:

> Having never debated and discussed how the world came to be as it is, the democratic citizen will not know what is worth defending, what should be changed, and which imposed orthodoxies must be resisted. . . . We are concerned also that among some educators (as among some in the country at large) there appears a certain lack of confidence in our own liberal, democratic values, an unwillingness to draw normative distinctions between them and the ideas of non-democratic regimes. Any number of popular curriculum materials deprecate the open preference for liberal democratic values as "ethnocentric." One widely distributed teaching guide on human rights accords equal significance to freedom of speech, the right to vote, and the guarantee of due process on the one hand, with the "right" to take vacations on the other.[23]

To improve education for democracy, the authors ask for better schools, and for a "more substantial, engaging, and demanding social studies curriculum for all our children." As for the preparation of teachers, we are given this nostrum: "And [curriculum reform] requires new approaches to teacher education, both pre-service and in-service, to help teachers present the revamped and strengthened curriculum."[24]

In *The Civic Mission in Educational Reform: Perspectives for the Public and the Profession*, Freeman Butts reviews what intending teachers should know about civic education. We are presented with fifty-three pages in Chapter Six, "Capstone for Educational Reform: Civic Learning in the Education of Teachers," only to end up with vague and unhelpful generalizations such as, "We need to develop a new conception of the civic mission of American education, one that Jefferson, Madison, Washington, and Adams would find congenial and yet that would be efficacious in coming decades."[25]

In an earlier essay, "The Revival of Civic Learning Requires a Prescribed Curriculum," Butts talks about everything but a prescribed curriculum, even joining (implicitly) with others in wondering about Jefferson's prescriptions. Jefferson prescribed the Declaration of Independence, *The Federalist,* the Resolutions of the General Assembly of Virginia in 1799 on the alien and sedition laws, and the valedictory address of George Washington. After listing these four works, Butts says: "Some historians have found it incongruous that Jefferson, the great proclaimer of intellectual and religious freedom, should have been willing to prescribe the texts for the study of the civil polity in his beloved university. But it is an interesting list of prescribed texts, which in the hands of scholarly and critical scrutiny could raise many of the basic issues of federalist and republican government, so long as prescribed *study* did not imply prescribed *believing*."[26]

There is a certain curious irony here: a prescribed curriculum is deemed necessary for civic learning, but at the same time the argument is made that intellectual and religious freedom necessarily precludes arguing that some texts might be prescribed.

Views from the Right

What do we find when we look for counsel from what we might roughly call the political right? We find indications of an awareness of the education/democracy connection, but the prescriptions for teacher education focus on either how bad teacher education is or on how much better teachers would be if they "knew their subject matter" or "majored in an academic subject." Thus, in *Academic Questions*, Jeffrey Hart bemoans the lack of civics knowledge of students in even the elite institutions such as his own (Dartmouth University) and, quite correctly I think, assigns part of the blame to the K-12 system: "It would do little good to sit down and design a sensible high-school course on, say, 'Introduction to American History.' There exist decent texts, and of course the obvious assigned readings. But the problem is that our secondary school teachers are not equipped to deal with such elementary materials. They produce students who do not know anything because the teachers do not know anything."[27] Hart suggests possible remedies, including, "Try to change the rules so that teacher certification requires an academic college major in a field of substance—history, English, math, science—rather than an 'education' major. Teachers should come to the classroom with *something* to teach, rather than a background in teaching *methods.*[28]

Similarly, Rita Kramer talks much of a common political culture, but in the end asserts that "everything you need to know about how to teach English—that can be taught didactically—can be learned within the framework of an undergraduate English major."[29] A critical question, of course, is whether majoring in history, English, math, or science will provide what teachers need in their repertoire in order to teach (and model and exemplify) what is needed. What does majoring in math do for one's understanding of the tension between rights and responsibilities? Between liberty and order? Between individual and state?

Similar arguments are made by the Holmes Group, as well as by the Carnegie Forum on Education and the Economy. *Tomorrow's Teachers* and *A Nation Prepared: Teachers for the 21st Century* grant the usual acknowledgment of the democracy/education relationship, but then suggest only that subject-matter knowledge be considered of primary importance.[30] They assume, apparently—and the assumption is untested—that majoring in one of the academic fields prepares one to teach and model and exemplify civic education.

Views from the Left

From what we might roughly call the left, we hear much concern about the relationship between democracy and education, and about the role of schools in creating a better and more authentic democratic social order. A typical recent example is *Teacher Education and the Social Conditions of Schooling*, in which Daniel Liston and Ken Zeichner write:

> While contemporary radicals are perhaps not as optimistic as some of the earlier proponents, many sense that our democratic way of life and that democratic forms of schooling are continually undermined by forces both internal and external to the institution of schooling. They will encourage students (and we will encourage prospective teachers and teacher educators) to elaborate and clarify their social beliefs and assumptions and to examine the ways in which larger societal forces obstruct and undermine our democratic way of life.[31]
>
> Minimally it seems that teacher educators must enable prospective teachers not only to formulate good reasons for their educational plans but also to identify those social beliefs and conditions of schooling that are obstacles to a democratic education.[32]

We have outlined substantive concerns (e.g., teachers' work, minority achievement in majority schools, and the gender dynamics of teaching) and examined specific issues (teaching as emotionally infused labor, the recognition and awareness of cultural differences, and teaching as a "woman's true profession"). A teacher education curriculum that includes these sorts of issues would, we think, better prepare prospective teachers for the reality of schooling and encourage a reflective examination of their social beliefs.[33]

In Henry Giroux's *Teachers as Intellectuals: Toward a Critical Pedagogy of Learning* we find similar talk:

> Teachers should become transformative intellectuals if they are to educate students to be active, critical citizens. Central to the category of transformative intellectual is the necessity of making the pedagogical more political and the political more pedagogical. Making the pedagogical more political means inserting schooling directly into the political sphere by arguing that schooling represents both a struggle to define meaning and a struggle over power relations. Within this perspective, critical reflection and action become part of a fundamental social project to help students develop a deep and abiding faith in the struggle to overcome economic, political and social injustices, and to further humanize themselves as part of this struggle.[34]

> [Transformative intellectuals] must speak out against economic, political and social injustices both within and outside of schools. At the same time, they must work to create the conditions that give students the opportunity to become citizens who have the knowledge and courage to struggle to make despair unconvincing and hope practical.[35]

In "Teacher Education and the Politics of Democratic Reform," Giroux and Peter McLaren want teacher education programs "to commit themselves uncompromisingly to issues of both empowerment and transformation, issues which combine knowledge and critique with a call to transform reality in the interest of democratic communities."[36] They want "a public philosophy that recognizes the boundaries between different groups, the self and others, and yet creates a politics of trust and solidarity that supports a common life based on democratic principles that create the ideological and institutional preconditions for both diversity and the public good."[37]

To do this, they suggest that a "revitalized discourse of democracy should not be based exclusively on a language of critique." What is also needed is "a language of possibility, one that combines a strategy of opposition with a strategy for constructing new social order." They argue that "educators need to define schools as public spheres where the dynamics of popular engagement and democratic politics can be cultivated as part of the struggle for a radical democratic state. . . . Schooling would be analyzed for its potential to nourish civic literacy, citizen participation, and moral courage. . . . [Teachers would learn] how important it is to use their skills and insights in alliance with others who are attempting to redefine the terrain of politics and citizenship."[38]

Later they state more specifically just how the terrain is being redefined: "Derrida, Saussure, Foucault, Barthes, Lacan, Gadamer, and Habermas are slowly finding their way into educational journals and have had the cumulative effect of marshalling a massive assault on dominant modes of educational theorizing and practice."[39] They tell us that to find our way across this new terrain of democracy and education, politics and citizenship, we will have to "selectively and critically appropriate key concepts in discourse theory, reception theory, poststructuralism, deconstructionist hermeneutics, and various other new schools of inquiry without becoming trapped in their often impenetrable language, arcane jargon, and theoretical cul-de-sacs."[40]

Whether or not the new social order, so reminiscent of George Counts, will have to wait for yet additional schools of inquiry in order to emerge is an open question. As for the present, it seems clear that some of those on the left have some notions of what that new social order is to be, but much deconstructionist hermeneutics will have to be brought to bear here to divulge what intending teachers should know.

Beyond considerations of centrists, those on the right, and those on the left, there is another position on democracy, education, and the preparation of teachers—a position not especially edifying, but useful to consider nonetheless. In *The Ennobling of Democracy*, Thomas Pangle expresses hope that teachers (and thus presumably future teachers) might appreciate the need for civic education. His hope, however, is highly qualified and his prognosis glum:

> The mass of the American citizenry, and especially those who choose the burdens of parenthood, seem more sensible, more responsible, and wiser in civic matters than the elites who dominate the universities; and teachers in the public schools, since they tend to live among ordinary folk and only spend a few years under the direct tutelage of the higher education establishment, remain somewhere in between. On the whole, I am inclined to think reasonable the hope that primary and secondary schoolteachers are not as alienated from the educational principles I have sketched as is sometimes suggested by the pronouncements of their "spokespeople." At the very least, I think we have to hope that the men and women who devote their lives to teaching will be willing to listen to and reflect upon calls for a return to our civic educational heritage, enlarged and enriched by a new infusion of classical republican inspiration.[41]

Here we have moved from the left's "language of possibility" and strategies of opposition to a language of hope: hope that somehow, willy-nilly, teachers will respond to calls for reflection on our civic heritage, and the hope that would-be teachers will not spend too much time becoming derailed by university-dominated teacher preparation programs.

Not all is quiet on the Western civic education front; not all are silent about what it is teachers should know. Mortimer Adler argues that teachers should receive the same kind of general, liberal, and humanistic schooling outlined in *The Paideia Proposal*, and asserts that what is required is

> the reading and discussion of the basic documents that throw light on the political principles of our republic. I have in mind such documents as the *Declaration of Independence*, the Constitution of the United States, the *Federalist Papers*, Tocqueville's *Democracy in America*, Lincoln's *Gettysburg Address*, Theodore Roosevelt's Progressive Party Platform of 1912, Franklin Delano Roosevelt's Message to Congress in 1944, and so on. These documents are not now read and discussed in the years of basic schooling. Most of our teachers have not read them, and, on a first reading of them, would not be able to understand them or to lead intelligent discussions of them.[42]

Some discussions of prescribed texts can be found, too, in Peter Pouncey's essay, "On a Background for Teachers," which prescribes for high school teachers familiarity with Herodotus, Thucydides, Fernand Braudel, and Isaiah Berlin, among others.[43]

Where does our consideration of what others have said about democracy, education, and teacher education leave us? At most, we can say there is unanimity over the decades and across the political terrain in arguing for a strong and positive relationship between democracy and education and the schools. There is unanimity in the recognition of the importance of the teacher in this relationship. As to how teachers might best be prepared to deal with our civic heritage and the enculturation of the young into that heritage, there is (with the exceptions noted here of Mortimer Adler and Peter Pouncey) unanimity in the silence. The silence is punctuated by vague nostrums about teachers having a good general education, by claims that majoring in an academic discipline is sufficient, by brave declarations of victory by the deconstructionists and the reconstructionists over the ruling class, by hopes that teachers will imbibe Plato if they can only be kept away from the universities. Yet, despite this occasional noise, there continues the silence, an unwillingness to argue that there are after all certain texts, certain fundamental notions that all teachers must have as part of their basic working knowledge if they are to fulfill their responsibilities as teachers in the American democracy.

We cannot here plumb the depths of the reasons for the silence. It is instructive, nevertheless, to note that the discipline of education is not peculiar in its unwillingness to argue for certain texts and fundamental notions. Thinkers in other disciplines have lapsed into silence when faced with similar questions. Perhaps the most salient example is the highly influential educational and political tract *Medical Education in the United States and Canada*, in which Abraham Flexner puts the matter this way:

> So far, we have spoken explicitly of the fundamental sciences only. They furnish, indeed, the essential instrumental basis of medical education. But the instrumental minimum can hardly serve as the permanent professional minimum. It is even instrumentally inadequate. The practitioner deals with facts of two categories. Chemistry, physics, biology enable him to apprehend one set; he needs a

different apperceptive and appreciative apparatus to deal with other, more subtle elements. Specific preparation is in this direction much more difficult; one must rely for the requisite insight and sympathy on a varied and enlarging cultural experience. Such enlargement of the physician's horizon is otherwise important, for scientific progress has greatly modified his ethical responsibility. His relation was formerly to his patient—at most to his patient's family; and it was almost altogether remedial. The patient had something the matter with him; the doctor was called in to cure it. Payment of a fee ended the transaction. But the physician's function is fast becoming social and preventive, rather than individual and curative. Upon him society relies to ascertain, and through measures essentially educational to enforce, the conditions that prevent disease and make positively for physical and moral well-being. It goes without saying that this type of doctor is first of all an educated man.[44]

What is noteworthy here is that in later chapters of *Medical Education,* Flexner is quite specific as to what the physician should know. It is, after all, the Flexner model of medical education that is still with us. The basic sciences, the chemistry, the biology, the anatomy, the clinical work, all are laid out in a straightforward manner; but as to what "goes without saying," that the doctor is first of all "educated," Flexner says no more.

If we wish to argue that teachers are important to democracy and education, we must break the silence and, as with Leo Strauss, define our powers by performing our tasks. My task here, I suggest, is to present a series of texts and fundamental notions that must be part of the repertoire of all teachers, part of their basic working knowledge of the political dimensions of teaching in a democracy. In doing so, I recognize the difficulty suggested so nicely by Samuel Johnson, who when asked, "Sir, what is poetry?" replied, characteristically, "Why, Sir, it is much easier to say what it is not. We all *know* what light is, but it is not easy to *tell* what it is."[45] At the same time, Johnson notes the need to get on with it: "We talked of the education of children; and I asked him what he thought was best to teach them first. . . . 'Sir, it is no matter what you teach them first, any more than what leg you shall put into your breeches first. Sir, you may stand disputing which is best to put in first, but in the mean time your breech is bare. Sir, while you are considering which of two things you should teach your child first, another boy has learnt them both.' "[46]

Let us then, in the final section, put on our pants and see what we have.

Fundamental Texts for Teaching in a Democracy

What follows is a listing of texts, allocated to twelve categories. Some of the texts are well known; for those that may be less familiar, some commentary is provided. Some of the texts are important in and of themselves. Obviously, if you wish to know something about the Constitution of the United States, you have to first read it carefully. Other texts could have reasonable substitutes, as long as the substitutes are primarily focused on the same basic theme. The total number of texts could be much larger, but it seems more reasonable to keep to a smaller number. Allan Bloom is helpful here: "Liberal education should give the student the sense that learning must and can be both synoptic and precise. For this, a very small, detailed problem can be the best way, if it is framed so as to open out on the whole." Bloom also suggests that the specific intention is to "lead to the permanent questions, to make the student aware of them and give him some competence in the important works that treat of them."[47]

It should be noted that many of the texts speak of far more than the rubric under which they are placed here. Thus, for example, Gertrude Himmelfarb's essay on liberty is offered, while John Stuart Mill's *On Liberty* is not; however, it will be difficult to give Himmelfarb a fair reading without dealing closely with Mill.

It should be noted, too, that the texts are not sufficient. The notion of a repertoire of working knowledge suggests skill and dexterity in bringing to bear on the teaching situation a wide variety of strategies, approaches, techniques, and practices. Surely, a good teacher will not find it appropriate that students engage solely in memorization and recall. At the same time, we cannot accept the notion that everyone has an innate sense of democracy, political constitution, and rights and responsibilities, and that everyone is thus free to engage in talk of these matters without expecting to do any heavy lifting. Mystery writer Harry Kemelman tells about his protagonist, Rabbi Small, dealing with college students during the first class session. The students are shocked to find that there will be required reading, and that there will be lectures. Why not have a discussion course, says one student. The rabbi considers, shakes his head, and says, "You mean that by combining your ignorance, you'll be able to achieve knowledge?" No, he says, "let's proceed in the traditional way. When you have some knowledge, then perhaps we can discuss its interpretation."[48]

Bibliographic data regarding the texts are included in the appendix to this chapter.

Constituting Ourselves Politically

There are, of course, many ways to approach the general notions of how we constitute ourselves politically. I begin with Plato and Aristotle, plus one general book about the Greeks, with the assumption that later political philosophers will be addressed in at least a modest way in other parts of one's undergraduate schooling.

Plato, *The Republic*

Aristotle, *Politics*

A. R. Burn, *The Pelican History of Greece* (a good one-volume summary of our political roots)

Democracy: Fundamental Conditions

Again, there are lots of choices for our approaches to studying democracy and the fundamental conditions necessary for democracy. These four titles have particular strengths; perhaps others would be seen as useful to other people.

Thomas Pangle, *The Ennobling of Democracy* (a philosophical analysis of "the civil duties and rights required in a healthy democratic republic")

Robert Putnam, *Making Democracy Work: Civic Traditions in Modern Italy* (an innovative and careful empirical study of the conditions and requirements of democracy)

Carol C. Gould, *Rethinking Democracy: Freedom and Social Cooperation in Politics, Economy, and Society* (an analysis of political constitution and freedom and economic constitution and freedom)

Jean-Francois Revel, *Democracy Against Itself* (explains why we cannot feel complacent about the survival of democracy)

The American Context

Understanding of the context of the American democracy can come through examination of a number of sources. I have included here some of the traditional fundamental documents, along with a basic history of the United States and five analytical texts.

The Declaration of Independence

The Constitution of the United States

The Federalist

Herbert J. Storing, *The Anti-Federalist*

George Washington's Farewell Address

Abraham Lincoln's Springfield Speech, 1857; House Divided Speech; and his Gettysburg Address, 1863

Alexis de Tocqueville, *Democracy in America*

Hugh Brogan, *Longman History of the United States of America* (a good one-volume history)

Ralph Lerner, *The Thinking Revolutionary: Principle and Practice in the New Republic* (an important analysis of Jefferson, Franklin, and Tocqueville; the matter of race; and the matter of commerce)

Mortimer Adler, *We Hold These Truths* (a short analysis of fundamental ideas pertaining to the founding of America)

Garry Wills, *Lincoln at Gettysburg* (an analysis of the Gettysburg address and its relationship to the Declaration of Independence)

Richard Hofstadter, *Anti-Intellectualism in American Life* (in conjunction with Tocqueville, a useful analysis of American character and anti-intellectualism)

Robert Nisbet, *The Present Age* (a short analysis of the vastly increased role of the state in twentieth-century America)

Law

Law is an important aspect of any civil society; America has in large part been shaped by law, by court decisions. The three texts indicated here provide a bit of introduction; some aspects of American law are covered in other texts (such as Ralph Lerner's "The Supreme Court as Republican Schoolmaster" in *The Thinking Revolutionary*).

Lawrence Friedman, *A History of American Law* (a one-volume basic history)

Marbury v. Madison; McCulloch v. Maryland; Dartmouth College v. Woodward; Gibbons v. Ogden; Lochner v. New York; Dred Scott v. Sanford

James Boyd White, "Constituting a Culture of Argument: The Possibilities of American Law," in *When Words Lose Their Meaning*

The Individual and the State

The tension between the individual and the state is an ancient theme. In addition to the texts offered here, one might want to consider the work of Gandhi and, say, Ibsen's *An Enemy of the People*.

Sophocles, *Antigone*

Henry David Thoreau, "Civil Disobedience"

Martin Luther King, Jr., "Letter from Birmingham City Jail," in *A Testament of Hope*

Freedom

According to Thucydides, the Spartan envoys responded to suggestions by a Persian satrap that they surrender to the Persian king with "had you known what freedom was, you would have bidden us fight for it." Freedom is a fundamental aspect of the human condition, surely a fundamental aspect of democracy.

Herbert Muller, *Freedom in the Ancient World, Freedom in the Western World,* and *Freedom in the Modern World* (a classic trilogy)

Donald Treadgold, *Freedom: A History* (a good one-volume history; useful to juxtapose to Muller)

Gertrude Himmelfarb, "Liberty: 'One Very Simple Principle'?," in *On Looking into the Abyss* (a critical analysis of John Stuart Mill's *On Liberty*)

Rights

As Kurland and Lerner point out (in the first text listed in this section), "a statement of rights is a claim, not a request. The language of rights is not that of supplication." They also say, "Claimants must be mindful of what is due them; governors must be reminded that they govern a people who know what is due them."

Philip B. Kurland and Ralph Lerner, *The Founders' Constitution*, Chapter Fourteen, "Rights" (annotated selections from documents relating to the founding of America)

Fyodor Dostoevsky, "The Grand Inquisitor," from *The Brothers Karamazov* (perhaps one of the strongest arguments against rights and for "miracle, mystery, and authority")

Mary Ann Glendon, *Rights Talk* (proposes ways of talking about rights that move beyond maximizing individual considerations)

Equality

Equality is as much a part of the political landscape as notions of freedom and rights. The three texts posed here provide the beginnings of an introduction. The Adams-Jefferson letters can be found in many anthologies (including Kurland and Lerner's); they are singled out because they provide a useful starting point, just as de Tocqueville was called upon in the list of works on the American context. I emphasize here a particular chapter because of the importance of dealing with egalitarianism that leads (perhaps) to a nation filled with a "flock of timid and hard-working animals."

Thomas Jefferson's and John Adams's letters on aristocracy: Adams, July 7, August 14, September 2, November 15, 1813; Jefferson, October 28, 1813, in *The Adams-Jefferson Letters*

Philip B. Kurland and Ralph Lerner, *The Founders' Constitution*, Chapter Fifteen, "Equality"

Alexis de Tocqueville, *Democracy in America* (see especially Volume 2, Part IV, Chapter 6, "What Sort of Despotism Democratic Nations Have to Fear")

Leadership and Power

In any regime, there are rulers. There are those who provide leadership, who one way or another assume considerable powers. How one gains power, and provides leadership, and what happens when leadership changes are questions fundamental to understanding and working in a democracy. The five texts listed here provide a variety of approaches to understanding the questions.

Niccolò Machiavelli, *The Prince*

Isaiah Berlin, "The Originality of Machiavelli," in *Against the Current* (a comprehensive review of the critiques of "The Prince")

Abraham Lincoln's "Perpetuation of Our Political Institutions"

Ralph Lerner, *Revolutions Revisited: Two Faces of the Politics of Enlightenment* (a careful look at Franklin, Burke, Tocqueville, and Lincoln)

Mary Beth Rogers, *Cold Anger* (profiles Ernesto Cortes and suggests another way to look at power, organizing the people, and getting things done)

Rhetoric and Politics

How we choose to talk is critical to how we choose to govern. The four texts listed here help make clear the connection.

Thucydides, *Peloponnesian War* (Books i, ii, iii, and v)

James Boyd White, "The Dissolution of Meaning: Thucydides' History of His World," in *When Words Lose Their Meaning*

Richard Weaver, "Edmund Burke and the Argument from Circumstance," "Abraham Lincoln and the Argument from Definition," and "The Rhetoric of Social Science," in *The Ethics of Rhetoric*

George Orwell, "Politics and the English Language"

World Politics and Nationalism

To understand the American democracy and political constitution, one must have some understanding of the dynamics of what goes on beyond the borders. Here the possibilities for texts are endless; I offer two that seem to provide particularly useful insights.

Edmund Stillman and William Pfaff, *The Politics of Hysteria* (provides the overall context for understanding the twentieth century and the peculiar role of Western civilization)

William Pfaff, *Barbarian Sentiments* (suggests fundamental conditions for national stability)

Democracy and Education

This is the topic at hand, and the texts are numerous. Four that help focus one's thoughts on the interplay between democracy and education are:

Horace Mann, "The Importance of Universal, Free, Public Education"

John Dewey, *Democracy and Education*

Robert Westbrook, *John Dewey and American Democracy*

Lorraine Smith Pangle and Thomas L. Pangle, *The Learning of Liberty: The Educational Ideas of the American Founders*

These, then, are the texts I offer. Would other texts be as useful or even better? Perhaps. We have here, at the least, a point of departure. You might feel that *Antigone* is not necessary to this list. Well and good, I might say: if *Antigone* is to go, what better, more useful text can you prescribe that delineates the tension between individual, state, and higher law? Perhaps you might want to come at the fundamental notion in a different way, say, through prescribing Freud's *Civilization and Its Discontents*; perhaps you might prefer Martin Luther, or Gandhi. Again, well and good. On the other hand, you might want to argue that the notion of tension between the individual and state (and higher law) or the tension between individual and group is, as a fundamental notion, unimportant to the education of educators in a democracy. Well and good: we will be in even deeper waters, but we should have a clearer idea of what we are arguing about than if we simply stayed with the usual nostrums.

If one accepts the fundamental claims as to the role of teachers in a democracy, and if one accepts the texts and notions offered here, then it is clear that there must be some fundamental changes in the ways educators are educated. Surely the civic education of teachers envisioned here cannot be accomplished solely within the confines of teacher education programs. Surely the moral and political matters cannot be covered in the typical potpourri "critical issues in education" course found in most programs. But can we really expect that a teacher preparation program can be extended to such a great degree that these matters can be carefully addressed? Most programs are already seen as too long, especially considering the pay received by the beginning teacher. If one cannot properly fit the consideration of the moral and political dimensions into the current program, and if one cannot extend the program in any significant way, where else can moral and political dimensions be addressed? In continuing education? Surely one cannot expect intending teachers to become facile in all these matters once they are out in the schools. There is too much pressure to deal with the practical and there is too little in-service money to cover what administrators and teachers think they need to deal with, let alone deal with Plato or *The Federalist* papers.

We have no other choice but to consider the arts and sciences—the locale for 75 percent of the intending teacher's time in higher education—as the fundamental place to provide the grounding in matters of the moral and political dimensions of teaching in a democracy. No other option makes serious sense. Educators in the arts and sciences must assume major responsibility for ensuring careful attention to the texts and notions prescribed here. And if other texts and other notions are deemed more appropriate to that civic education, then let the discussion begin. Those in education, those responsible for the education of educators, must assume their own major responsibilities, first for reviewing the texts and notions, and then for initiating the discussions with their arts and sciences colleagues—formidable tasks. Again, with Leo Strauss, "We cannot define our tasks by our powers, for our powers become known to us through performing our tasks."

Appendix: Bibliography of Prescribed Texts

Adams-Jefferson Letters. In Lester J. Cappon (ed.), *The Adams-Jefferson Letters.* Chapel Hill: University of North Carolina Press, 1987.

Adler, Mortimer J. *We Hold These Truths.* New York: Collier Books, 1987.

Aristotle. *Politics.* Many editions.

Berlin, Isaiah. *Against the Current: Essays in the History of Ideas.* New York: Viking Penguin, 1980.

Brogan, Hugh. *Longman History of the United States of America.* New York: Longman, 1985.

Burn, A. R. *The Pelican History of Greece.* New York: Viking Penguin, 1985.

Dewey, John. *Democracy and Education.* New York: Free Press, 1966.

Dostoevsky, Fyodor. *The Brothers Karamazov.* (R. Pevear and L. Volokhonsky, trans.) New York: Random House, 1991.

Federalist, The. Many editions.

Friedman, Lawrence. *A History of American Law* (2nd ed.). New York: Simon & Schuster, 1985.

Glendon, Mary Ann. *Rights Talk: The Impoverishment of Political Discourse.* New York: Free Press, 1991.

Gould, Carol C. *Rethinking Democracy: Freedom and Social Cooperation in Politics, Economics, and Society.* Cambridge: Cambridge University Press, 1988.

Himmelfarb, Gertrude. *On Looking into the Abyss.* New York: Knopf, 1994.

Hofstadter, Richard. *Anti-Intellectualism in American Life.* New York: Knopf, 1964.

King, Martin Luther, Jr. *A Testament of Hope: The Essential Writings of Martin Luther King.* San Francisco: HarperSanFrancisco, 1991.

Kurland, Philip B. and Ralph Lerner. *The Founders' Constitution: Major Themes,* Vol. 1. Chicago: University of Chicago Press, 1987.

Lerner, Ralph. *Revolutions Revisited: Two Faces of the Politics of Enlightenment.* Chapel Hill: University of North Carolina Press, 1994.

Lerner, Ralph. *The Thinking Revolutionary: Principle and Practice in the New Republic.* Ithaca, N.Y.: Cornell University Press, 1987.

Lincoln, Abraham. "Perpetuation of our Political Institutions." In Don Fehrenbacher (ed.), *Speeches and Writings,* Vol. 1. New York: Library of America, 1989.

Machiavelli, Niccolò. *The Prince.* (H. C. Mansfield, Jr., trans.) Chicago: University of Chicago Press, 1985.

Mann, Horace. "The Importance of Universal, Free, Public Education." Many editions.

Muller, Herbert J. *Freedom in the Ancient World.* New York: Harper, 1961.

Muller, Herbert J. *Freedom in the Modern World.* New York: Harper, 1966.

Muller, Herbert J. *Freedom in the Western World.* New York: Harper, 1963.

Nisbet, Robert. *The Present Age: Progress and Anarchy in Modern America.* New York: Harper & Row, 1988.

Orwell, George. "Politics and the English Language." In S. Orwell and I. Angus (eds.), *In Front of Your Nose: The Collected Essays, Journalism and Letters of George Orwell, 1945–1950,* vol. 4, ed. 1. New York: Harcourt, Brace, Jovanovich, 1968, pp. 127–140.

Pangle, Thomas L. *The Ennobling of Democracy: The Challenge of the Postmodern Age.* Baltimore, Md.: Johns Hopkins University Press, 1992.

Pangle, Lorraine Smith, and Thomas L. Pangle. *The Learning of Liberty: The Educational Ideas of the American Founders.* Lawrence: University Press of Kansas, 1993.

Pfaff, William. *Barbarian Sentiments.* New York: Hill and Wang, 1989.

Plato. *The Republic.* Many editions.

Putnam, Robert D. *Making Democracy Work: Civic Traditions in Modern Italy.* Princeton, N.J.: Princeton University Press, 1993.

Revel, Jean-Francois. *Democracy Against Itself: The Future of the Democratic Impulse.* New York: Free Press, 1993.

Rogers, Mary Beth. *Cold Anger: A Story of Faith and Power Politics.* Denton: University of North Texas Press, 1990.

Sophocles. *Antigone.* Many editions.

Stillman, Edmund, and William Pfaff. *The Politics of Hysteria.* New York: Harper, 1964.

Storing, Herbert J. (ed.) *The Anti-Federalist: Writings by the Opponents of the Constitution* (Abridged ed.). Chicago: University of Chicago Press, 1985.

Thoreau, Henry David. "Civil Disobedience." Many editions.

Thucydides. *The Peloponnesian War.* Many editions.

Tocqueville, Alexis de. *Democracy in America.* (G. Lawrence, trans.) New York: Anchor, 1969.

Treadgold, Donald. *Freedom: A History.* New York: New York University Press, 1990.

Washington, George. *Farewell Address.* Many editions.

Weaver, Richard M. *The Ethics of Rhetoric.* South Bend, Ind.: Regnery/Gateway, 1953.

Westbrook, Robert B. *John Dewey and American Democracy.* Ithaca, N.Y.: Cornell University Press, 1991.

White, James Boyd. *When Words Lose Their Meaning: Constitutions and Reconstitutions of Language, Character, and Community.* Chicago: University of Chicago Press, 1984.

Wills, Garry. *Lincoln at Gettysburg: The Words That Remade America.* New York: Simon & Schuster, 1992.

Notes

1. Plato, *Laws* (644a), translated by T. L. Pangle (Chicago: University of Chicago Press, 1988).

2. Abraham Lincoln, "To the People of Sangamo County," in *Speeches and Writings*, edited by D. Fehrenbacher (New York: Library of America, 1989), vol. 1, p. 4.

3. John Adams, letter to Thomas Jefferson, June 19, 1815, in *The Adams-Jefferson Letters*, edited by L. J. Cappan (Chapel Hill: University of North Carolina Press, 1987), p. 443.

4. *The People Shall Judge*, edited by the staff, Social Sciences 1, The College of the University of Chicago (Chicago: University of Chicago Press, 1949), p. vii.

5. Ralph Lerner, *The Thinking Revolutionary* (Ithaca, N.Y.: Cornell University Press, 1987), p. 61.

6. Leo Strauss, "Jerusalem and Athens: Some Preliminary Reflections," in *Leo Strauss: Studies in Platonic Political Philosophy* (Chicago: University of Chicago Press, 1983), p. 147.

7. Richard Hofstadter, *Anti-Intellectualism in American Life* (New York: Knopf, 1964), p. 299.

8. Thomas Jefferson, "A Bill for the More General Diffusion of Knowledge," in *Writings*, edited by M. D. Peterson (New York: Library of America, 1984), pp. 365–373. For a useful discussion, see Lorraine Smith Pangle and Thomas L. Pangle, *The Learning of Liberty: The Educational Ideas of the American Founders* (Lawrence: University Press of Kansas, 1993), Chapter Six. See also Ralph Lerner, *The Thinking Revolutionary*, Chapter Two.

9. George Washington, "First Annual Address to Congress," in *The Writings of George Washington*, edited by J. C. Fitzpatrick (Washington, D.C.: Government Printing Office, 1939), vol. 30, p. 493.

10. Benjamin Rush, "A Plan for the Establishment of Public Schools and the Diffusion of Knowledge in Pennsylvania," in *Essays on Education in the Early Republic*, edited by F. Rudolph (Cambridge, Mass.: Belknap Press of Harvard University Press, 1965), p. 21.

11. Noah Webster, "On the Education of Youth in America," in *Essays on Education in the Early Republic*, edited by F. Rudolph (Cambridge, Mass.: Belknap Press of Harvard University Press, 1965), p. 59.

12. Webster, "On the Education of Youth in America," p. 57.

13. Robert Coram, "Political Inquiries: To Which is Added, a Plan for the General Establishment of Schools Throughout the United States," in *Essays on Education in the Early Republic*, edited by F. Rudolph (Cambridge, Mass.: Belknap Press of Harvard University Press, 1965), p. 126.

14. Samuel Doggett, "A Discourse on Education," in *Essays on Education in the Early Republic*, edited by F. Rudolph (Cambridge, Mass.: Belknap Press of Harvard University Press, 1965), p. 160.

15. Robert Maynard Hutchins, *The Higher Learning in America* (New Haven: Yale University Press, 1936), pp. 114–115.

16. Hutchins, *The Higher Learning*, p. 131.

17. Robert Maynard Hutchins, *No Friendly Voice* (Chicago: University of Chicago Press, 1936), pp. 130, 131.

18. Ryland W. Crary (ed.), *Education for Democratic Citizenship*, Twenty-Second Yearbook of the National Council for the Social Studies (Washington, D.C.: National Education Association, 1951), p. v.

19. John J. Patrick, *Political Socialization of American Youth: Implications for Secondary School Social Studies*. Research Bulletin No. 3 (Washington, D.C.: National Council for the Social Studies, National Education Association, 1967), p. 28.

20. Patrick, *Political Socialization of American Youth*, p. 62.

21. Patrick, *Political Socialization of American Youth*, p. 66.

22. American Federation of Teachers, *Education for Democracy: A Statement of Principles* (Washington, D.C.: American Federation of Teachers, 1987), p. 9.

23. American Federation of Teachers, *Education for Democracy*, p. 10.

24. American Federation of Teachers, *Education for Democracy*, pp. 20–21.

25. Freeman Butts, *The Civic Mission of Educational Reform: Perspectives for the Public and the Profession* (Stanford, Calif.: Hoover Institution, 1989), p. 272.

26. Freeman Butts, "The Revival of Civic Learning Requires a Prescribed Curriculum," *Liberal Education*, 1982, *68*(4), 318. For a discussion of Butts's views of civic learning, see also "Teacher Education and the Revival of Civic Learning: A Reprise of Yesteryear's Theme," *Journal of Teacher Education*, 1983, *34*(6), 48–49; Joe R. Burnett responds in the same issue, pp. 50–51. It is interesting to note that although the theme of this issue of the *Journal of Teacher Education* is "The Civic Education of the American Teacher," only one of the twenty-one authors (Mortimer Adler, as we shall see) addresses the question of what should be part of the intending teacher's working knowledge of civics and democracy.

27. Jeffrey Hart, "Reform Must Begin with K-12," *Academic Questions*, 1993, *6*(4), 87–88.

28. Jeffrey Hart, "Reform Must Begin with K-12," pp. 88. Emphasis in original.

29. Rita Kramer, *Ed School Follies: The Miseducation of America's Teachers* (New York: Free Press, 1991), p. 219.

30. Holmes Group, *Tomorrow's Teachers* (East Lansing, Mich: Holmes Group, 1986); Carnegie Forum on Education and the Economy, *A*

Nation Prepared: Teachers for the 21st Century (New York: Carnegie, 1986).

31. Daniel Liston and Kenneth M. Zeichner, *Teacher Education and the Social Conditions of Schooling* (New York: Routledge, 1990), pp. 49–50.

32. Liston and Zeichner, *Teacher Education and the Social Conditions of Schooling,* p. 93.

33. Liston and Zeichner, *Teacher Education and the Social Conditions of Schooling,* p. 117.

34. Henry Giroux, *Teachers as Intellectuals: Toward a Critical Pedagogy of Learning* (Granby, Mass.: Bergin & Garvey, 1988), p. 127. See also Henry Giroux and Peter McLaren, "Teacher Education and the Politics of Engagement: The Case for Democratic Schooling," *Harvard Educational Review,* 1986, *56*(3), 213–238.

35. Giroux, *Teachers as Intellectuals,* p. 128.

36. Henry A. Giroux and Peter McLaren, "Teacher Education and the Politics of Democratic Reform," in *Teachers as Intellectuals,* by H. A. Giroux, p. 166.

37. Giroux and McLaren, "Teacher Education and the Politics of Democratic Reform," p. 172.

38. Giroux and McLaren, "Teacher Education and the Politics of Democratic Reform," pp. 172–174.

39. Giroux and McLaren, "Teacher Education and the Politics of Democratic Reform," p. 165.

40. Giroux and McLaren, "Teacher Education and the Politics of Democratic Reform," p. 166.

41. Thomas Pangle, *The Ennobling of Democracy: The Challenge of the Postmodern Age* (Baltimore, Md.: Johns Hopkins University Press, 1992), p. 181.

42. Mortimer J. Adler, "Understanding the U.S.A.," *Journal of Teacher Education,* 1983, *34*(6), 36–37.

43. Peter Pouncey, "On a Background for Teachers," in *Against Mediocrity: The Humanities in America's High Schools,* edited by C. E. Finn, Jr., D. Ravitch, and R. T. Fancher (New York: Holmes & Meier, 1984), pp. 133–153.

44. Abraham Flexner, *Medical Education in the United States and Canada,* Bulletin no. 4 (New York: Carnegie Foundation for the Advancement of Teaching, 1910), p. 26.

45. James Boswell, *Life of Samuel Johnson* (Oxford: Oxford University Press, 1970), p. 744.

46. Boswell, *Life of Samuel Johnson,* p. 319.

47. Allan Bloom, *The Closing of the American Mind* (New York: Simon & Schuster, 1987), p. 343.

48. Harry Kemelman, *Tuesday the Rabbi Saw Red* (Greenwich, Conn.: Fawcet Crest, 1973), pp. 50–51.

Afterword

In his or her own way, each of the contributors to this book has tried to say what is important about the topics of democracy, education, and schooling and the relationships among them. The relative emphasis varies, of course, both because of the particular topic each author was invited to address and because of differences in temperament and belief. It is not my intent here to try to bring the several and varied sentiments of the contributors into some sort of synthesized whole or a new conceptual system. Nor is it my intent to summarize: such a summary, however effectively written, is part of the preface to these essays, and the views of the world in the preceding pages can speak well enough for themselves.

Nonetheless, it seems to me, and I trust to the reader, that despite differences in emphasis and perspective, the contributors offer us a remarkably consistent view of the world. That view centers on the importance of the individual human spirit, the importance of the human community, and the importance of being a free, responsible individual with a mind and conscience of one's own. It is a view that is summarized by Nathan Tarcov in his presentation of the classical standards of democracy at its best, a summary that I recapitulate here in numbered form:

1. A willingness to teach and learn in debate before taking action
2. A collectivity that surpasses even the few best in deliberation by each bringing his or her own share of virtue and prudence
3. Rule of law as a product of popular deliberation
4. A liberal tolerance and openness
5. Encouragement of virtue through distribution of office and honor on the basis of ability to benefit the community
6. The flourishing of a fundamental diversity of human types
7. A receptivity to elements of other regimes
8. A liberty that fosters sentiments of friendship and community

To these eight points, a ninth must be added. Mary Catherine Bateson reminds us "that the unit of survival is the species in its environment, and that the species that destroys its environment destroys itself."

How might readers react to this view of the world? In the preface it was suggested that at least two groups of people might look askance at a work on democracy, education, and schooling, one group thinking the volume redundant, the other thinking it just plain wrong. For those who think the volume redundant, in that they agreed with the basic premises and thought such matters settled, it might be hoped that what this volume does is offer a way of viewing and talking about the world that does more than reinforce beliefs already well situated. The collective intent of the volume is to reexamine the familiar, and by sustained holding of the familiar in new and different ways, to lead to a better and deeper understanding of the ideals and the challenges of democracy, the role of education, and the role the schools play. It is not enough simply to say that democracy is a good thing and that schools should support a democratic society. If one is going to deal with these matters, one had best be armed and clearsighted about what one believes.

As for those who disagree with the basic premises of democracy and who have a deep distrust of the people—those who in the end side with the Grand Inquisitor—there is little in this volume that will lead to an epiphany. It is asking too much of one slim volume to alter fundamental beliefs.

Perhaps there is another group of readers, however, who have found something more in this volume. Between convinced democrats and equally convinced antidemocrats range a good number of people who with complacency and inertia accept the prevailing political structure in America. But complacency and inertia are hardly sound building blocks for a democratic society, as we have seen, and there is always the danger that a complacent people can be moved by fear, insecurity, and uncertainty to reject democracy in favor of something far worse. Francis Fukuyama's notion of the "end of history" has perhaps been misinterpreted, but if a liberal representative democracy is indeed the ultimate and best end of history, there surely are enough examples of failed democracies and enough real and growing threats to civic democratic society in our time to make us question whether the end is in sight.

The "new world order" (how quickly that phrase moved in and out of our consciousness!) is in fact a world hardly stable and secure, as will be suggested by even a cursory review of civil, ethnic, and religious strife. The odds of survival for fledgling democracies trying to emerge from autocratic regimes are not good. As several authors in the book have noted, we must acknowledge the severe challenge posed by Robert Putnam in his claim that democracy can only thrive in a society that possesses a goodly amount of trust, exchange, and social capital, none of which are created by fiat or ukase.

Within America, the danger to democracy stems not from difficulties of emerging from autocracy, but (as has been well documented in hundreds of analyses) from fear, uncertainty, growing lack of trust, and unwillingness to accept the legitimacy of societal institutions. Based on his years of observing political strife in China, Theodore White concluded that we choose government and surrender some of our freedoms to protect ourselves against random violence, from dangers we cannot otherwise cope with. Real or perceived—and who is to gainsay the difference in effect— fear of unknown, unpredictable threats to one's basic safety and well-being poses a genuine threat to the political order. The need for security, stability, and predictability is real, to be sure, even part of the human condition. The question remains how much of one's fundamental freedoms one is willing to trade to meet that need. The people of Singapore apparently are willing to trade a good deal (as are others who wish to do business in Singapore: witness the performance of the *International Herald Tribune* in allowing its reporters to be fined and having its executives extend deepest apologies to the Singapore government for having the audacity to criticize the Singapore judiciary). The Grand Inquisitor is still with us, austere, quietly watching, offering us Singapore as proof of what we really want.

It is to the disenchanted and the tired, those who are beginning to suffer from failure of nerve, those who are beginning to believe that maybe our democracy is, in the end, not worth the price they think they must pay, that this volume might offer even more than it might to the already convinced. What we have tried to offer, at the very least, is some clarity of vision and some understanding of what is at stake, what we think is worth struggling for, and what the trade-offs are. In part, then, this volume offers some means for achieving better clarity of political discourse. Armed with such an understanding, one will be more likely to view critically, for example, arguments for dismantling America's public school system in favor of private schools. If one thinks that democracy is important, and that schools are important for enculturating the young into the habits of mind necessary to maintain our democracy, then one certainly has to question the arguments for privatizing schools based solely on efficiency in producing workers. And thus, for example, one will look carefully at propositions for national standards and (in effect) a national curriculum, to see whether such propositions support or threaten achievement of the classical ideals of democracy.

Beyond clarity of discourse, however, this book offers what we hope is a persuasive case for the democratic ideals and for the willingness to struggle for those ideals and to accept the challenges they embody. A similar case must be made for all citizens by our schools. As Tocqueville reminds us, "if we do not succeed in gradually introducing democratic institutions among us, and if we despair of imparting to all citizens those ideas and sentiments which first prepare them for freedom and then allow them to enjoy it, there will be no independence left for anybody, neither for the middle classes nor for the nobility, neither for the poor nor for the rich, but only an equal tyranny for all."

We must succeed in introducing democratic institutions among us (and working for a world in which others are free to do the same), and we must do so, as Tocqueville emphasizes, for *all*. Beyond that we must succeed in rejecting the argument of the Grand Inquisitor; we must reject the blandishments of miracle, mystery, and authority.

These tasks, in an uncertain world, may seem beyond us. We can only proceed with them, for—again recalling the wise words of Leo Strauss—"We cannot define our tasks by our powers, for our powers become known to us through performing our tasks."

—R.S.

Name Index

A

Aaron, M., 175
Adams, John, 25, 36, 90, 245, 254, 266, 272
Adams, Samuel, 36
Adan, Jane, 67
Adler, Mortimer J., 96, 121, 122, 259, 260, 264, 270, 273, 274
Aikin, Wilford M., 206
Alexander, Karl L., 178
Ancess, Jacqueline, 151, 180–181
Anderson, Charles, 216–217, 218, 224, 227, 228, 236, 242
Anthony, Susan B., 191
Apple, Michael, 179
Appleby, Joyce, 35
Arendt, Hannah, 182, 206, 209
Arias, Beatriz, 175
Aristotle, 9–14, 19, 21, 27, 29, 31, 32, 34, 214, 215, 231, 233, 242, 263, 270
Armour-Thomas, Eleanor, 160, 176

B

Bacon, Francis, 229, 243
Baker, Jean H., 147
Bakhtin, Michael M., 47, 50, 51–52, 67
Baldwin, James, 182–183, 191, 206
Banks, James A., 175–176, 193, 208
Banner, James M., Jr., 195, 201, 208, 209
Barber, Benjamin R., 88, 95, 96, 97, 112, 121, 122, 125, 126, 127, 135, 145, 146, 148, 195, 207, 208

Barilli, Renato, 241
Barr, Rebecca, 176
Barthes, Roland, 258
Bateson, Gregory, 75, 86
Bateson, Mary Catherine, 69, 75–76, 86, 276
Battistoni, Richard M., 138–140, 145, 148, 149
Bazerman, Charles, 239–240
Beiner, Ronald, 206
Bender, John, 240
Bennett, William, 94
Benson, Lee, 150
Berends, Mark, 178
Berlin, Isaiah, 260, 267, 270
Bernard, Henry, 129
Bizzell, Patricia, 241
Black, Edwin, 221, 242
Bloom, Allan, 262, 274
Bloom, Benjamin S., 121
Boswell, James, 274
Bowers, C. A., 86
Boyer, Ernest L., 134, 148, 179
Brady, Marion, 209
Braudel, Fernand, 260
Brint, Steven, 148
Brogan, Hugh, 264, 270
Brophy, Jere, 178
Brown, J. Stanley, 133, 147
Bruner, Jerome, 66
Bryk, Anthony, 180
Bugnion, Jacqueline, 124
Bull, Barry L., 95, 121–122
Burke, Edmund, 3, 34, 267
Burke, Kenneth, 234, 243

Burn, A. R., 263, 270
Burnett, Joe R., 273
Burnham, Walter Dean, 147
Butts, Freeman, 254–255, 273

C

Callan, Eamonn, 149
Callicles, 225, 226
Campbell, John Angus, 211, 243
Carter, Jimmy, 120
Church, Robert L., 147
Climacus, Johannes, 224
Clinton, Bill, 126, 145–146
Cmiel, Kenneth, 240
Cohen, David K., 177, 179
Coleman, James S., 104, 123
Coleridge, Samuel Taylor, 43, 65
Coles, Robert, 60, 62, 68
Columbus, Christopher, 224
Conley, Thomas M., 240
Cooper, Eric, 178
Cooper, James Fennimore, 33, 36
Coram, Robert, 251, 272
Cortes, Ernesto, 267
Counts, George S., 141, 149, 258
Crary, Ryland W., 273
Cremin, Lawrence A., 122, 147, 183, 206
Croly, Herbert, 149
Cuban, Larry, 117, 123
Cubberly, Ellwood P., 132, 147
Cusick, Philip, 176

D

Dahrendorf, Ralph, 227
Darling-Hammond, Linda, 151, 174, 175, 177, 178, 179, 180–181
Darwin, Charles, 77, 225
Davis, Donna G., 178, 179
Debs, Eugene V., 191
Delpit, Lisa D., 201, 209
De Romilly, Jacqueline, 239, 240
Derrida, Jacques, 258
Dewey, John, 136–138, 141, 142, 145, 148–149, 150, 167, 180, 184, 185,

186, 188, 190, 194, 197, 206, 207, 208, 209, 210, 246, 268, 270
Diamond, Martin, 36
Dietz, Mary, 208
Dillon, George L., 240, 242
Dillon, J. T., 208
Dizard, Jan E., 68
Doggett, Samuel, 251, 272
Dostoevsky, Fyodor, 266, 270
Dreeben, Robert, 176
DuBois, W.E.B., 187, 205, 207
Dunn, James, 34

E

Eckstrom, Ruth, 178
Eder, Donna, 179
Eliot, Charles W., 162
Elshtain, Jean Bethke, 190, 207
Emerson, Ralph Waldo, 68, 130, 146, 191
Epstein, David F., 36
Ericson, David F., 34, 35
Erikson, Erik H., 93, 121

F

Falk, Beverly, 180–181
Farrar, Eleanor, 177, 179
Farrell, Thomas B., 240
Farson, Richard, 86
Felmlee, Diane, 179
Fenstermacher, Gary D, 106, 112, 123
Ferguson, Ronald F., 160, 176
Fine, Michelle, 176, 180
Finley, Merilee K., 179
Finn, Huck, 56, 64
Fisher, Walter R., 239
Flexner, Abraham, 260–261, 274
Foucault, Michel, 258
Franco, Paul, 34
Franklin, Benjamin, 90, 264, 267
Fraser, Nancy, 192, 208
Freud, Sigmund, 51, 268
Friedman, Lawrence, 265, 270
Friedrich, Paul, 34
Fuch, Lawrence H., 208

Fukuyama, Francis, 276
Fuller, Buckminster, 74
Fuller, Steve, 226, 240, 243
Furet, François, 34

G

Gadamer, Hans-George, 210, 258
Gadlin, Howard, 68
Gaia, 74
Galston, William, 146
Gamoran, Adam, 176, 178, 179
Gandhi, Mohandas, 265, 268
Gardner, Howard, 174, 178, 181
Garver, Eugene, 226, 235, 240, 242, 243
Gay, Geneva, 176, 179–180
Giddens, Anthony, 50, 53, 67
Gilbert, Neal, 240
Giroux, Henry, 257–258, 274
Glaser, Robert, 173–174, 180, 181
Glendon, Mary Ann, 56, 68, 206, 266, 270
Goldstein, Barry, 159, 176
Good, Thomas L., 178
Goodlad, John I., 87, 121, 122, 123, 124, 176, 179, 180
Gorgias, 214, 225
Gould, Carol C., 263, 270
Gould, Stephen Jay, 177, 178
Graham, Patricia Albjerg, 147
Grant, Ruth W., 35
Grayson, 60, 64
Green, Philip, 188, 207
Greene, Maxine, 121, 209
Grimaldi, William M. A., 242
Gross, Alan G., 240
Guiton, Gretchen, 179
Gutierrez, Ramon, 67
Gutmann, Amy, 67, 174, 175, 208, 209

H

Habermas, Jürgen, 258
Hackney, Sheldon, 144–145, 150
Hall, G. Stanley, 162
Hallinan, Maureen T., 179, 180
Hamilton, Alexander, 30, 31, 32, 33,

34, 36, 90, 128, 135–136, 141, 145, 146, 153
Hanna, Paul R., 209
Harding, Vincent, 188, 207
Harkavy, Ira, 150
Hart, Jeffrey, 255, 273
Hartman, William T., 176
Hermes, 5
Herodotus, 260
Herzberg, Bruch, 241
Hess, Karl, 189–190, 207
Hiatt, Diana Buell, 123
Higgins, Ann, 209
Hilliard, Asa G., 177
Himmelfarb, Gertrude, 262, 265, 270
Hobbes, Thomas, 100
Hoffman, Eva, 44–45, 64, 66
Hofstadter, Richard, 249, 264, 270, 272
Holmes, Stephen, 34
Hooks, Bell, 207
Hopps, Don, 123
Howland, R. L., 241
Hubbell, Harry, 213, 241
Hunt, Maurice P., 205, 209
Hutchins, Robert Maynard, 123, 252, 273

I

Ibsen, Henrik, 265
Ijsseling, Samuel, 239
Isocrates, 213, 214, 215, 216, 218, 222, 223, 225, 226, 227, 237, 241, 242

J

Jacoby, Russell, 207
Jaeger, Werner, 242
Jarratt, Susan C., 240, 242
Jay, John, 34, 90
Jefferson, Thomas, 24, 29, 33, 36, 90, 94, 128–129, 134, 136, 138, 141–142, 143, 145, 146, 149–150, 153, 154, 161, 165–166, 195, 249–250, 254–255, 264, 266, 272
Jesus, 90, 101

Johnson, Samuel, 237, 261–262
Jonsen, Albert R., 239, 240
Joubert, François, 111

K

Kahn, Victoria, 242
Kamin, Leon, 177
Kant, Immanuel, 43, 44
Karabel, Jerome, 148
Karoly, L., 179
Katznelson, Ira, 146
Kaufman, Julie E., 177, 179
Kemelman, Harry, 262–263, 274
Keniston, Ken, 86
Kennedy, George A., 240, 241
Kennedy, Paul M., 102, 122
Kenny, John, 34
Kerr, Donna H., 37–38
Kierkegaard, Søren, 224, 228–229, 243
Kimball, Bruce A., 239, 240, 242
King, Martin Luther, Jr., 191, 265, 270
Kliebard, Herbert M., 177
Kohlberg, Lawrence, 205, 209
Kornhaber, Mindy, 174, 181
Kozol, Jonathan, 159–160, 176, 177
Kramer, Rita, 255–256, 273
Kramnick, Isaac, 35
Kurland, Philip B., 266, 270

L

Lacan, Jacques, 258
Ladson-Billings, Gloria, 208
Lasch, Christopher, 148
Lawson, Hal A., 123
Lear, Jonathan, 34
Lee, Gordon C., 175
Lee, Valerie, 180
Leech, Geoffrey N., 241
Leff, Michael C., 220–221, 235, 242
Lentz, Tony M., 239
Lerner, Ralph, 34, 35, 247, 264, 265, 266, 267, 270, 272
Levi, Edward H., 235, 243
Levine, Daniel O., 148

Lightfoot, Sara Lawrence, 163, 177
Lincoln, Abraham, 140, 149, 245, 259, 264, 267, 270, 272
Lippmann, Walter, 127, 146
Liston, Daniel, 256–257, 274
Locke, John, 19–24, 26, 30, 31, 35–36
Loh, Wallace D., 110–111, 123
Lonergan, Bernard J. F., 237, 242, 243
Lovejoy, Arthur O., 86
Lovelock, James E., 74, 86
Luther, Martin, 268
Lynd, Helen, 132, 147
Lynd, Robert, 132, 147

M

McCloskey, Donald N., 240
McCraw, Thomas K., 121
McDaniel, Janet E., 207
McDermott, John, 64, 68
McDill, Edward L., 178
McGuffey, William, 131
Machiavelli, Niccolò, 14–18, 19, 20, 30, 35, 39, 235, 267, 270
MacIntyre, Alasdair, 40, 66
McKnight, Curtis C., 175
McLaren, Peter, 257–258, 274
Madaus, George F., 178
Madison, James, 26, 28–29, 30, 31, 32, 34, 90, 128, 146, 195, 254
Manin, Bernard, 34
Mann, Horace, 129–130, 146, 268, 270
Mansfield, Harvey C., Jr., 35
Mare, Robert, 178
Martin, Jane Roland, 55, 56, 68
Mathews, David, 209
Mattson, Kevin, 150
Megill, Allan, 240
Meier, Deborah W., 121, 140–141, 144, 149, 150
Mercer, J. R., 177
Messerli, Jonathan, 146
Metcalf, Lawrence E., 205, 209
Mill, John Stuart, 43, 65, 66, 262, 265
Miller, Carolyn, 242

Miller, Peter, 34
Monfort, F., 175
Morrison, Toni, 207
Muller, Herbert M., 262, 270
Murchland, Bernard, 195, 208

N

Nasaw, David, 133, 147
Nelson, Jack L., 210
Nelson, John S., 240
Newman, John Henry, 236, 243
Newman, Vicky, 123
Newmann, Fred M., 205, 209
Nietzsche, Friedrich, 65
Nisbet, Robert, 264, 270
Noddings, Nel, 67, 121

O

Oakes, Jeannie, 160–161, 176–177,
    178, 179, 180
Oakeshott, Michael, 97, 105–106, 121,
    122, 123, 205
Ogbu, John U., 166, 178, 180, 208
Oliver, Donald W., 205, 209
Omi, Michael, 207
Orfield, Gary F., 175
Orwell, George, 267, 271
Orwin, Clifford, 34
Otis, James, 36

P

Paine, Thomas, 25
Paley, Vivian Gussin, 48–50, 58, 59,
    64, 66, 67
Pangle, Lorraine Smith, 36, 146, 268,
    271, 272
Pangle, Thomas L., 35, 258–259, 263,
    268, 271, 272, 274
Parker, Walter C., 182, 207, 209
Patrick, John J., 273
Pera, Marcello, 239
Percy, Walker, 66
Pericles, 2–6, 16, 20, 30
Perry, Imani, 179
Persell, Caroline Hodges, 176

Pfaff, William, 268, 271
Pharoah, 217
Phenix, Philip H., 99, 122
Phillips, Anne, 189, 207, 208
Piche, Dianne M., 175
Pippin, Robert B., 34
Plato, 6–9, 19, 34, 214, 215, 216, 217,
    225, 226, 244, 260, 263, 269, 271
Pocock, J.G.A., 35
Polakow, Valerie, 59–60, 68
Polus, 225
Potter, Alonzo, 146
Poulakos, John, 215, 242
Pouncey, Peter, 260, 274
Powell, Arthur G., 177, 179
Power, F. Clark, 209
Prelli, Lawrence J., 240
Press, Gerald, 241
Protagoras, 226
Puckett, John L., 150
Pullin, Diana, 176
Putnam, Robert D., 57–58, 68, 109–
    110, 123, 263, 271, 277

Q

Quintilian, 220–221, 242

R

Rahe, Paul A., 35
Rawls, John, 39, 56, 66
Ray, John, 34
Redfield, James, 34
Revel, Jean-François, 263, 271
Rist, Ray C., 177, 180
Rodriguez, Richard, 45–46, 64, 67
Rogers, Mary Beth, 267, 271
Roland, Alan, 50, 52–53, 67
Romer, Roy, 94
Romulus, 16
Roosevelt, Franklin Delano, 259
Roosevelt, Theodore, 259
Rorty, Richard, 191, 207
Rosenbaum, James E., 177, 179
Ruderman, Richard, 34
Rush, Benjamin, 250, 272

S

Sagan, Carl, 238
Sagan, Eli, 50, 51, 67
Said, Edward, 207
Sale, Kirkpatrick, 68
Sandel, Michael J., 123
Sanford, Alan, 86
Sarason, Seymour B., 121, 122
Saussure, Ferdinand de, 258
Scheffler, Israel, 96, 122
Schiappa, Edward, 213–214, 241
Schiller, Herbert I., 64, 68
Schlesinger, Arthur, 193, 208
Schofield, Janet W., 175
Schwab, Joseph J., 185–186, 207
Scott, James C., 46, 67
Scott, John T., 34
Sedlak, Michael, 147, 176
Seigel, Jerrold E., 239, 241
Selvin, Molly, 179
Shaver, James P., 205, 209
Shelley, Mary, 185
Sherk, John, 178
Short, Michael H., 241
Silard, John, 159, 176
Simons, Herbert W., 240
Sinclair, R. L., 178
Sizer, Theodore R., 176, 197, 209
Skinner, B. F., 100–101, 122
Smith, Mary Lou, 180
Snyder, Jon, 177
Socrates, 5–6, 101, 226, 251
Soder, Roger, 244
Sophocles, 265, 271
Sorensen, Aage B., 177, 179
Stanley, William B., 208
Stapledon, Olaf, 101–102, 122
Sternberg, Robert J., 178
Stillman, Edmund, 268, 271
Storing, H. J., 264, 271
Stourzh, Gerald, 36
Strauss, Leo, 34, 122, 248, 261, 269, 272, 278
Struever, Nancy S., 239
Sullivan, B. Todd, 146
Sunstein, Cass, 34

T

Talbert, Joan E., 179
Tallmon, James Michael, 239
Tarcov, Nathan, 1, 35, 36, 275
Taylor, Charles, 66, 67, 208
Taylor, William L., 175
Tennyson, Alfred, 246
Thales, 237
Theobald, Paul, 123
Theuth, 217
Thoreau, Henry David, 68, 265, 271
Thucydides, 2, 5, 34, 260, 265, 267, 271
Tocqueville, Alexis de, 57, 106, 151, 153, 175, 189, 259, 264, 266, 267, 271, 278
Toulmin, Stephen, 239, 240
Treadgold, Donald, 265, 271
Trimble, K., 178
Tyack, David, 155, 175, 177
Tyler, Ralph, 116

U

Ulich, Robert, 121
Untersteiner, Mario, 239
Useem, Elizabeth L., 179

V

van der Post, Laurens, 111, 123
Van Winkle, Rip, 56
Veblen, Thorstein, 234
Velasquez, Eduardo, 34
Vickers, Brian, 239, 240
Villegas, Ana Maria, 178
Viviano, Frank, 123
Voegelin, Eric, 243
von Foerster, Heinz, 86

W

Wagar, W. Warren, 99, 122
Walzer, Michael, 143, 145, 150
Ward, Edward J., 143–144, 145, 150
Washington, Booker T., 187
Washington, George, 90, 128, 146, 250, 254, 264, 271, 272
Watson, Bernard C., 177

Weaver, Richard M., 267, 271
Webster, Noah, 131, 250–251, 272
Weir, Margaret, 146
Weisenthal, Simon, 233
Wellberg, David E., 240
Welter, Rush, 130, 146
Welty, Eudora, 149
West, Cornel, 179, 207
Westbrook, Robert B., 125, 147, 148, 268, 271
Westbury, Ian, 240
Wheeler, C., 176
Wheelock, Anne, 179
White, James Boyd, 265, 267, 271
White, Theodore, 277
Whitehead, Alfred North, 237, 243

Whitson, James A., 208
Wilkof, Neil, 240
Wills, Garry, 264, 271
Winant, Howard, 207
Winnicott, D. W., 47, 67
Wolfe, Alan, 62–63, 68
Wood, Gordon S., 35

Y

Yalom, Irvin D., 68
Young, Michael F. D., 187, 207

Z

Zeichner, Ken M., 256–257, 274
Zieba, Maciej, 243

Subject Index

A

Accelerated Schools Program, 169
Access: aspects of, 151–181; background on, 151–152; bureaucracy and tracking as barriers to, 161–169; to democratic community, 166–169; to empowering knowledge, 162–166; and landscape of inequality, 154–161; opposition to, 183; policy for, 169–174; and recovering democracy, 152–154; and school restructuring, 172–174
American Association for Retired Persons, 82–83
American Federation of Teachers, 253–254, 273
Apprenticeships, and schooling, 118
Aquarium, as ecological system, 75–76
Aristocracy, and meanings of democracy, 3, 33, 34
Articles of Confederation, 26
Assessment, in restructured schools, 173–174
Associations: democratic community in, 167–168; multiple, in curriculum, 198–199
Athens, and imperial democracy, 2–6

B

Brown v. Board of Education, 154
Bureau of Indian Affairs, 45
Bureaucracy, as barrier, 161–169

C

Carnegie Forum on Education and the Economy, 256, 273

Carnegie Foundation for the Advancement of Teaching, 134
Catholic Church, 46
Change, and ecology, 71, 73–77, 85. *See also* Reform
Chicago, and inequalities, 159, 161
Chicago, University of, readings from, 245–246, 272
Children: as advocates for ecology, 69–70, 81–82; in democratic process, 79–83; metaphorical stories of, 49–50; nurturance of, 48–51
Civic community: features of, 57–58; nurturance in, 63–66; and self-interest, 110
Civic education: curriculum for, 195–199, 201; marginalized, 134; reconstructing, 135–141, 148, 149; and teacher education, 254–255, 259, 273
Civic literacy, dearth of, 125–126
Civitas: and democracy, 88, 89, 121; laws of, 100
Coalition of Essential Schools, 169, 172
College Board, 176, 179
Colorado, University of, National Center for Atmospheric Research at, 82, 86
Commission on the Reorganization of Secondary Education, 183, 206, 209
Common schools, in public schooling, 129–131, 137, 147
Communitas, and democracy, 98
Community: access to democratic,

166–169; and arts of judgment, 225–229; civic, 57–58, 63–66, 110; competence and differentiated consciousness for, 236–239; and critical reason, 221–225; deliberation in, 226–227; democracy and education related to, 87–124; and democratic education, 111–120; education for freedom and, 98–103; educative, 116–120; horizontal relationships in, 108–109; and human conversation, 103–106; issues of, 103–111; and mastery, 218–221; nurturance in, 56–58; political and social democracy for, 107–111; and practical reason, 217–236; sense of, 28

Community Civics (CC) course, 183, 202–204

Community schools, in public schooling, 142–144, 150

Community service, and schooling, 117–118

Competence: for community, 236–239; for discussion, 200–201

Computer metaphor, and nurturance, 43, 46, 52, 66

Concreteness, fallacy of misplaced, 237–238

Consciousness, differentiated, for community, 236–239

Constitution, 89–90, 128–129, 259, 264

Constitutionalism, in history of democracy, 21–22, 31–32

Constraints, and creativity, 230–234

Conversation: human, in community, 103–106; pedagogical, 120

Council for Basic Education, 195

Creativity, as applied judgment, 230–234

Critical thinking: and community, 221–225; disinterest in, 94

Curriculum: aims of, 194–199; aspects of, 182–210; background on, 182–185; conclusion on, 204–206; deliberation for, 185–188, 204; differentiated, 187–188; interactions in, 199–201; as morally justified, 50; planning for, 183–184; principles for, 196–199; problems approach in, 201–204; and social aims, 188–194; standards for, 205

Cybernetics, and ecology, 73–76, 86

D

Dartmouth College v. Woodward, 265

Dartmouth University, and civic education, 255

Declaration of Independence, 24–25, 26, 32, 89, 254, 259, 264

Deliberation: in community, 226–227; concept of, 185; and content selection, 186–187; and creativity, 232; culture of, 236–239; and curriculum, 185–188, 204

Democracy: and access to education, 151–181; afterword on, 275–278; American, beginnings of, 24–34, 127–129; American, and public schooling, 125–150; American, recovering, 152–154; in American context, 264; analysis of meanings of, 1–36; and art of rhetoric, 212–217; and arts of judgment, 225–229; background on, 1–2; children in, 79–83; and classroom oratory, 211–243; creative, 190–192; and critical reason, 221–225; criticisms of, 6–9, 26–27, 29, 33; curriculum for, 182–210; dangers to, 277; and ecology, 69–86; education and community related to, 87–124; educative contingencies for, 100–101; essence of, 103; of human spirit, 89; imperial, 2–6; kinds of, 11–12; liberal, and curriculum, 189–190, 192–194; and liberalism, 19–24; logic of, 126; and mixed polity, 9–14; modern, 13–14, 16, 17, 20; moral arts of, 105, 114–115; multicultural, 192–194; and nurturance, 37–68; participatory, 12, 137, 139, 141, 189–190; in personal relationships, 53–54; political, 88–92, 107–111; and practical reason, 217–236; preserving, 12–13; and republics, 14–18; revitalizing publics for, 141–145; social, 88–89, 92, 95, 104, 107–111; standards of, 14, 275–276; tension in, 88; texts for teaching in, 262–269; truths in, 89–90; universalism in, 32; ward system for, 142

Discussion, face-to-face, in curriculum, 197, 199–201

Diverse perspectives, in curriculum, 198, 199

Diversity, cultural, and curriculum, 192–194

Domination, and nurturance, 38–39, 40, 46–47, 53–54, 56–57, 66

Dred Scott v. Sanford, 265

E

Ecology: aspects of, 69–86; background on, 69–73; and change, 71, 73–77, 85; and children in democratic process, 79–83; conclusions on, 83–86; and education, 77–79; empirical, 71–72; environmentalist, 72–73, 81, 83, 84; and epistemological change, 73–77; issues of, 70; systems view of, 72, 73–74, 75–76, 84–85; and values education 70–71, 80; views in, 71–72

Education: access to, 151–181; afterword on, 275–278; aims of, 96, 122, 138, 153–154, 236–239, 247; aspects of democracy and community in, 87–124; background on, 87–88; balance in, 92–98; context of, 88–92, 97; democratic, 111–120; and ecology, 77–79; in history of democracy, 4, 8, 13, 20–21, 25, 33–34; for individual freedom and common good, 98–

103; industrial, 131–133, 137, 162–163, 168; and liberty, 95–98; moral role of, 97, 122; and public schooling, 125–150; texts on, 268; and training, 93–95. *See also* Civic education; Higher education; Schooling; Teacher education

Educational Testing Service, 175

Eight-Year Study, 183–184

Election, in mixed polity, 11

Empowerment: and access to knowledge, 162–166; and mastery, 218–221

Equality: meanings of, 14; natural, 19–20; policy for, 169–174; political, 58; texts on, 266

Equity, intergenerational, 82–83

Ethical norms, and judgment, 225–229

Executive, energetic, 30

F

Families: nurturance in, 55–57; and schools, 114, 123

Federalist, The, 26–33, 34, 36, 90, 248, 254, 259, 264, 269, 270

Federative power concept, 23–24

Financing schools: equalizing, 170–172; inequalities in, 157–158, 159–160, 165

Freedom: and democratic education, 91, 95–98, 103–104; individual, 98–103; texts on, 265. *See also* Liberty

G

Gibbons v. Ogden, 265

Government: end of, 20; forms of, 9, 15, 22–23

Great Neck, spending in, 159

Greece, ancient: meanings of democracy in, 2–14; rhetoric in, 212–217, 225–226

H

Health and human services, and schooling, 117, 123

High schools, comprehensive, 132–134

Higher education: art of rhetoric in, 212–217; aspects of classroom oratory in, 211–243; background on, 211–212; cagey students in, 215–216, 217, 224; competence and differentiated consciousness in, 236–239; and creativity, 230–234; democratic community in, 217–236; mastery in, 218–221; mindlessness in, 236; suggestions for, 216–236; teacher education in, 244–274

Holmes Group, 256, 273

Hudson Institute, 175

Humanism, lawsuit against, 76

I

India, nurturance of self in, 52

Individualism: and democratic education, 91–92, 95, 98–103, 107–108; and liberal democracy, 193; texts on, 265

Industrial education: and access, 162–163, 168; in public schooling, 131–133, 137

Inequality: and access to education, 151–181; in classrooms, 211; landscape of, 154–161; results of, 155–157, 170; sources of, 157–161

Infants, nurturance of, 47–48

Infrastructure, and community, 103–104, 107, 119–120

Internships, and schooling, 119–120

Italy, regional governments in, 57, 109–110

J

Japan, nurturance of self in, 52

Judgment: applied, creativity as, 230–234; arts of, 225–229; in public speaking, 220–221, 229

Justice, in history of democracy, 10, 12, 17

K

Knowledge: access to empowering, 162–166; repertoire of working, 262–263; in tension with imitation and transcendence, 234–236; theoretical and common-sense, 237–239

Knowledge-in-use, in curriculum, 197, 206

L

Lau v. Nichols, 154

Law, texts on, 264–265

Leadership, texts on, 267

Liberalism: in history of democracy, 19–24; and nurturance, 39, 40–41; warm and cold, 227–228

Liberty: and education, 95–98; meanings of, 14; natural, 19–20; political and civil, 31. See also Freedom

Listening, and nurturance, 41, 48–50, 66

Lochner v. New York, 265

M

McCulloch v. Maryland, 265

Marbury v. Madison, 265

Markets, and nurturance, 43–44, 46, 62–63

Mastery, and telos of community, 218–221

Metaphors: and children's stories, 49–50; and ecology, 73–77

Minorities, and access to education, 151–181

Mirroring, and nurturance, 41–42, 44–45, 46–47, 60

Monarchy, and history of democracy, 23, 25

Morality: arts of, in democracy, 105, 114–115; and curriculum, 50; and education, 97, 122; and fear, 51; and nurturing, 64

Mt. Edgecombe BIA School, 45

N

National Association for the Education of Young Children, 171

National Board for Professional Teaching Standards, 171

National Center for Atmospheric Research, 86

National Center for Education Statistics (NCES), 158

National Commission on the Reform of Secondary Education, 148

National Council for the Social Studies, 253

National Council of Teachers of Mathematics, 171

National Education Association, 133, 183, 201, 206

National Education Goals, 170

National Endowment for the Humanities, 144

National Governors' Association, 94, 121, 180

Nationalism, texts on, 267–268

New Jersey, spending in, 157

New York City, and inequalities, 159, 160

Niles Township High School, 159

Nurturance: aspects of, 37–68; background on, 37–39; conditions for, 55–63; immediacy of, 38; for intervention with targeted populations, 60–63; mapping needs of, 39–41; moral meaning of, 64; and nature of the self, 44–54; and needful others, 59–60; of self, 41–44; suggestions on, 63–66

O

Oligarchy, and history of democracy, 9–14, 34

Oratory, teaching, 211–243

P

Participation: in democracy, 12, 137, 139, 141, 189–190; in ecological concerns, 69–86

Pennsylvania, civics students in, 126

Philadelphia, community schools in, 142, 150

Phronesis: and art of rhetoric, 212, 216, 223; and curricular principles, 196, 206

Play, and mastery, 219–221

Political art of science, in mixed polity, 12–13

Political correctness, and intergenerational conflict, 80

Polity: mixed, 9–14; texts on, 263

Power: in history of democracy, 4–5, 9, 19, 21, 24, 29–30; texts on, 267; and trust, 48, 54

Presbyterian Church, 45

Problems of Democracy (POD) course, 183, 185, 201–204, 205

Progressive Education Association, 183

Progressive movement, and public schooling, 131

Public schooling: and American democracy, 125–150; as American experiment, 153; background on, 125–127; civic education reconstructed for, 135–141, 148, 149; compulsory, 113–115; and discussion, 200; history of, 127–135; revitalizing, 141–145; shortcomings of, 126–127

Public speaking, teaching, 211–243

R

Rationalism, and democratic education, 90–91, 99, 102

Reality, sense of, in classroom, 219, 222–224

Reason: critical, 221–225; practical, 217–236

Reflective citizen action, in curriculum, 197–198

Reform: and classroom oratory, 211–243; curricular, 182–210; of teacher education, 244–274

Relativizing moment, experiencing, 225–229
Religion, and democratic education, 90, 99, 102, 120
Representation, in American democracy, 27–29
Republic: and American democracy, 25, 26–27; democratic, 16; imperial, 14–18; and liberalism, 19, 35; procedural, 105; and sense of the community, 28
Rhetoric: concept of, 212–215; and democracy, 212–217; and ecological education, 85; teaching, 211–243; texts on, 267
Rights, texts on, 266
Rochester, social centers movement in, 143–144, 150
Rome, republic of, 15–16
Rules, in public speaking, 220–221, 229, 235

S

Scandinavia, welfare states in, 62–63
School Development Program, 169
School for Individual and Community Development project, 205
Schooling: afterword on, 275–278; compulsory public, 113–115; and pedagogy of the poor, 59–60; restructured, 118–120; voluntary attendance at, 114–116. See also Education; Public schooling
Schools: common, 129–131, 137, 147; community, 142–144, 150; confidence in, 117; custodial function of, 112–113, 114; as instruments, 40, 92, 116; mission of, 90, 112–116; and nurturance, 48–51; private, 113, 115–116; as public spaces, 143; restructuring, 172–174
Science, experiencing in, 42–43
Second International Mathematics Study, 154–155

Segregation, and inequalities, 158–159
Self: conditions for nurturing, 55–63; cultivation of, 48; dialogic character of, 52–53; nature of, 44–54; nurturance of, 41–44; theories on, 50–54
Sheldon Jackson School, 45
Singapore, freedoms surrendered in, 277
Slave quarters, nurturance in, 47
Social aims, and curriculum, 188–194
Social capital, and community, 104–105, 108, 120
Social centers movement, 143–144, 150
Social fabric, and nurturance, 51
Social services: and nurturance, 61–63; and schooling, 117, 123
Sparta: contrasted to Athens, 3–4, 5, 8; and freedom, 265; republic of, 15–16
Stability, need for, 30–31
Standards: for curriculum, 205; of democracy, 14, 275–276; for opportunity to learn, 171–172
Student achievement, and inequalities, 160–161
Subject/object split, in classrooms, 222–225, 237
Switzerland, and early childhood education, 118

T

Teacher education: aspects of, 244–274; background on, 244–245; centrist views of, 252–255; changes in, 269; domains of, 113; grounding of, 247–249, 269; leftist views of, 256–260; rightist views of, 255–256; texts for, 262–269; views on, 249–262
Teaching: approaches to, and inequalities, 164–165; political agents in, 245–249; standards for practice in, 171–172

Teaching the aim, in curriculum, 196–197, 199, 206
Tennessee, humanism lawsuit in, 76
Testing, and inequalities, 163–164
Tlingit Indians, 45, 46
Tolerance, and democracies, 3–4, 5–6, 8
Tracking, as barrier, 161–169, 187–188
Training, and democratic education, 93–95
Trust, and power, 48, 54
Tyranny, in history of democracy, 7, 12, 14–18

U

United Kingdom, mixed constitution of, 25, 26, 31

Utah, spending in, 157

V

Values: democratic, in curriculum, 198; education in, and ecology, 70–71, 80
Virtues: in American democracy, 25, 28, 33; in imperial democracy, 2–3; in imperial republic, 17–18; in liberalism, 19, 20–21; in mixed polity, 8, 10–11, 13

W

William T. Grant Foundation, 124, 175